chicks laying nest eggs

Chicks

laying nest eggs

HOW 10 SKIRTS BEAT THE PANTS OFF WALL STREET...AND HOW YOU CAN, TOO!

karin housley

CROWN
BUSINESS
NEW YORK

Published by Crown Business, New York, New York.
Member of the Crown Publishing Group.

Random House, Inc. New York, Toronto, London, Sydney, Auckland
www.randomhouse.com

CROWN BUSINESS and colophon are trademarks of Random House, Inc.

Printed in the United States of America

Design by Lindgren/Fuller Design

Library of Congress Cataloging-in-Publication Data
Housley, Karin.
 Chicks laying nest eggs : how 10 skirts beat the pants off Wall Street . . . and how
you can, too! / Karin Housley.
  p. cm.
 1. Investments—Handbooks, manuals, etc. 2. Women—Finance, Personal—
Handbooks, manuals, etc. 3. Investment clubs—Handbooks, manuals, etc.
 I. Title.
 HG4527 .H67 2001
 332.6'082—dc21   00-065584
ISBN 0-609-60697-2

10 9 8 7 6 5 4 3 2 1

First Edition

For all the Dianes of the world

Contents

Diane's Story

Hey Karin, it's me . . . Diane. Even though we've been friends forever, what you don't know is that I'm a financial wreck. I can't even believe I just told you that. I hear that you and your friends have started some kind of investment club. Do you really know what all that stock market stuff means? I don't, and I feel like I never will. If I even catch a glimpse of a *Wall Street Journal,* I pick up an *Enquirer* and "Rub the Blue Dot." Please, please, please, can I join you? And if I can't join your club, could you please tell me how to start one of my own? I know I'm not stupid; I just need to learn.

You know that I've been a schoolteacher for the last fourteen years and my students think that I know everything, but I have no idea what my investments are or what they are doing. Excuse me, let me back up, I do have some idea. These nice people come to visit me at school every year and tell me how they think I should invest my money, which "plan" I should put it in and how they will do their best to make it "work" for me. Do they charge me for this? I don't know. What are they doing with my money? I can't tell, no matter how many times I read the reports they send me. Oh, help me. It all looks so difficult.

I have picked up a couple of financial books, but six pages into them, I'm bored—and if I'm not, I can't understand a word they're saying. Can

you Chicks really speak plain English when you're talking about investing?

I'm doing okay with my financial situation right now, but when it
comes to retiring, I have *no idea* where I'll be, and I want to make sure I
won't have to live through a Minnesota winter after age sixty. I *need* to do
this. Can you help me?

Financially Frustrated in St. Paul,

Diane

P.S. By the way, I am not going to retire for years. I am
still very young. I am. I am very young.

Introduction

I know what you're thinking: Yeah, yeah, another investment book. Another author peddling ten steps to becoming a financial wizard— another "You *Can* Be a Millionaire" infomercial in print. I'll bet you're already figuring that this is going to make finance sound exciting for the first four pages, then lose you right after page five. That's not going to happen. I've read those "other" finance books. Lots of 'em. The last thing I want to do is be another dust collector on your shelf. I've done my darnedest to make sure this book isn't like anything you've ever read before. Here, you're going to watch ten women change their lives by changing the way they look at investing. How'd we do it? We started an investment club, studied a bit, and laughed a lot as we helped one another over the tough spots.

Starting or joining an investment club is going to be the most eye-opening experience you've ever had. You're going to figure out how to make your money work for you in ways you never dreamed of, without spending a lot of time. We've learned that the stock market has been the greatest engine for wealth creation on the planet, and "the guys" have been keeping it to themselves for too long. It's our turn, and an investment club is the perfect way to learn to safely navigate it. (Oh, and it's kinda fun . . . but don't tell the guys that part.)

This book is designed to be the simplest-ever step-by-step guide to learning how to invest in the stock market. It has to be, because it's the way *my* investment club learned. And I guarantee you that we made every mistake, every misstep conceivable, before we got together. I'm going to start from day one of the Chicks Laying Nest Eggs Investment Club and show you how we got to the point where our portfolio (don't worry, you'll find out what that is) has more than doubled the market (and you'll understand how great that is).

I'll teach you the basics of what the market is and how it works, how to start your own investment club and eventually buy stock in some good companies. So you don't have to worry about how you can fit this into your too-busy schedule, I'll show you how to get a computer and get your club online. Getting online will enable you and your club to meet anytime, anywhere, without even getting out of your pajamas (not that I don't ever get out of my pajamas. Come on. Not me. Puh-lease).

You'll learn how to make your monthly meetings fast and investing fun. This, mind you, while you are still able to watch the *Today Show,* put in a fifty-hour workweek, read your *People* magazine front to back, nurse the baby, and whip up dinner.

Buying a stock is actually just buying or owning a piece of a company. Instead of buying a pair of Gap jeans and feeling like you own a part of the company, you can actually *buy* a piece of the Gap (that's a share or shares of stock) which will make you a part owner of the company! Your goal is—and if you have invested in or bought a piece of a good, strong company, your end result should be—for the piece to be worth more the day you sell it than the day you bought it. That's a profit, and that's what this book is all about (with a couple of song lyrics thrown in.).

We are not going to talk about realizing the profit potential of market upticks due to metaeconomic gobbledygook. What did I say? Metaeconomic upticks? The Chicks talk about investing in everyday English. We have to, because this is the only language we know.

This book is for every woman, as the time passed long ago when any of us could afford to be ignorant about our finances. Need I go into the story of my auntie Eileen, who was widowed and clueless at the age of forty? Or should I tell you of my twenty-three-year-old baby-sitter, who's looking for a rich man to marry, and until she finds him, will continue to spend every penny that she's earned? How about my girlfriend who has let her financial situation spiral so out of control that she doesn't even know if she and her husband have any investments because he supposedly takes care all of that "stuff"? Or my neighbor who left his wife with only $65 in the checking account and moved out of the state with the perky young thing who lived next door? If I didn't get a move on it, this could have been me. Don't let it be you. (Tip: try to stay perkier than your neighbor.)

I don't want to scare you, but you have to do something now. I was so panicked a few years ago that I bought every investment book I could find at my local bookstore. I wanted to learn it all, every last thing about investing. Peter Lynch, Warren Buffett, Charles Schwab, Suze Orman, and the Motley Fool: I read them *all*. And yes, I did learn some things . . . but there I sat.

Even after I finished reading, I didn't do anything. I sat on my duff and let our "professionally managed" investment portfolio and our professional investment manager continue to intimidate me. I had the knowledge but didn't have the nerve to use it.

That reminds me of how I learned to knit. (Lame, I know, relating investing to knitting. If I could relate it to chess, I would.) I could have read four hundred books on how to knit-one, pearl-two, but until I actually picked up the needles and yarn, I never would have made that sweater with the yellow smiley face in the center. I had the book with the sweater's pattern; I just wasn't doing it. You have to do it to learn.

Which brings me to why an investment club is the best way for a woman to learn about investing by doing it. We are women. We need human contact and validation. We like to know that others think like us, and we need their feedback. God gave us the gift of gab, and here is the perfect place to use it. I needed to talk about investing with someone like me before I could make a move. So I gathered a bunch of my girlfriends and started the Chicks Laying Nest Eggs Investment Club. This was the only way I could have gone from on-my-butt-and-doing-nothing to learning and doing: I was on my way to becoming a Chick! Girls just wanna have fun, but Chicks wanna learn something along the way. And when it comes to investing, we'd like to make a few bucks as well.

Chicks are confident in their knowledge of both past and future investments; we can make sound decisions regarding them and have fun doing it. This book is for any woman who wants to learn how to invest in the stock market and has no idea where to start.

You're going to learn how our group went from ten fairly clueless women to a bunch of Chicks able to answer, without hesitation, "What stock would you invest in tomorrow?" I'll share our story and teach you how to start yours. You might even end up watching financial TV in the morning and understand what they are saying! It's a struggle at my house—Katie and Matt or Maria Bartiromo and Joe Kiernan. (CNBC personalities are becoming cult icons, at least inside my four walls.)

Even if you don't think this is the best time for you to invest in the market, it is. There never is a "best" time, and how long have you waited already? How has all the waiting worked for ya? I know you've already tried these techniques: "I'm going to read that book and figure this out all on my own . . . next week" or "I'm going to sit down with a financial planner and have him explain what he does" or "I'll start putting money away after *this* paycheck." Forget it. Get your friends together and just do it. You'll learn about the stock market, and what your investments could and should be doing, faster than you ever imagined. Even if you have no money right now, invest a little through the club every month, whether it's $10 or $50, and simply learn about the market. Then when you do have some cash to put away, you'll know exactly what to do with it.

With this book, you won't need a lot of time to learn about the stock market. I'll give you enough basics to get started, and as you go, you learn more—on your way to becoming another investment club success story, or retiring when *you* want to. Start with this book, a three-hour read, and then spend a little time each month on your research. You'll be amazed at your results. With a club, your research time is multiplied by the number of members in the club, so you get the benefit of their research too.

What snowballed out of our club knowledge was that each of us now uses the Chicks as our think tank for personal investments. We invest on our own, in addition to the club, but we get our information from club discussions and figure it into our own personal purchases. What better than real-world women discussing their beliefs about a company and bouncing ideas off one another? Would you rather discuss with a man behind a desk who has no idea what kind of jeans his kids wear, whose wife does the back-to-school shopping, or still doesn't have a home computer because he sits in front of one all day at work? You make the call. I cannot begin to tell you what investing in the stock market—without the guidance of a broker, husband, father, or so-called expert—does for a woman's self-esteem. Bring it on, chica!

I am not going to teach you how to read and track a stock hourly, how to buy and sell a stock within the same day, or become so obsessed with the stock market you don't have time for dinner with your dad. Those books are probably on the bookstore shelves next to mine, but stay clear. They're not for you, as you want to continue to have a life. I will not pretend to know everything about the market, because I don't, but the beauty of it is, you don't have to. Just learn the basics and start doing it is the best advice I can give. I wish I had figured this out ten years ago and written this book then for me to buy and read.

Many people will claim that the individual investor or little investment clubs of the world can't possibly do better than the big Wall Street firms. But you can, and we are. The Chicks Laying Nest Eggs Investment Club has consistently beaten the market since we began—a feat 90 percent of the mutual funds are unable to boast. The funny thing is, it was easy. (What the market is and what the percentages mean is explained very plainly later in the book.) The investments that I have made on my own, because of the club, have also beaten the market. Thank you, Chickies!

Of course, there will be skeptics. The last thing the financial world wants to see is the individual learning too much, asking too many questions, and demanding answers.

If this were another "Read my investment philosophy and good luck to you" kind of book, it would not have been worth my time to write, or yours to read. This book will get you into action. By the end, you will be running for the hills with your girlfriends in tow, ready to take the plunge and invest in the stock market. Like the Nike ad says, *just do it.* Just get going, get started, buy the yarn, and see what happens from there. It's a continual learning process, but when you put that sweater on, whoa, baby . . . strut it.

Now go, go, just do it. I'll be the needles, you be the yarn.

1

I Am Woman...
Hear Me Roar

Don't compromise yourself, you are all you have.
— JANIS JOPLIN

We're women—and down through the years, investment decisions haven't typically been ours to make. The financial world is male-dominated, and I think they'd like to keep it that way. Enter: Chicks. I don't want to be the one to break it to you, but it's about time you get a financial hold on your "stuff" before it's too late. I could run the divorce statistics and show you how women fare after a marriage ends, but it's just too plain old scary for me. I hate that 50 percent of all wedded blisses end in divorce. (Oops, sorry, it's the only stat I'll throw at you.)

I'm going out on a limb here, but I'm pretty sure that most women get the short end of the stick when the bliss goes missing. We all know that it is entirely possible that one day our husbands could be gone. Would you know what to do? Do you know enough about your family's investments to make future investments on your own? Why not?

No band of gold on your finger? You haven't taken the plunge into couplehood yet? Still holding out for Prince Charming with all the cash? This book is for you too, because he doesn't exist. And if he did, he wouldn't be looking for a dependent and financially insecure woman. He'd want an unattached Chick willing to sign a prenup. So come prepared, bring your ammunition to the table, and *then* fall in love.

You have to take control of your life and your finances and be responsible for your future. No one will do it for you or take care of you. Not your dad, not your husband, and not your wealthier-than-snot uncle in Fiji. If and when you do waltz down that aisle, you don't want your financial future to be the reason you are saying "I do."

Too many of us have no idea what to do with our money—how to invest it, or how to tell if it could be doing better. Worse yet, you might even *avoid* putting money away because you don't know where to put it. It's time you got your head out of the sand, opened your eyes, and got a grip. This is your future too, and *you* should be in control. The hardest part about investing as a woman is that you aren't always taken seriously. (Please don't throw stones.) We've come a long way, baby, but until the world sees that women can bring home the bacon *and* fry it up in the pan, we will be met with resistance when entering an otherwise male-dominated territory. But this isn't the world's problem, it's ours, women, and we need to get past it. I can complain till I'm blue in the face that my financial planner wasn't speaking my language, or that he wasn't taking enough time to explain things, but it's not going to get me anywhere. My point is, I let him talk this way to me. Not once did I say, "Stop, back up, I want to really understand this and you are making no sense." My solution was to smile and say, "That looks great."

How is it that we can juggle five schedules, hold birthday parties for twenty screaming kids, keep up with every new John Grisham and Danielle Steel novel while managing to count fat grams for the whole family and still be unable to say what we really think? We cook, we clean, we know that Downy in the rinse cycle is better than Bounce in the dryer, we drive carpools, we pay bills, and we squeeze in a Tae-Bo video before the sun comes up. We take care of our aging parents, we put sunscreen on everyone's backs, we volunteer at church bazaars, we have careers, we *give birth,* and we can even hold a conference call from a cell phone while changing the oil in the car. Amen! I am woman.

Then why do we always seek validation from others? We are amazing enough on our own—why do we need someone else to back up our ideas? Do you think it's in our genetic fingerprint? Were we born meek, or have we just been trained for a couple of centuries to neeeeeed others' approval?

We tend to blame the men in our lives. We say, "Oh, my husband doesn't think I should go back to work this soon after the baby" or "My father says I should buy a Ford even though I really want one of those cute little Volkswagen Bugs." If you want and think you should go back to work, state your case, Chicky. Be confident in what you believe and know . . . and go get that Bug. Mine's red.

This is your bacon we're talking about here. You should decide how you want it cooked. Flabby and disgusting or extra crispy and ready for the English muffin? Are you just flippantly tossing your cold hard cash into "a plan" that some executive from the company recommended? Doesn't that go against everything that you believe in? Tsk-tsk. What happened to that "You Go Girl" attitude? If you keep putting money blindly into that fund, let me sell you my mint-condition Ford Pinto. Do you think Mary Tyler Moore had Murray manage her cash? Exactly.

I realize we are not talking about whether you want a blue or black Bug; this is your future. But because it *is* your future, it may seem scary to have it all in *your hands*. It's another responsibility you aren't sure you can handle. Remaining ignorant and letting someone else decide your future seems like the logical choice. Not so, and this must end. The only reason it seems like such a huge undertaking and looks so scary is that you don't know a thing about it. You probably don't even know where to start learning. Believe me, when you get over this hurdle, you will welcome the challenge of planning your future, and even enjoy it.

There is probably nothing more important in life—oh wait, there is: your health, your family's health, a Starbucks coffee—okay, a couple of things more important, but your money is right up there at the top. It's time to get your feet wet, learn a bit about the stock market, and figure out what your future looks like or could look like. Once you learn, who cares what everybody else thinks? You might even be able to teach them a thing or two, though they would claim they already knew it.

My editor says I tend to ramble, so I will summarize at the end of each chapter:

0   We are amazing.
0   We are clueless.
0   Think about what you want.
0   Voice it.
0   Do it.
0   Grrrrrrrr.

Put Your Money Where Your Mouth Is

Those who are really in earnest must be willing to be anything or nothing in the world's estimation.

— SUSAN B. ANTHONY

Before you go any further, I'm guessing that you want to make sure this will be worth your time. What is so great and unique about a bunch of women getting together and jabbering over the Internet? Big deal, you say? What have the Chicks bought, and how well has it done? What did we compare it to? In this chapter, I am going to put our money where our mouth is and tell you how our stock portfolio has performed (and that doesn't mean at the ballet). I'm going to strip the stock market down to all you need to know to understand and measure a portfolio—just enough to get your interest piqued.

Stupidity confession: I had no idea what any of this chapter meant before joining the club. For instance: What on God's green earth is a stock portfolio? My mind would draw a blank. Or what is a percentage return? What is the market? What is the S&P 500? What do you mean, compare my percentage returns to the market? I was totally clueless. Stay with me here, because *I know now!* It's easy. It's *all* easy, but no one will ever let you in on that secret in plain English. (Or maybe you already know this stuff, and I've just totally embarrassed myself in front of the world.) For those of you who are like I was, I'll give it to you in Chicks lingo.

First of all, our main goal in forming this investment club was not to become millionaires. It was not even our aim to smash the market. Our main objective was to learn.

Stop right there! Karin, you must tell them what "the market" is before you can compare it to our stuff. Explain this first, then tell them about our success.

Aha, yes, thank you, Chick Kristin. I tend to get ahead of myself when I mention the words "smash" and "market" in the same sentence. The market is the benchmark that most investors (including the Chicks) measure a stock portfolio's percentage returns against. When I say "portfolio," it is simply the word people use when talking about all of their stocks combined. It's as if they had put them in a folder or a three-ring binder— a portfolio. For Chicks, this market benchmark is the S&P 500. The S&P 500, or Standard and Poor's 500, is simply five hundred of the largest companies in the United States, gathered into an imaginary little portfolio, with a title slapped on it—*The S&P 500*. Among the S&P 500 biggies are McDonald's, Coca-Cola, General Electric, Microsoft, and America Online. There are 495 more companies (and if you want to know what all five hundred of them are, you can find them at our website), but that's it, five hundred humongous companies under one S&P 500 roof. And that's our benchmark, the thing that we measure our gains and losses against. How so?

Each and every day, the average worth of the five hundred companies goes up or down, depending on their stock price. To use it as our benchmark, we take the average of those companies over a specific period of time. Well, it's not *exactly* like that: they complicate it a bit more by giving some companies more weight in the index. The bigger they are, the more weight they carry; but to keep things simple, let's say they all are given equal weight within the index. For example, if the McDonald's market cap (market cap is explained later, but it's the company's current value) is $50 billion, America Online is valued at $130 billion, and General Electric is valued at $520 billion, those three companies' average worth is $233 billion:

$$50 + 130 + 520 = 700; 700 \div 3 = 233$$

So let's pretend on Day One their average is $233 billion. Day Two, their worth goes up a bit, and they're worth $240 billion. By the end of the week, their average worth is $280 billion. Remember, on Day One, they were worth $233 billion, and at the end of the week, they were worth $280 billion . . . that is an increase of 20 percent (the easy math instructions come later).

So in that week's time, our pretend three-company market has had a 20 percent gain. (That would be a very good week, not to mention a very good year, but again, this is a simplified example.) The S&P 500 averages them pretty much the same way, but with all five hundred companies. Using the S&P as your benchmark, you can compare your portfolio to the S&P's gain or loss during the same time period. (The Chicks compare the two twice a month.)

I don't want to confuse you, because I know it's been a long time since you've pulled out that calculator, and even worse, I'm throwing foreign words at you. But just take a deep breath and say to yourself, "Karin Housley was the dumbest woman on earth when it came to numbers, the stock market, and trying to figure out how much to pay the babysitter.* If she can do it, I am sure I can."

Let me do a simple sample, Simon, and you will realize your potential. Let's say in June 1995 you had $7,000 you wanted to invest in the stock market. You could either pick your own stocks or put the money into an S&P 500 fund. You chose to pick your own stocks but want to compare it to the S&P 500 just to make sure that your little portfolio has beaten it.

Here is what you bought (because you were a Chick long before I was):

$1,000 of America Online
$1,000 of Dell Computer
$1,000 of General Electric
$1,000 of Home Depot

---

*$6 per hour × 4 hours = $24

$1,000 of Coca-Cola

$1,000 of McDonald's

$1,000 of Pfizer (this is a pharmaceutical company and your husband
was a doctor on TV, so you decided to research it)

Your original $7,000 investment is now worth (and this is not made
up): $126,000. Can you even? If you invested $7,000 in 1995 in those companies, that is what it would have been worth today. Now, here comes
my little math assignment. What would your percentage gain be?

Tap. Tap. Tap.

I'm waiting. You can go get that calculator now.

Here is how you would figure that out:

$$\$126,000 - \$7000 = \$119,000$$

($119,000 is how much you would have made off your original invest-
ment.)

$$\$119,000 \div \$7,000 \text{ (what you started with)} = \$17$$

Then you need to change it to a percentage:

$$\$17 \times 100 = 1700 \text{ percent}$$

Ta-da! Your portfolio has increased 1700 percent in five years. Not bad,
Chicky.

Now, how about the S&P. What would your money be worth had
you put it into the S&P? (I know this too, because I am no longer the
dumbest woman in the world.) Your original $7,000 put into the S&P
500 would today be worth $19,250.

You knew I'd ask. Get the calculator. I'll wait. What would the percentage gain be had you put your money in the S&P 500 over the past
five years?

Answer: $19,250 − $7,000 = $12,250 (that's how much you would
have made).

$$\$12{,}250 \div \$7{,}000 \text{ (what you started with)} = 1.75$$

Remember, you need to change it to a percentage.

$$1.75 \times 100 = 175 \text{ percent}$$

Yippee! Your imaginary Chick portfolio did 1700 percent over five years compared to the market's 175 percent. That is your goal as a Chick: to beat the S&P—the market.

You can find the S&P every day in the little box in the bottom corner of your finance cable channel. It will tell you if it has gone up or down (green or red is how I figure it out) and by how much. When you track your portfolio online, the calculations are done for you, but don't you ever let that little handheld solar baby get that dusty again.

Now, what I just said about the S&P is *huge*. Reread it. That may be the single most important thing you can learn in this book—what the market means and how to use it as your benchmark. It will also allow you to start an impressive dinner conversation with the stuffiest potatoes you sit down to dine with. All you have to do is ask someone how his portfolio (think three-ring binder) has done against the S&P 500 (think the average growth of a lot of big companies). You will first blow the socks off the guy next to you, and second cause Miss Hoity-Toity across the table to choke on her Cornish game hen.

Mutual Fund

Now, if your goal is to beat the market, or get a little bit better return than the market's average, you should first look at how the mutual fund industry has done against the S&P 500. I'm going to be brief about mutual funds because I don't enjoy them. Every time I see one of their "stretch-the-truth-and-skew-the-numbers" commercials, I get a headache. You've seen them: "Our fund got a solid 33 percent over three years, beating all of our competition."

What do they mean by 33 percent? Does that mean that each year they got 33 percent? If you had invested $1,000 in their fund, would you have $1,350 at the end of the first year? Then 33 percent more each year after? Not usually. It most likely means that they got 10 percent per year and have compounded the interest, so in total, they got 33 percent. Let me explain briefly. Pretend you invested $1,000 in this fund, and the first year you made 10 percent.

Ten percent of $1,000 is $100. At the end of the first year, you have $1,100. Let's say the next year you also got a 10 percent return in interest.

Ten percent of $1,110 is $110. Add this to your balance:

$$\text{you have } \$1,100 + \$110 = \$1,210.$$

In the third year you also got 10 percent.

Ten percent of $1,210 is $121. Add this to your balance, you have $1,210 + $121 = $1,331. Now, you started with $1,000 and ended up with $1,331. That's a difference of $331. So if you want to turn that into a percentage gain number, divide what you made by what you started with:

$$\$331 \div \$1,000 = .331$$

To turn that into a percentage, multiply it by 100. (You learned how to turn decimals to a percentage in fifth-grade math, but I always forget, so I'm refreshing you too.)

$$.331 \times 100 = 33 \text{ percent}$$

The moral of the story is, the mutual fund got 10 percent *a year*, compounded annually, not 33 percent, like they misleadingly claimed. It had a *total* return over three years of 33 percent. If they really got 33 percent a year, at the end of three years it would be worth $2,353. Quite a difference. Buyer Beware.

I'll give you what I think you need to know about mutual funds, which is the second most important thing you can learn in this book—what mutual funds are, and how they perform vs. the market.

Most mutual funds are made up of stocks picked by a fund manager, although some mutual funds include bonds, property, and whatever else that company's hired professional lumps together in his three-ring binder. And they always have a great (or greatly intimidating) name: the Brown & Company High Growth Fund Class A, or the Adviser Opportunities Class T, the More Bang for Your Buck Value Fund, the Managed Growth and New Opportunities Fund, and the list goes on. Then they spend a lot of money advertising their fund, as their goal is to sell it to you. It would be like the Chicks packaging our stock picks, putting them into the Nest Egg Growth with a Ton of Class Fund Portfolio, and reselling a portion of it to you. We would of course have to charge you a fee—say, 2 percent of whatever you give us to invest. And after all that, you would entrust us to pick stocks we felt were going to do the best in the upcoming years. But you won't have to do this, because by the end of this book, you'll be able to do it yourself—and do it better than the suits at the funds.

In the eighties and nineties, owning mutual funds was supposedly "the" way to go. All the commercials, all the fancy investment houses with the big names, and all the men in suits pitching why they have the most profitable mutual fund and why it's suited just for you. Money was pouring in to the mutual fund industry. What were they going to do with it all? I'll tell you.

There are laws designed to regulate mutual funds, and they require that each fund be diversified. A single fund is not allowed to own too much of one company, so they buy stock in small start-up companies, large established companies, rich companies, poor companies, beggar-man-and-thief companies, drug companies, European companies, television stations, wheat farms, gold mines, Pokémon cards, et cetera. They can't miss an industry, a country, or a product. It's like if you couldn't decide what you want to order off the menu, so you order everything; you will be sure to have tasted the best dish, but you had to stomach the worst entrée too. If you'd asked your waiter, he would have told you their house specialty was the prime rib. Think of a mutual fund as the menu, a very expensive way to dine, and think of me as your waitress. Since we have different taste buds, the final decision is up to you.

Now, if a mutual fund packages the good with the bad, how well do you think it performs? Average? Nope, not even average. More than 90 percent of the mutual funds available underperform or do worse than the market's average. They are actually selling a product that doesn't perform as well as the market's average . . . and they get paid for it! That's like sending your child to a $40,000-per-year private school when that institution's test scores don't even meet the country's average: ludicrous, and none of us would even think of doing it—yet we own mutual funds.

If you do own a mutual fund, ask your financial adviser how it has done this past year versus the S&P 500. Keep that information in mind as you read this book. Matter of fact, when he tells you how well it has done over the past five years, compare that to what our pretend five-year portfolio did earlier. Imagine if you had given your money to someone to handle and they put it into a mutual fund that ended up getting an average of 8 percent (pretty decent in the mutual fund world) per year. At the end of five years, it would be worth $11,755.

So, I ask you, if you had $7,000 to invest today, and someone told you that in five years it could be worth either $10,285, $19,250 or $119,000, which would you choose? (You don't have to get your calculators out on this question: Would you rather have $10,000 or $119,000?)

You could go back many many years—to the beginning of the stock market, or the mutual fund, and the stock market numbers will consistently beat the mutual funds. Take General Electric, for example. If you had invested $1,000 in GE in 1990 today it would be worth $8,000! Or how about this: if you had invested $1,000 in Microsoft in 1990, today it would be worth $35,250! The stock market has, year-in-year-out, beat the mutual funds. There is a very good reason for you to become Chicky and not trust that every chef is going to take care of you.

What the Chicks originally thought was that we would be a success as a club if we could beat a mutual fund's returns. We learned after reading a little that doing this was too simple. How hard is it to get a tan in the Bahamas? Exactly.

Let's try and get the market's average return! Let's mimic the S&P 500! We read a little more, talked amongst ourselves, and decided that anyone can do that. You don't even need to read a book to get the market's average.

You can actually buy a piece of the S&P 500 called an S&P Index

Fund; it holds stock in every one of the five hundred top companies and resells them to you. The most popular is the Vanguard Index Trust 500 Portfolio. Buy that, and you get the market's return, or the market's average. Does that make any sense? You can buy a piece, a small piece of each of the five hundred companies, so your percentage return for the year will be almost exactly what those companies attain. (I say *almost* exactly, because you pay a small fee to buy it.) Brilliant idea. This is still a mutual fund, but it's the only one you should consider having a piece of, because it keeps the fund manager honest by making sure that he never has to make a decision between stock A and stock B, between buying dependable old General Electric or the latest Internet flash in the pan.

Buying a Vanguard 500 stock fund, or a piece of the five hundred largest companies in the U.S. going by another name, is like taking home the silver medal. It's a great end result in the Investment Olympics. Your mother would be proud. A mutual fund might net you a bronze. But, I say to you, would the U.S. women's soccer team be happy going home with the silver? A silver medal does not a Wheaties box make.

What fun is settling for the silver medal? What fun, and how much will you have learned if you simply buy a piece of the S&P? You can stop right here if that's your goal, and your end result will still be great, better than a bronze mutual fund, but what knowledge will you have gained about the market? Why brag about watching a foreign film when you didn't understand a word? If you're anything like us and you plan on investing in the stock market, you want to know why, and how it works, before you drop a penny. That way, when you do beat the market, you can take some credit for it. Stand tall, girl. Go for the gold!

Let me indulge for one more moment in explaining the market, and then I promise to move on. If you kept your money in the bank, you could get around 2 percent interest per year. If you put it in a money market account, you get around 5 percent. (No medals given for those two.) You could buy a mutual fund and go home with the bronze: yee-haa. Now, if you put it into the S&P 500 ("the market"), you'd get that year's market return, averaging over the history of the market, around 11 percent. In 1999, the market's average return was 21 percent. Imagine if you had dropped $10,000 into the S&P 500 fund at the beginning of that year. At the end of the year, it would have been worth $12,000. In the bank it would have been worth $10,200, and in a money market, $10,500. If you compounded that over the next ten years, the S&P fund's $10,000 would be worth $67,269, the bank's $11,949, and the money market's $16,288.

Hey, Karin, can we get back to what the Chicks have done? Remember . . . put our money where our mouth is?

Oops, sorry, I get lost in deep compounding interest thoughts, it's just so dang exciting. Anyway, the Chicks' goal was to beat the market. Whatever the market was doing when we invested, we wanted to beat it. If the market was getting 5 percent per year, we wanted to get 6 percent. If the market was getting −5 percent, we wanted to get −4 percent. (There will be some down years. Remember: historical average is +11 percent.) If the market was getting 21 percent, we wanted to get 22 percent.

Now to the good stuff: the Chicks Laying Nest Eggs (say to yourself, "ten clueless women until they joined a club") have managed to beat the market this past year. In our first year, when the market did 21 percent (remember, we'd be happy to get 22 percent), we got 53 percent! In a year! Fifty-three percent without a broker or financial adviser, and without spending a ton of time! Can you say *smash*?

We realize that's a little extreme, but we beat the market. Mission accomplished. But an even greater accomplishment is that we know *how* we beat the market, what we own, and why we own it. Even if we had gotten a 22 percent return, we would have been thrilled. No college class, financial adviser, or book would have taught us all that. We had to do it, to learn.

Though it might make my next book a best-seller, I'm not going to pretend that the Chicks will continue to get those kind of returns, but we've been lucky to have invested in the market during a good swing and in some pretty strong companies. It's up to you: you can put your money in the bank, a money market, a mutual fund, an S&P 500 fund, or directly into the stock market. Bronze, silver, or gold? Ask yourself what Kristi Yamaguchi would do.

Below is what the Chicks have bought, and how our portfolio (three-ring binder) has done long-term vs. the market (big companies' average growth) during the same time period. As you can see, we have more than doubled what we would have done by buying the no-brainer S&P stock. And quite frankly, Scarlett, you should give a damn!

THE CHICKS' PORTFOLIO (THREE-RING BINDER)

Company	Date Bought	Chicks' Original Cost	Worth	Chicks' Value Change in Dollars	Chicks' Value Change in %	S&P Value Change in %
America Online (AOL)*	Dec. 1998-	$1,547.48-	$4,257.36	$2,709.88	175.12%	21.09%
Cisco (CSCO)	Mar. 1999-	$1,472.23	$3,146.64	$1,674.41	113.73%	10.09%
Nokia (NOK)	Aug. 1999-	$1,537.36-	$2,713.68	$1,176.32	76.52%	4.50%
Pfizer (PFE)	Oct. 1998-	$1,992.23-	$2,677.80	$685.57	34.41%	40.53%
Coke (KO)	Oct. 1998-	$1,917.23	$1,753.20	$164.03	−8.56%	40.53%
Gap (GPS)	June 1999	$1,523.36	$707.25	$816.11	−53.57%	8.92%
Oracle (ORCL)	Dec. 1999	$1,563.75	$2,705.20	$1,141.45	72.99%	−1.01%
General Electric (GE)	Mar. 2000	$1,414.73	$1,783.20	$368.47	26.05%	1.97%
Sun Microsystems (SUNW)	June 2000	$1,592.48	$1,935.00	$342.52	21.51%	−4.00%
Yahoo (YHOO)	Sept. 2000	$1,502.54	$1,056.25	$446.29	−29.70%	−7.35%
TOTAL		$16,063.39	$22,735.58	$9,525.05	41.54%	13.09%

*These abbreviations are called ticker symbols. It is how each company is identified on the stock exchange, by their assigned lettered symbol.

Don't let the 41.54 percent and the 13.09 percent confuse you. This is now halfway through our second year, and our portfolio continues to grow, while the market has slipped a little. Our 53 percent is now 41 percent, and the market went from 21 percent to 13 percent. Now look hard at those last two columns. Pretend this was *your* money. If you had put your $16,063.39 into the S&P 500, you'd have $15,432.00. That's great, but it's not gonna get us to sing your anthem. The Chicks' portfolio has netted a whopping 42 percent! Our $16,063.39 is now worth more than $22,000! Oh say can you see?

I'm telling you this to give the Chicks some credibility, perk up your ears a bit, and get you to read on. I want to say again, this end result wasn't our intention or our main goal. We wanted to beat the market by a hair to consider our venture successful. The knowledge, the fun, and the confidence gained have more than paid off for us. Those are things that mean the most to us as women: learning and having fun; the market smashing is just a bonus, but a fruitful one at that.

We did this by creating our own investment philosophy, which I'll teach you in the Chicks' Dozen chapter (page 132). The Chicks' philosophy doesn't require a lot of time on your part, in either purchasing a stock or following a company. We are long-term buy-and-holders; matter of fact, we are buy-and-hold-on-to-ers." We buy every three months and don't spend a ton of time in between checking on what we've purchased. We are so confident about acquiring a company that we only have to check on it every three months after we've bought it. Although, after a while, you find yourself interested in anything that is being written or spoken about your "baby." Who says you can't get emotional about your companies? It's okay to get a peacock-perky feeling about a three-ring binder.

The bottom line is, we didn't want our real lives to change a lot (we didn't have time), so this is what works for us. We wanted simple, easy, fun, and market beating by a feather. We have succeeded, and you can too!

So that's the Chicks' portfolio in an eggshell. We had a percentage return that beat the market during the same time period (any time period—one year, two years, et cetera). If this makes sense to you, you are already way ahead of where the Chicks Laying Nest Eggs were when we started the club. Uh-oh, my crystal ball is calling, let me look . . . aaahhh, yes, I can see you're just itching to get started. Let's begin the training program in your quest for the gold right now. Break a leg, Chicky! You are going to be great at this.

Chapter Summary

O No one was dumber than I was when it came to the stock market.
O Market smashing can be done, even by women in pajamas.
O Bronze, silver, or gold?
● Five hundred companies' average is your benchmark (S&P 500).
● Historical average per year of the S&P 500 is 11 percent.
O Mutual funds can cause migraines.
O Chicks 67, market 19 . . . Chicks win gold!
O Peacock-perky.

C3

Me

I had some dreams, they were clouds in my coffee.
— CARLY SIMON

How did the Chicks get here? Well, my ignorance about my family's personal investments had been irritating me for years. Every time I opened up a newspaper, it seemed like the stock market was up a record amount, and every time I turned on the TV, someone was telling me that he'd just made a killing. My husband and I had mutual funds coming out of our ears and employee benefit plans that were benefiting someone, I think, but how would I ever know? Financial statements filled with numbers would come monthly, and I would toss them in the garbage. I used to open them, read the quarterly statements, percentages, balance sheets, income statements, annualized returns, and I would get nothing out of them but frustration. Yeah, the numbers were getting bigger, but compared to what? Were we doing well or okay or . . . what?

I would call our financial planner. "Steven, what does all of this mean?" I would ask. His answer was always the same: "Soy planificador financiero. Nunca entenderá ni siquiera una palabra que yo digo mientras que estás vivo."* What? Steven was born and raised in New Jersey,

---

*Translation: "I am an investment adviser. You will never understand a word I say as long as you live."

24

so I should be able to comprendé. My degree was in communication, for goodness' sake, but I couldn't understand his. I'd hang up convinced I was stupid. I was still using my fingers to count up the cards at the black-jack tables, so how the heck could I ever understand this stuff?

Years went by (like twelve of them) before I opened a "How to Invest in the Stock Market" book. I read it, thought it sounded like a great idea, but how could I, the five-foot domestic engineer, knee-deep in to-do lists, figure out how to invest in the stock market? Where would I start, and where was I going to find the time? Keeping the checkbook balanced was enough of a challenge. Like many women who can barely find time for their yearly Pap smear, I went back to molding the kids' Play-Doh and left the real dough for the guys with suits.

I did sneak in one little stock transaction. It was a tip from a friend of a friend's aunt who worked for the company. This was my chance. I was going to do it, I was going to invest. I was going to make a ton on this new start-up long-distance telephone company. One month after I put the money in, half of it was gone. My stock market days were over. I needed to get back to my *Martha Stewart Living* magazine. I had napkins and tablecloths to coordinate. This I could do.

I spent two more years tossing financial statements and diapers into the garbage. I was happy. Dumb and ignorant, but I told myself I was happy. What more was there to life? I had kids, a husband, a house, and some cash stashed away. I didn't need to understand where our money was and what it was doing. It was doing as well as everybody else's money, I think. If only I didn't have to get that statement in the mail, I wouldn't have had to stare my ignorance in the face every month.

When our fourth baby was born, I looked at this little munchkin and thought, what is more important than this, my family, their future, and finding a good baby-sitter? *Their future.* Will there be enough money for all of these little guys to go to college? Of course there will be. I mean, Steven says there will be. But how do I really know? Should I trust every-one else to make these decisions for us? I wouldn't let anyone pick the kids' pediatrician for me, or the schools they attend, or the neighborhood we live in; why would I let anyone choose what our future will look like? On top of that, I'm letting them choose without even asking a question.

I'm every financial planner's dream. Send them a monthly check and they are on their way (to Tahiti, I imagine).

I've talked with some money managers/financial consultants/investment advisers (they call themselves so many different things, it only adds to my confusion), and they didn't seem like rocket scientists. I just didn't understand their jargon. The worst part was when I saw Joe, a guy who went to my high school, now working for an investment bank. I knew something had to give. I mean, seriously, Joe? Joe, who took six years to finish high school, is managing money?

Man, I had to get those investment books out again, tackle them, sleep with them, live and breathe them. I had to figure this out.

It was then that my own personal little sun started to shine. I was able to raise kids without being a child psychologist! I knew how to jump-start my car without a man—I mean manual. Heck, I was the general contractor (GC in construction lingo, and I'm proud that I now know that) on the complete remodel of my house. The stock market couldn't be any harder than that.

I was smelling the coffee! I didn't need a Ph.D. in cash or a grandfather on Wall Street to be able to know how to invest, and neither do you. (Of course, you can spend lots of time and money and go to college to get a business degree. Go ahead, you decide, but this book is a lot cheaper, and it'll only take you a few hours to read. Let's see, a $24.95 book and three hours, or $48,000 and four years. Hmm.) If you know something about anything, you can invest. I just needed to apply the same basic principles of my life to investing. I dusted off the books.

I had all the books, boy, did I have all the books, and I read them until I could understand them and I could even tell you about them over coffee, but I still wasn't doing anything. I sat on my rear, spineless and scared, and moped about our miserable returns. (At this point, those financial reports began to make sense, and the picture wasn't all that pretty.) What good was the knowledge when I wasn't doing anything with it? Aha: brilliant idea #6,342 in my life. I'd solicit the help of my girlfriends, ask them to join a club, and maybe that would propel me into at least buying my first stock. Believe me, it was not because I was bored, I already had a pack of children, a husband who was rarely home, and a graduate degree in the works . . . but somehow, I needed more. Maybe it was greed. Thank goodness I had nine greedy and clueless friends who were dying to make sense of this stuff too. I picked up the phone.

Chapter Summary

O Even a domestic engineer can invest.
O I bought a lot of books.
O You don't have to be a child psychologist to raise good kids.
O Apply your basic principles of life to investing.

4

You're Invited

You see a lot of smart guys with dumb women, but you hardly ever see a smart woman with a dumb guy.
— ERICA JONG

When I was thinking about getting an investment club together, I didn't have ten close friends who lived in the same city. I blame it on my husband's "up and move every two years" hockey career and not my hermitlike tendencies.

Over the years, I had collected a great crew of friends in the various cities we'd lived. My sister lived in Atlanta, my mom lived in Phoenix, Cheryl in L.A., Susie in St. Louis, and so on. It became instantly apparent that getting everybody to monthly meetings would be a little complicated.

One look at airfares, and I realized that the online alternative was really the only way to go. I'd been in a chat room or two and spent some time watching the message boards on the Motley Fool.* That gave me the idea to do most of the work on the Internet and get everyone to meet face-to-face once or twice a year. I drafted an e-mail, swearing that we were going to have some fun and maybe even make some money (and promising instructions later), and sent it off. I only hoped they didn't think I was bonkers.

---

*It was there that I'd see people from across the country discussing different topics. It was a gathering place of ideas, on the Internet.

They didn't! They were all dying to learn—both about the stock market and the online world. We were ten women, all a little anxious but ready to rumble, um, yeah, rumble something.

Most of these women had never met; I was the common denominator (more math). To introduce everybody, I sent out e-mail biographies. You can read the original short bios below. Let me introduce them in order of age, only because my mother would like to be first. I'll oblige. After all, she did give me life.

Jeanette—60-something, St. Paul, MN/Scottsdale, AZ: Mother of three girls (I'm in the middle), tax expert (I love her, but that's why she was invited in the first place), Arizona Snowbird (that's the term for folks who live in Minnesota during the summer and Arizona in the winter), married to my dad, Pete. She has had perfect attendance at an affiliate of the American Lutheran Church since birth, so don't argue with her about wine and wafers, you'll never win. She's worked at H&R Block forever and is now a bigwig. Loves bridge and golf. No, loves bridge and golfs just to see my dad every once in a while. And she's the person we have to be the nicest to, since she will be handling all of our money.

Julie—46, Edina, MN/Scottsdale, AZ: Julie's another Arizona Snowbird and a friend of my mother's but is closer in age to me (does that mean I'm old too?). Both my little sister and I baby-sat for her son when he was young (and she was young too), and we thought she was cool. We tortured him. I hope he's forgotten. Julie can beat the pants off any man on the golf course, as long as they play at the one she owns. Julie was in an investment club that folded not too long ago. They just bought what some guy told them to. This club will get more of her time if we can convince her to put down those dang clubs. Julie is a closet tour guide for any city you want to visit: she's been everywhere and knows everyone. She owns and runs a golf course in Minnesota in the summer, and golfs in Arizona in the winter. Tough life she has.

Susie—42, St. Louis, MO: Mother of three. I met Susie at Mike Ditka's Restaurant in Chicago. I lived in Winnipeg at the time (1991). Over a few

Coors Lights (at least for me—she drank skim milk and Kahlua, don't ask how I remember), I begged her to get me out of Winnipeg. She works in my husband's business and has this kind of power. We soon after moved to St. Louis. Susie has been known to lie to her husband on their vacations and say she is at the Laundromat when really she's gambling at an Indian reservation casino. Allen can't figure out why he never gets that lucky with the change machine when he does his laundry. Susie ran a couple of hockey tournaments that were semisuccessful: the Olympics in Japan and the World Cup in North America.

Lynn—41, Afton, MN: Lynn had a party at her house in 1995, and through a friend of a friend, I was invited. Got there, loved her, loved her hair, loved her shoes, and loved her boat. I wanted to be her. So I bought the same boat and went to the same hairdresser, but Macy's was out of the shoes, so I bought the house two doors down. After that day, she decided to become a real estate agent. Go figure. Lynn is married to Craig, who operates on people's bones, my husband's included. They have five children, are the godparents of our baby—like they need another—and Lynn teaches my kids to water-ski in her spare time. She lived in her garage for a year. Don't ask.

Karin—34, St. Paul, MN: Master Delegator (me).

Cheryl—34, Los Angeles, CA: I met Cheryl in 1992 in a . . . ahem, a nightclub in Buffalo, New York. She was some big soap star doing a charity golf tournament. I asked her if her hair was naturally that red or did she have to apply a lot of expensive products? We've been friends ever since. Cheryl has one bun in the oven and one hatched egg in the nest, a little boy and a little girl. She has stopped talking about her dog, thank God. She has been known to buy the same clothes I have. Seriously. We will show up to dinner wearing the same thing. She says it's coincidence, but I keep looking over my shoulder at Nordstroms—she must be buying the security videos. She has done some investing and knows more about it than I do, though I'm not sure if her investments are successful. She never tells me that part.

Jana—31, Atlanta, GA: My little sister. Jana wanted to change her name to Jana Lynn after her divorce—true story, Jana Lynn, with no last name, like Cher. Jana has a teeny-tiny baby who should be my god-daughter, but isn't. Jana lives with Mac, and he wants part of this invest-ment club thing too, but no way, too many muscles for us Chicks. Besides, his real name is Richie, and that would get confusing. I don't have any stories about Jana, and I should just leave it at that. Okay, just one and then I have to move on. When she was little, we used to call her "baby boy." We would run around the house and scream, "BABY BOY, BABY BOY." Now, this scarred her so terribly that when we watch the videos of her parachuting out of airplanes, we can hear her scream-ing, "STOP CALLING ME BABY BOY, STOP CALLING ME BABY BOY!" Wow, some people have no sense of humor. Jana works for a computer software corporation, talks on the phone a lot, and sends important e-mails to the wrong people.

Lorene—30, Annapolis, MD: I met Lorene when I lived in Annapolis. Our husbands worked together. She barely made it out of her house, as she was so busy trying to keep her four children's names straight. She wears black bras and Bebe suits. She owns more Bebe clothes than all the malls in Maryland. She has a striking resemblance to Jackie Kennedy Onassis, but the similarities stop there. We have to watch this girl, she just spent five hours trying to get her sound card working on her new laptop only to find out she had forgotten to turn up the volume. In her spare time, she paints all of her walls. Then she paints all of her furni-ture. Then she repaints her nails. I keep trying to get her to go out and be a little social: her idea of that is to be the room mother at school. I'm still working on her, but I might need some help. Lorene just went back to school to get her degree—in what, she isn't sure—but it got her out of the house. It's a start.

Megan—29, Portland, ME: Megan's husband plays professional hockey. His nickname is Killer, but they gave that to the wrong spouse. I've seen videotapes of her in the stands fighting with the fans. Don't cross Megan. If she wants to invest in "Dorothy the Tornado Predictor," we drop the whole nest egg into tornado predictors—even if Helen Hunt won't endorse them. Megan has two children, little girlies. I can only imagine what they have in store for her. Killer and Killer reproduce . . . oh dear. Watch out, Roller Derby fans. I've never met anyone who can organize a charity event in two weeks from a neighbor's house (hers was out of commission due to ice storms), while her daughter was in and out of the emergency room, and still manage to come out with $200,000 to give away. She almost put it into tornado predictors, but the charity contract was already signed. My dad says Megan is intense. That's a good word for her. She looks like an intense Connie Stevens. She hates when I say she looks like Connie Stevens, but she does.

Kristin—29, Pittsburgh, PA/Atlanta, GA: I met Kristin when I flew to Atlanta to help my sister deliver her baby. I was still nursing my baby, who had to come along. Kristin, being the kind, genuine, and caring person she is, took care of her. She didn't even complain when my starving baby wouldn't take a bottle for hours. I wish I could find something sneery to say about Kristin, but I can't. She's just that good. I mean, come on, she's from Appleton, Wisconsin. She was even Miss Appleton once, and then went on to the Miss Wisconsin pageant. She forgot to use Stick 'Em to cement her bathing suit to her caboose, the only reason she lost, or so I am told. Kristin is self-employed and does very well for herself, but I'm not sure what she does. Something with computers and training, or computers and sales, or computers and consulting. Oh well, it's that alley and she's up it. Kristin is fluent in Spanish, in case we ever make enough money for a trip to Madrid.

Phew . . . that's it: the Chicks Laying Nest Eggs Investment Club.

chick chat

*Some say our national pastime
is baseball. Not me. It's gossip.*
— ERMA BOMBECK

Now that you've met the Chicks, you can take a peek into our Chick Chat message board. Our board is the diary of the club. It's the place where we go and post about the companies that we own, would like to own, or would just like to talk about. Sometimes we get sidetracked and talk about our personal lives and our feelings about world events. I can't help it, but I want to know what is happening in Megan's life. I want to know what the people in Minnesota think of Jesse "The Body" Ventura being their governor. I want up-to-the-second coverage of Cheryl's labor and delivery. Again, we're women, so chatting and bonding is important to us.

The message board is our lifeline. Until we got the Chicks Laying Nest Eggs website up, our message board was on the Motley Fool website. Since the day we started our club, part of my daily routine was to check it, read the posts (messages) that interested me, and respond when so inclined. This was not required to be a member in good standing in the club, but it slowly became habit for all ten of us.

Let me explain a message board and how it works. It would be like a big piece of paper on your refrigerator. You walk by and write a message on the paper that says:

Dear Family: If one more person leaves their dirty dishes in the sink, I'm going to hop in my car and never come back. Ashley...don't forget your soccer game tonight at 6:00 p.m. Love, Mom.

Then your husband walks by the refrigerator. He writes:

Honey: Relax. Notice my dishes? Aha... I washed them. Don't leave us. Ashley, I will drive you to your soccer game. Love, Dad.

Then Ashley comes home, reads the messages, and continues on the slip of paper:

My soccer game was canceled. I'm going to the mall with Leah. Sorry about my dishes, I'll do them when I get home. XOXOXOX, Ashley

This is exactly how a message board works on the Internet. It is an ongoing log of communication. The Chicks' message board is our "Dear Abby" for both personal and investment-related topics. We've been known to ask, "What is the DJIA [Dow Jones Industrial Average] again?" "What time does the market open in Mountain Time?" "Could someone please help me figure out General Electric's balance sheet?" Or "Could anyone give me some tips on how to keep a two-year-old from getting out of her new big bed?"

The history of our club is all on our message board. You'll find some of our posts scattered throughout this book. What you'll see is that our lives are *not* all about investing, and neither is this club. Investing is a small portion of our lives, as it should be. You should buy what you believe in and put it to rest. You may come to your investment club for the financial education and the profits, but the bonds you form there—and the posts about everything in the world—are what will keep you coming back. While you read, you can see how the board works and what its role is in the give-and-take process that makes our club, and every investment club, work. Warning: message boards are addictive.

(You will notice a couple of asterisks before some posts. This is how we distinguish an investment club–related post from a personal story. Only the posts with asterisks are required for a club member to read. When you're in a hurry, you'll do anything to get *just the facts*.)

TITLE: **COMPANY PURCHASED
By: Karin

Hey Chickies! You found our message board! We can post all of our investment-related topics here, and our not-so-investment-related stuff too. Just be sure to check in once a week to see what's happenin'.

Okay, we bought Coke and Pfizer. I am surprised my mother didn't post anything. Hmmmm. I think she was a little stressed about her Europe trip . . . she left this morning. She and my dad are on a ship for two weeks—or at least that's what I think she said. I wasn't listening, as I was more concerned about the price we bought Coke and Pfizer at.

Here's the scoop. We bought thirty shares of Coke at 63.25. We bought twenty shares of Pfizer at 98.625. Netty actually did this online for a $19.73 purchase fee. It took her the whole day, but she did it! Send her an e-mail, as it was her greatest feat to date (next to getting my dad to go to Norway again).

Proud daughter,
Karin

TITLE: RESPONSE TO COMPANY PURCHASED
From: Susie

Congratulations, Jeanette! If you can do it, any of us can. I'm going to go open an online account right now. I should have made my own personal trade by the time you get off the ship. I hope you aren't too seasick, I know how you love the fjords.

Susie

5

Dealing with Mars

The thing women have got to learn is that nobody gives you power. You just take it.

— ROSEANNE BARR

Just when you were about to jump into the stock market pool, you ran into the man of the house. Now what are ya supposed to do?

Don't get me wrong. I love men, especially the one I barely cook for. But I have a feeling this book wasn't a gift from a member of the opposite sex—unless you have one of those sincere, sensitive guys. If a man did buy you a book on teaching a woman how to be independent and invest for herself, I'd be careful—Ally McBeal might steal him. It was you who bought this book, right? Y-O-U . . . you! I love independent women! Women who can think for themselves, ask questions, and make decisions based on what they know, not on what someone else tells them. Watch us for a little while longer, then follow through and do what you want to do . . . and don't leave us sitting on your bedside table like that pile of pictures in the drawer waiting for you to put them in an album.

First hurdle? That resistance thing. You know, the people who aren't going to be as gung ho about your decision to try your hand at something new as you are. We need to be careful how we approach the subject, or your excitement will be squelched before you can get to the next chapter.

You can't just blurt out at the dinner table, "Oh, honey, I think I might start doing a little investing on my own and then compare it to how well our mutual fund is doing." Bad idea. Tiptoeing is best: "Um, honey, how's the chicken? I couldn't decide if I should marinate it in the honey mustard or the lemon pepper vinaigrette tonight. Oh hey, I was reading over our financial statements from the Huey, Dewey, and Louie Fund, and I really don't understand all of it. Do you? I was thinking I should read a book about this stuff, see what our money is doing. You know, just in my spare time, after I put the kids to bed, get the laundry put away, and wrap all the Christmas presents. I found this book that Vicki told me about, so I was thinking I might read it, and, well, maybe try a little investing on my own, or in a club or something."

If he looks up from the newspaper, give him two points. If he looks you in the eye when he responds, give your man a ten. Here's how it's likely to go, though. "Ah, yeah, go ahead dear, that's great. What did you say again, you want to read about investing? Sure, no problem, here's the business section." Hmph. The real conversations will begin when you actually start putting away a little nest egg of your own. Just remember, buckle down and be strong.

Also, I think there are some men left out there who still feel the need to control the "manly" things. I know, I know, call me Gloria Steinem, but they feel they should still wear the pants in some arenas, especially the ones with dollar signs. The financial field is prime "guy talk" territory.

For these guys, women trying to play their game isn't revolutionary, it's a *revolution* (or revolting, you choose). What more are women going to ask for? First they wanted to vote, then a career with equal pay, and then they wanted to split up the household chores. What trousers are left for him and only him to wear? Isn't it enough that he changed a couple of diapers last year? Pass him the Virginia Slims.

Your starting or joining an investment club may not be a big deal to your significant other. Nor will buying your first stock or two and starting to speak about a company's earnings. But chances are, a day will come when the man of the house—or one of his buddies—will decide that he needs to reassert the masculine role of family financial wizard.

Don't think that your logic and great results will be enough to stop this herd of bulls. Once your club is up and running, and you have a couple of successful buys, the men in your life may bring out the big horns—the "it's a more complicated game than you think" horns.

Not long ago, I was sharing the Chicks' story with a male neighbor. He was silent as I went on and on about our exciting newfound hobby. I told him what it has done for us, and what we've learned. After about half an hour of my delirious rambling, he said, "Well, what do your girls think of the Federal Reserve announcement today?"

"The what?" I replied.

"The announcement, the decision handed down from the Fed today. It could affect the market enormously. Who in your club is watching that? Who reports on what Alan Greenspan says? If the market falters, you can say good-bye to all your profits. Who is in charge of timing the purchases of your club? Maybe you should read a bit more about how the real professionals do it. Matter of fact, here are a few of the books I've read. Take them home, then we can talk."

I almost crumbled, but then I managed to come back with "We don't figure timing into our purchases. We look for good companies with good management that we love and believe in, invest in them on a regular basis, and let the rest take care of itself."

"Oh, that's how you girls do it. Buy what you love. Interesting," he replied. "So you'd buy Starbucks just because you enjoy a morning coffee with cream and sugar? Cute, but you don't take into consideration when the best time to buy Starbucks would be? Did you know that you would have much more success as an investor if you watched the trends of each stock to see when a company is overvalued? Which, by the way, is a time to sell; undervalued is a time to buy."

Even as I felt myself shrinking to the size of my pinky, I whispered, "You see, we believe in long-term buy and hold. We want to have a life outside of sitting in front of the television, on the phone with a broker, or on the computer tracking our companies hourly. We want to bring our kids to the park. We want to take vacations. We don't want our investments to consume us."

I was getting louder.

"We want our financial planning to take up a small portion of our lives. We want to be comfortable with it because we understand what we have and why. We feel you don't need to know *everything* about the market, all those numbers, every company's P/E ratios, what the Wall Street whiz kids say are market trends of the day, or what Alan Greenspan says. We know all that affects the market temporarily, but over the long run, the buy-and-hold approach beats all. We've done the numbers, and we know.

"Besides, we barely can keep track of our children's vaccination schedule, much less a stock market sale. So, yeah, maybe your portfolio does do better than the market average, but I also see that you're at work until seven P.M., haven't taken your wife out to dinner in years, and your kids have no idea that you know how to play basketball. But congrats to you and your superior knowledge. Oh, by the way, Mr. Murray, I'd like to see your percentages after you've figured in all of your broker's commissions." Advantage—Chick Karin.

It's a man's world, and we just live in it . . . or so they think. I surveyed the spouse or significant other of each Chick to see what he *really* thought when he was approached by his Venus. What did he think when she said she was going to join an investment club and learn something about the market? It's interesting to see how their tunes have changed after they've seen a successful transformation, our commitment, and that it just isn't another flippant social activity (though sometimes we want it to be). I wanted you to hear from some real men on what you might have to deal with, what we dealt with, and how we overcame any hurdles. (The key is to let him continue to think that it's his world; then, when you start getting smashing results, hand him some books and tell him to start his own club.)

I'll start with my husband, since he was first to get the news. Here was the conversation:

Me: I am going absolutely berserk trying to figure out these portfolio summaries from Steven. Adam keeps telling me that he got 54 percent last year and we got 8 percent. How did he do that? Hello . . . are you listening? I just e-mailed all my friends and asked them to join a club with me to help me learn.

Phil: That's great, tell them I said hi.

(A week later)

Me: Okay, I've got ten people, we are going to Minnesota in May for our first meeting. We are reading some books and are going to discuss them at the meeting. I think we can do this. I think this is going to be great for our financial future.

Phil: You're what? Who's gonna watch the kids? Do you really have time for all of this? Well, I hope this isn't going to consume you, you don't need to add anything else right now.

That was Phil's introduction to the club, and, well, yeah, it's kind of consumed me, but it didn't have to. I *love* it! Here is Phil's take on it after the fact:

> Seriously, I didn't want Karin involving herself in one more thing. I had a career that was pretty demanding, and I needed to depend on her to carry most of the family and household responsibilities. I know it was pretty selfish of me, but she had been doing it all these years, and I didn't think she had time for another distraction. She was still trying to get her master's degree on the side, so adding this investment club stuff was a bit even for me to handle. I just didn't see her needing anything else, and I was sure this was just another avenue where she could go out with her girlfriends.
>
> Now, I realize, I was wrong. I was not wrong in wanting her to cut down on some of her activities, but I was wrong about us not knowing about our investments. In this short amount of time, she has taught us so much, and as an end result, our financial future looks much brighter. I still can't believe some of what we are doing with our money, but it makes so much more sense than what we were doing.
>
> I still wish she would slow down a bit, but I can't complain, 'cause it is actually paying off. I'm very proud of her.

Isn't he just the cutest? From thinking I'm a Chatty Kathy to being proud. Every once in a while, I smirk while I thank him for letting me live in his world.

Jana's life partner, Mac, e-mailed me this:

I'll bet you never in your wildest dreams thought that I would e-mail you about the investment club. You know I was a little skeptical. I was sure that Jana thought investing in the stock market was a game and wouldn't ever take it seriously. But now, thanks to the club, Jana is teaching ME a few things. Now we both discuss what we invest in for our 401k's. She has her way to do her research, and I have mine. We compare notes. (To date we are neck and neck in the Who Got the Better Returns Race.) We discuss what stocks we should purchase for our children, allowing them to grow for college.

The whole club thing seemed a little weird to me in the beginning, just because I didn't get it. I thought it was an excuse to take a trip twice a year. I didn't think you guys would come this far in such a short time. I had no idea that she was going to learn this much and be so good at it. If everyone in the club has this kind of knowledge, you guys are really a success.

Jana went to learn and enrich her life by meeting new people and furthering her education. She has worked very hard and enjoyed all these women. Her knowledge on researching stocks and companies is amazing, and I am proud of her dedication to this club.

Karin, I hope this helps, don't tell Jana because I will never be able to kid her again about these "girls' night out/trips/meetings" again. Maybe one in Hawaii next year with the husbands?

Our newly engaged Chick has a hip, happenin' fiancé, Tim, who e-mailed me this:

I absolutely loved the idea when I first heard it. I supported Kristin 110 percent about joining. I truly believe that more women should learn about the stock market and be able to invest their money wisely. I think what you have all done is fantastic and I wish nothing but better things for you all. I love that you are all getting the word out there.

I have been a member of a stock club for two years now. The way we choose our stocks is a little research by one or two individuals and then we take a vote. A little different than Chicks Laying Nest Eggs. But what I like best is that I can communicate with Kristin about the market, different companies, and planning our future together.

And what did I say about a man wanting an independent and financially secure Chick? Point proven.

Chapter Summary

- O Men are sensitive.
- O They pretend not to be.
- O They hate new ideas, especially if it takes time away from them.
- O They will try to discourage, or at least belittle.
- O Do it anyway. Their big picture comes into focus eventually.
- O Peacock-perky . . . oops, that was the other chapter.

chick chat

TITLE: **MEETING SUNDAY NIGHT
From: Karin

Hey guys, just wanted to remind you that at nine P.M. EST we have our meeting tomorrow night. Here is the agenda:

9:00 P.M. Cock-a-doodle-doo . . . meeting starts.

9:05 P.M. Treasurer's Report—Chick Jeanette

9:10 P.M. Chicken Scratcher's Minutes Need Approval—Chick Jana

9:15 P.M. Assign people to track our new companies. Any takers? We have Pfizer and Coke. To begin with, maybe we should have two people. One does the numbers . . . this requires about an hour every three months. The other keeps us up-to-date on the news releases.

9:20 P.M. We need to discuss where we will have our next face-to-face meeting. Please post which city you would like to have it in and why. What are your free dates in February? (This is the month we decided on at the last meeting.)

9:30 P.M. Discuss future purchase. What companies are you interested in researching? Post to the message boards your choice and why. We will volunteer at this time and assign each girl a company.

9:35 P.M. Adjourn.

TITLE: MEGAN'S WORLD
From: Megan

I know I have been MIA for a while, so I thought I would give you a little update on my situation. A couple of Thursdays ago (these days, that's about as specific as I can get), Kevin signed a hockey contract in Vegas and we packed up some stuff and Kevin and the girls flew out and I drove fifty-two hours with a U-Haul on the back. They put us up at some gross hotel and finally moved us into a slightly better hotel where we remained for ten days. No computer, etc. Soooo sorry! Then we moved into our house and have been here a little over a week, and we are all trying to adjust: McKenna at eighteen months to a big-size bed—which means several trips up in the night—and Lexy starting school and dance, all in unfamiliar surroundings three thousand miles from home while someone else rents out our home in Maine for nickels—which is about what the new salary amounts to! ANYWAY, I will do my best to get my stuff done, otherwise please bear with me as I try to get my feet on the ground. Also, the next meeting is at dinner hour in my new time zone. I will try my best to focus, but I might have to cut up someone's spaghetti. Can you tell I'm streeeeeeeeesssssssed?

ZGhost,
Megan

TITLE: **S&P REPORT
From: Cheryl

First, let me congratulate those of you posting earnings and research! Job well done, gals, and I really enjoy reading it! Thanks so much!

Here is the S&P report ending this week:

Coke (KO) is up 8.25% since date of purchase.
Pfizer (PFE) is down 1.19% since date of purchase.

Portfolio total is up 3.8% versus the S&P 500 totals of 8.86%. So what if we are losing, we just bought. Patience is, patience is, patience is, UGH, I can't remember how that saying goes.

Stuck,
Cheryl

Calling All Friends

*If you want something said, ask a
man. If you want something done . . .*
— MARGARET THATCHER

I have to be honest with you here, I tried four times to start investing
on my own. I got the game of golf down before I could finish reading an investment book. My light was on and I was home, but I
needed Robert Palmer to sing it to me, live. It didn't matter which investment book I had, the effect was the same. I'd pick up the book, start it,
and suddenly I'd get an inexplicable urge to change the sheets on all the
beds in the house, paint the entryway (again), or crack open an ice-cold
beverage. It was overwhelming, and even though the "I Am Woman" in
me knew I was capable, I wasn't getting it done.

It's kind of like the weight-loss thing. Don't even ask me how long I
have been meaning to lose those few extra pounds. Every time I put a
fork to my mouth, I think about Oprah walking out onstage, pulling the
wagon of lard behind her. Yet I still insert the fork.

Aha! I had the solution. One of the big reasons people are successful
with their weight-loss program is that they go to work out at a gym where
there are, you got it, other people. People who are expecting them, friends
they've made there. Not convinced? Then think about Weight Watchers.
They must have made something like a billion dollars off of helping people *help one another* lose weight.

I had to find someone who could support me in this quest for investment knowledge. I had to find my biggest fan, someone who thinks the world of me, someone who does everything I say, someone I could boss around. I asked my little sister. Sure enough, she fell for it. Poor girl, she had no idea what she was getting into.

All Jana and I knew was that we wanted to learn (and that with the next family wedding coming up soon, we could impress the pants off those genius cousins of ours if we could talk about something other than what Britney Spears was wearing at the Grammys). Shoot, we *had* to know a little about the market. Of course we did. We knew something. We knew we could get the freshest organic broccoli every weekend at the farmer's market across town. Could *our* two heads really be better than one? Could ten be better than two?

A club doesn't mean thirty people; heck, you can have four or five if you want. You just need someone besides yourself to bounce stuff off of. You need to be able to ask questions and feel comfortable doing so. If you're worried about whether or not your questions seem too silly, who better to ask than your friends? I wouldn't recommend asking your neighbor the investment guy, he's going to suggest something you should buy, through him of course, for a fee. Ugh, fees, we'll discuss them later: interesting subject, if you like *War and Peace*. Seriously, though, I see only one way for a woman to begin investing successfully—an investment club. I know there are women who have done investing on their own and beat the market, and kudos to those three. Women are social beings. We like people. We like to talk. We like validation of our ideas. With those overflowing plates already in front of us, learning how to invest in the stock market looks like an insurmountable task to tackle alone. Why do it alone, when (start humming here) You've Got a Friend?

We chose to be an all-women club. We were thinking if we are going to be together for the next ten, twenty years, let's do more than learn about the stock market. Let's travel together, have our own golf tournaments, or take Vegas excursions. (Investment Club in Vegas—oxymorons are alive and well and living on the Vegas strip.) We call the twice-a-year trips our annual and semiannual meetings, or that's what we tell our husbands. These are our girls' only getaway retreats . . . with a little stock talk tossed in. Let me tell you, the annual meetings are reason enough for you to start a club. (Wink wink.)

We've had many face-to-face meetings that have left us cracking up hysterically. (Get it? Chicks, eggs, cracking up? I'm sorry, I had to put that joke in this book somewhere or my eight-year-old said he wouldn't dance with me at his wedding.) The bonding may be the best part of an investment club. Have you ever noticed that people are willing to tell you anything about themselves—from their favorite soap to their sex life— before they'll talk about their money? We've discussed everything in our posts or face-to-face, including our money. And a lot of it is stuff we'll never forget, like when Lisa* ever so timidly showed off her new Victoria's Secret "water bra," or when Darlene couldn't stop doing her chicken dance, or when Ann hit the first golf ball of her life. Or those warm, fuzzy moments, like when Corey announced she's getting married or you attended a member's labor and delivery via the Internet. Awww . . . so sweet. (No, there was no video.)

Okay, enough schmaltz. What I'm trying to get across here is that the investing part is easy, but it isn't all you'll get out of a club, and sometimes it's not even the most important part. Be open to any direction your club might take, but make sure it's fun, or it won't last.

Okay, Sure, I'll Start a Club . . . But How?

The most important thing in starting an investment club is to connect with the right people from the beginning. I can't stress enough that the beginning is the single most crucial moment. If not well thought out, it could be the beginning of the end. So when choosing your members, think hard, harder than you did when you took those SATs. The last thing you want is someone who says yes to your club only because it was you who asked them. You want people who are interested in investing, interested in learning about the market, if not downright excited.

---

*Names were changed due to possible embarrassment.

Make a list of ten friends whom you would like to ask. Then rate them on a scale of one to five, one having the most similar beliefs and energy level as you. (Also, put a one next to the best baker in the group. Every club needs a baker.) Phone all of the ones on your list first. These are the people you want in your group, the go-getters, the "I love learning something new and I was just thinking about doing it after I kick up my heels" kind of friends. Call them up and say something like "Hey, I was just thinking about starting an investment club. I have no idea what I'm doing, but I want to learn. I have this book and I think I can get this going. You should go buy it, it's called *Chicks Laying Nest Eggs* and it's worth every penny. I really am interested in learning about the stock market, and I was just wondering if you are too or would like to learn. I'm tired of not knowing a thing, and at every get-together I've been to lately, someone is talking about America Online and their earnings. What the heck are earnings? I want to know what the S&P 500 is, or what the Dow Jones blah-blah-blah is. What do those ticker symbols mean, anyway? I want to form a club with people who are just as interested as I am, but I want it to be fun too. Do you think I'm nuts? Probably, but I'm thinking we can learn a bit about the stock market and get together once a month. Barb is heading up the treats committee, and you know what she can do with a little flour and sugar. Whatd'ya think?"

Rate each person again based on how she answered your initial call. Some will turn you down flat in the first two minutes. Fine. Don't beg. They wouldn't make it for the long haul anyway and would only end up making you miserable. Don't take it personally, and don't hold it against them. It just isn't for some people. They'll regret it after hearing you talk about what you've learned, or seeing people ask you for advice, or hearing through the grapevine about the club's market-beating returns. Not to mention the rip-roarin' trips your club has been taking together. Hold the snickers and tell them they could start their own, yours is already through those infant stages. Did someone say Snickers? Be right back.

Mmmmmmmm . . . 14 grams.

By now your list might have narrowed down to seven or eight. If these people are serious and really excited, count them in. One or two of these super-dee-duper excited friends (I've been watching way too much

Barney) might even mention that she has another friend or family member who is dying to be part of an investment club. Talk to this person on the phone and be the judge of her excitement. Does she really want to commit? Is she really interested in learning about the market or just looking for someone else to invest her money and not do any work on her own? You want people who are fun, bright, exciting, and willing to do their share of the work. You want people who can get along. You want people you like and who you think the others will like. Don't spend hours telling people how great it will be. The people you want are the ones who *know* this is an awesome opportunity and are dying to get started.

As for how many members should be in your club, this is totally up to you. We have ten members and prefer to keep it that way, since everything is easily divisible by ten, i.e., club earnings, profits, and restaurant bills. No need to bring out the calculators in this club.

The only reason to have more than two or three people is to have enough members so the workload doesn't become a burden. The flip side is if you get too many members, you're not going to get to know one another that well. Plus, it gets too easy for some of the people to dodge their share of the work. That means they may not learn what they need to, and that's not what this project is supposed to be all about.

Tip: When making up your list of prospective members, put a bonus star next to the fun ones; they'll get you through any flat market years and, even more important, boring flight layovers.

If I haven't said it enough already, picking the right blend of people will be your most important move in getting your club going. If you have the slightest hesitation about someone, you are probably correct. Someone told me on my wedding day, "If there is anything that bothers you about your fiancé today, don't think that getting married will make it better. It will only get worse." This goes for an investment club member too. So think about it long and hard before asking someone who is questionable. You can't divorce an investment club member, but she can still leave and take part of the cash. Put the thinking cap to good use on this step.

Chapter Summary

O Investing alone is not fun.

O Start a club with friends, but don't beg.

O A club should have the right blend of butchers, bakers, and candle-
stick makers.

O Heed advice given on wedding days.

O Remember the annual meetings.

chick chat

TITLE: MEGAN'S WORLD
From: Megan

Kevin was hit in the face with a slap shot Friday night. He broke his
orbital bone and shattered his zygomatic arch . . . it took two plates and
twelve screws and forty-plus stitches to put him back together. The
doctor said an eighth of an inch higher and he would be dead. He is on
strict bed rest for two weeks (not that he'll notice, he's so drugged up),
so needless to say, I may not be making the Sunday-night chat. Will
read the minutes when I can, but I am doing this on my own, with my
kids, and I am a little stressed. Can things EVER run smoothly for the
Kaminskis??? (Yes, we could pick a really incredible stock and make
millions.)

OnMyKneesPryng,
Megan

TITLE: **S&P REPORT
From: Cheryl

Oh my goodness, Megan! So sorry to hear about Kevin. Yes, things will
run smoothly for the Kaminskis . . . soon, we pray!

Okay, gang . . . here is the S&P report ending this week:

Coke (KO—as in knockout) was up 11.49%
Pfizer (PFE) was up 9.29%
The S&P 500 was up 11.49%
Our portfolio as a whole is up 11.46%. The S&P leads by a hair.

FYI, the baby is engaged and ready to go. I don't know if I can wait much longer. I'm soooooooooo huge!!!!!!

Waddling like a penguin,

Cheryl

TITLE: **JESSE "THE BODY" VENTURA
From: Lynn

Did I type Jesse "The BODY" Ventura? Woops. I meant Jesse "The GOVERNOR" Ventura. Do you think one of us should e-mail him and ask about his latest headlines? Tsk-tsk. And to think he's a Lutheran. Anyway, to make this post worthy of the asterisk, did anyone see that the WWF is going public? Does this work for the "buy what we know" category? I mean, Jesse is our governor. Maybe I'll start watching the stuff on TV to get a feel for it. Nah. Mind if we steer clear of this one?

Lynn

TITLE: **NEXT MEETING
From: Jana

I just got off the phone with Karin. She is trying to see if she can go three days without getting on the Internet. It's her own personal twelve-step program. Instead, she just called me and told me to post this. Would this qualify me as an enabler? Anyway, she doesn't want us to forget about the meeting next Sunday at nine P.M. Megan, she said you were excused. Sooo sorry to hear about Kevin.

Here are the assignments we should all have done by the day before. Research these companies and pull them through the Chicks' Dozen.

Susie—Anheuser-Busch
Lynn—Medtronic

Kristin—Oracle
Julie—Ann Taylor
Jana—General Nutrition Centers (GNC)
Karin—Bebe
Megan—Gap
Cheryl—AOL
Jeanette—GE
Lorene—Abercrombie and Fitch

Flock Frolic

*I'm so excited, and I just can't hide it; I'm about to
lose control and I think I like it.*
— THE POINTER SISTERS

You're ready to take the plunge. You're going to do it, start your own investment club. You have a list of friends who are as excited as you. What's next, Captain Karin? Tell me more! First, get yourself a cup of tea, take a breath, and get ready to schedule your first face-to-face meeting with your Sister Chickies. There's a ton to get done at this first meeting, from discussing how much and how often to invest to deciding on your club's name, but after we walk through what needs to be done, you'll see that it's all stuff that you can accomplish pretty easily. I think that your first step in getting your club off the ground successfully is—I'm a little reluctant to even write it— for you to tell all your prospective members to go buy this book and read it before you get together.

I may be tooting my own horn, honking my own beak, but I'm serious. It really could make a huge difference when you get together for your first meeting if all your members are on the same page, riding the same wave. A huge problem with investment clubs is that each member comes to the club with an opinion about how all this should work, and everyone thinks her idea is the cat's meow. It might very well be, but it doesn't make for a cohesive group.

Trying to start a club when the group hasn't agreed to some basic principles—or at least a notion of the way the group's going to work—is an awful lot like being invited to a card party and not being told what game you were going to play until you got there. You accepted the invitation thinking it was a bridge club, Dori thought it was a hearts party, Chrissie wanted to play euchre, and then there's Katharine, who will play only Uno. It becomes a problem, especially when the hostess has blackjack tables set up, and some of you didn't bring any money.

If you've all read this book, your expectations are on the table before the hand is dealt, no hidden jokers. If some of your friends don't agree with the basic philosophy, they can go start their own club. This doesn't mean that your meetings have to be exactly like the Chicks' meetings, or that your investment philosophy has to match ours; *Chicks Laying Nest Eggs* was meant to be a starting point, no more and no less. From here you can go anywhere you want. If everyone has read this book, it will help move the first meeting along, because you'll all have some shared information. This is especially helpful if the first meeting is, for some of your Chickies, the first time they've met. Let this book be the icebreaker. Here are a couple of one-liners:

- ◊ What do you think of the Chicks' operating procedures?
- ◊ What do you think of the long-term buy-and-hold philosophy?
- ◊ How long do you want to hold a stock before considering a sell?
- ◊ Can you believe they own Cisco?
- ◊ Who's Cisco?
- ◊ What kind of cell phone do you own? A Nokia? I didn't know they were public in the United States.
- ◊ Didn't you think that author was psycho?

Having everyone read the same book helps to get the first meeting going in the right direction, and avoid a *Titanic* mess. (Didn't you just love that little Leonardo?) I apologize for my deep desire to be a best-seller. Seriously, though, you will be ahead of 90 percent of all the other clubs out there. (And most definitely ahead of where the Chicks were at our first meeting.)

Where to Meet

Where should this first gathering take place? Where should you flock together, birds of a feather? (Dr. Seuss is my middle name.) I would suggest that your first meeting, even if you are going to be a computer-only club, happen face-to-face. This way, everyone gets to meet, get a feel for one another, and put faces to the names. If there's ever a meeting that's important to be there for, it's the first one. Even if it means flying halfway across the country, it will be worth your time (and money).

The meeting can be in someone's living room or a restaurant, or you can do like we did and hold it on a pontoon boat. Really, we did. Why not enjoy a meeting? Why not catch some rays while all in the same boat? The two-Chicks-with-one-stone idea. The meeting should be *casual* and set that tone from the get-go. Your members should look forward to the meeting not only for what they can learn, but as a real break from their routine, their girls' night out.

Life is too short to attend another stuffy meeting. Even some of those home parties are a bit much: "Everyone go around the room and tell us a little bit about yourself, your makeup likes and dislikes, how many candles you currently own, and whether or not your plastic containers are missing any lids." I'm sorry, but I can't do another one of those.

Your meeting should have a relaxed, Independence Day atmosphere, not an "open your checkbook and sign away the kid's college fund" feel. I agree that your money is serious stuff, as it should be, but this meeting should be a celebration of your independence. Remember all those teachers who tried to tell you how much fun learning should be? I think they were onto something, especially when what you're learning means that you are no longer going to be a slave to your investment ignorance.

There are a few definite no-nos for meetings. There shouldn't be a conference table in sight. A couch, a coffee table, and a refrigerator make for a successful meeting. (We had life jackets and a cooler, same thing.) A friend of mine booked a suite at a hotel for her first club meeting. They all hot-tubbed, sauna'd (if that's a word), swam, and broke up the meeting over two days. They'll be together forever. Also, be sure to alert the

members—no words can be spoken that contain more than seven letters. (Monotonous, macroeconomics, irrefutable, mastication, and hem-
orrhoid are offenders.) No kids. No excuses. No name tags. And NO, I
repeat, NO brokers. NO brokers.

Now that you've gotten your meeting place figured out and reserved,
it's time to organize. If you are the person in charge of getting everyone
together, you must put a little thought into your first meeting. You need to
have a plan. Women like organization. We follow directions, heck, we even
ask for directions. The agenda from the first Chicks Laying Nest Eggs
meeting is below. Remember that this is only an informational meeting. An
informal meeting where you're going to get to know one another, gather
facts, discuss goals, and divulge investment knowledge (if any). Discuss
each of the points below, but make no decisions. People need to go home
and mull over this stuff before committing. If everyone has time to think it
through, by the next meeting, you will have complete commitment.

Chicks First Flock Frolic Agenda

Get a drink and some snacks before hopping aboard.

1. Introduce yourselves
2. Amount of monthly dues
3. How often to buy a stock
   How often would you be able to invest in the market if you had $25 or
   $50 per member? Discuss different scenarios. How often do you want
   to be able to buy per year? (We spend $1,500 every three months—or
   as close as possible—$50 per month × 10 people = $500 × 3 months =
   $1,500, which we spend on a company that we vote on.)
4. Discuss computer availability for each member and whether she
   spends time on the Internet
5. Discuss investment philosophies
6. Discuss online discount brokers
   Anyone using one already? Anyone want to research them for the
   next meeting?

7. Discuss potential names for your club
8. Drink and dessert break (Lynn's cheesecake with fresh raspberry topping)
9. Membership count

   Is there a limit? Do we want an even ten? Do we want an odd number to break a stock vote tie? Does it matter? Do we need to call some more people?

10. Discuss operating procedures (if time permits)
11. Discuss duties of the officers
    A) President—Head Hen
    B) Vice president—Second Chick in Charge
    C) Secretary—Chicken Scratcher
    D) Treasurer—Egg Carton
12. Next meeting(s)

    Would you like to meet only face-to-face, only online, or a combination of both? What days would work best for people?

13. Adjourn

This simple agenda will help everyone get to know the other interested members and a direction your club would like to go. Some women may not like the chemistry happening, or the philosophy, or the dessert. That's what this first meeting is about . . . getting a feel for the whole idea.

That's it—the first meeting. Not all that difficult, now is it?

Let's look a little more closely at each of these agenda items and where they should take the group.

1. Introduce Yourselves

It's fun to find out who traveled the farthest, but what you really want to hear is what everybody knows about investing. You need to get the members to tell what investment knowledge they have and where they got it. Ask each of them: Who does the saving in your house? What do you want to get out of an investment club?

2. Amount of Monthly Dues

How much do you want to invest and how do you want to do it? There are two ways to approach this.

A) Contribute an equal amount every month.
B) Contribute different amounts every month, depending on each individual's choice.

The Chicks chose option A, and I think you should too, at least in the beginning. Keep it simple. Contribute the same amount, because this makes it much easier to do the bookkeeping, and it also helps each member get the hang of how it all works. In a year or two, the club may become the main source of investing for each member. In that case, each member can decide how much she wants to invest every month (anything from $50 to $50,000), but in the beginning, everyone putting an equal amount in the pot every month works best.

Besides, the Chicks felt that if we all contributed different amounts, it would create an imbalance. If Megan has $20,000 invested in the club and Lorene has $3,000, Lorene may feel that Megan's stock choice carries more weight, which might influence her voting decision or her overall status in the club. At your first meeting, make the decision to each contribute the same amount for the first two years, then the subject can be discussed again at that point.

How much per month? This subject might be touchy, as someone may only want to invest $20 per month, and the person next to her might want to contribute $100. Tread lightly so you don't offend anyone. If you make the amount too small, nobody will care enough to put time into the research and work necessary to make the club a success. On the other hand, you don't want to break anyone by making the dues too large.

The Chicks ended up agreeing on $50 per month. Fifty dollars per person a month amounts to $600 a year, enough money to make the research each month worth it. Add it all up and it means that as a group we have $6,000 a year to invest.

To some members, $50 a month will be like picking up another lipstick or two: not a big deal if it goes missing, there are more in the drawer. How is this club thing going to benefit them if their $600 won't make or break them? Hold your horses, they too have a reason for being a part of the club. For $50 a month, they get an investment think tank made up of their peers; they get to learn step by step *how* to invest their oodles and oodles, then use this newfound knowledge to start their own personal portfolio.

Option B, putting in unequal amounts—as I said above, I'd steer clear of this in the early days, but if you insist, there is investment club software that I will tell you about in Chapter 17 which can help you deal with the accounting.

If making this decision gets sticky, or if you notice that someone in the group is looking a little uneasy at this juncture, suggest that each member write a comfortable amount on a slip of paper (anonymously). Then you can get a general consensus of what the monthly dues should be.

3. How Often to Buy a Stock

First, at this initial meeting, decide *not* to buy a stock for at least two months. It will take this long to open a brokerage account, get enough collective money and deposit it, and to do a little research. Then, after that, how often your club buys a stock will depend on how much each person decides to invest monthly. The unwritten rule is, have the cost of the purchase of your stock be 1 percent or less of the amount you are investing. If you decide on a discount broker (more on discount brokers in chapter 17) that charges $10 to buy a stock, you want to invest at least $1,000. If you are happy with a discount broker that charges $15 a trade, then you need $1,500 to invest.

With a ten-member club and each person contributing $50 a month, getting $1,500 together will take three months. This is how the Chicks do it; it gives us a month and a half of downtime to rest on our laurels, and then we can use the next month and a half to gear up for our next purchase. We invest four times a year, keeping things simple and financially comfortable for everyone, and you should too.

4. Discuss Computer Availability for Each Member

I'm sure that before your first meeting, everyone will have decided the Chicks are so inspirational that they will have already completed all of the necessary steps suggested, how to get online being one. All of your wanna-be Chicks will have a computer and be Internet-savvy. Am I right or am I right?

What? Did you say not yet?

At this point in your first meeting, it's important to be aware which members are online, who is going to get online, who needs help getting online, and who thinks she's never, ever going to get online. There is room for everyone in the club; no need to discriminate against the computer illiterates. If, though, after two years, they still haven't bothered to figure out how to log on, drag their hinies down to the public library, introduce them to the free Internet service, and show them exactly how simple this all is (and it really is simple).

5. Discuss Investment Philosophies

After you learn who is and isn't online, it's time to start the real investment talk. The books I mentioned earlier—anything written by Peter Lynch, Warren Buffet, or the Motley Fool—are great places to start the conversation. Maybe someone in your club has read something else she found informative. Convince her to report to the club about what she's learned. If you've all finished reading *Chicks Laying Nest Eggs,* you could discuss the philosophies summarized in this book. Is this where you want to start? Is the Chicks' long-term buy-and-hold approach one you want to use? Does anyone want to read and report on one of the other books to kick off the next meeting?

Even though all the books and investors I've mentioned so far have a lot that they can teach you, I want to ring the Fool's bell a bit here. The Chicks chose to read the *Motley Fool's Investment Workbook* before our first meeting. It's a basic, easy-to-read financial investment workbook, and even though there's more in it than just the Fool's basic investment strategy, the additional information won't hurt. There's enough in this book to get you started, but if you want to get some added oomph, go the extra nautical mile. Discuss at this time whether you want to do any more reading; if yes, who reads what, or will you all read the same book? It's all up to you!

Now is the time: Are you going to go with the Chicks' Dozen philosophy or wait another couple of months to come up with your own ideas about how and why and what to invest in? It wouldn't be a bad idea to start with the Chicks' philosophy, just to get going, then reevaluate after a year or two.

6. Discuss Online Discount Brokers

There are many good online discount brokers. We haven't gotten to the broker chapter yet, but when we do, you can decide who would like the job of picking your broker and taking care of that business. Have one person in your club (preferably the person who will be your treasurer) research and report at the next meeting which two discount brokers were her favorites and why. There are plenty of places where you can find out other people's experience with the various online brokers —the Chicks Laying Nest Eggs website (www.chickslayingnesteggs.com), the Motley Fool website (www.fool.com), or AOL Keyword: Personal Finance. Your choice may come down to the broker having a local office near your treasurer's house, or the people at the office being especially friendly, or the fact that their website was the simplest to use or offered the best service. (This last one was the reason for the Chicks' choice.)

7. Discuss Potential Names for Your Club

Now the meeting gets fun. I love this part, the high-diving off the ship into the sea of excitement. Naming the baby. Be creative. Be silly. Be original. Be fresh. A couple of the names we threw out were the Laptop Stockettes, the Merlot Only Investment Club, We Are Clueless and Proud of It Investors, and the Investors Need Vegas Every Spring Time (INVEST) club. Chicks Laying Nest Eggs won, though, and it makes for a much better book title.

Just brainstorm into the drink and dessert break and bring a list of choices to your next meeting.

8. Drink and Dessert Break

Get someone else to make you a cheesecake with fresh raspberry topping, we're going to keep Lynn. No other instructions needed.

9. Membership Count

How many people do you want to have in your club? Is this important to you? You don't want too many, because you lose the personal side of the club, but fewer members makes for a tougher workload. Discuss among yourselves.

10. Discuss Operating Procedures

Everyone should have read this book (hopefully *enjoyed* it) and looked over the Chicks' operating procedures. These need to be discussed, not at length because it is a lot to go over at your first meeting, but they need to be reviewed. At our first meeting, we had no idea what kind of guidelines we wanted to set up. Matter of fact, we didn't even know that we needed some. The one thing you *do* need to do and understand is *commitment*. At our first meeting, we ended up signing a piece of paper that looked like this:

1. We commit to a three-year partnership.
2. We will contribute $50 a month.
3. We will invest in good companies for the long term.
4. We will travel twice a year for face-to-face meetings.
5. We will reinvest dividends.

6. We will try to learn something at every meeting.
7. We will diversify our portfolio.
8. And, above all, we will have Fun.

That was it. I look at it now and see that it's no wonder we struggled a bit in the beginning. Go over the Chicks' operating procedures (in chapter 16). Everyone should make notes of what they have questions about or how they would like to change the rules to fit your own group for the next meeting. Maybe you can get it all done at this meeting, but I doubt it. (The Chicks just talked too much or took more than one dessert and drink break.)

Hey, Miss Karin, it wasn't US who talked too much or who had more than one dessert/drink.

Yeah, yeah, whatever.

11. Discuss Duties of the Officers

Now you need to elect officers. Probably the person who had this club idea in the first place should be the president (by the way, you can get creative with the naming of your officers too: I am the president, a.k.a. Head Hen). Your president can appoint someone who she thinks would make a good vice president, and then your other officers could volunteer. You will need a treasurer and a secretary. The treasurer usually deals with the broker. You could also have an appetizer/dessert committee, a club historian, a photographer, and a travel planner. The possibilities are endless. Depending on your operating procedures, these positions could be rotated every year, every other year, or every five. This isn't set in stone, and on my land, I prefer sand.

12. Next Meeting(s)

Where do you want to hold your next meetings? Online? Face-to-face? Do you want to be mostly online, or would you prefer to see one another once a month? Maybe every two or three months? Maybe a girls' week-end twice a year? Our club chose to meet face-to-face twice a year. We wanted to really get to know the members and make these club meet-ings a mini–girls' getaway. (A Scottsdale trip, a Minnesota golf trip, these were all investment club–related, all business.) I would recommend that you meet twice a year in person, at least in the beginning. It helps to keep everyone thinking the same, and to give your club a good strong core. But if you're only going to meet face-to-face twice a year, you need to get those monthly online meetings going.

Then talk about a time and day each month that you will meet via computer. Some groups may prefer to have all meetings in person, which is great if distance and time permit, but you should discuss dates for that too. We have found that it is easiest to always have the meetings on the same day each month, like the first Monday or Wednesday of the month. We chose the first Sunday night of every month at nine P.M. EST (unless it falls on a holiday weekend). Since it is a regularly scheduled event, we have put it in permanent ink in our calendars, and we don't need to wait for a phone call confirming the time or day. Discuss with your club which day/night of the week works best for all of you. You need to find a time that everyone is able to make it. Emphasize during the discussion that after the first few months, your online meetings will take no longer than an hour. The one-hour online meeting is a rule of ours, and most meet-ings are no longer than thirty minutes. In the same amount of time it takes me to dry my hair, I have been to and from an investment club meeting.

Karin, you didn't tell us that you were drying your hair during meetings!

I only did that once, but I had to! I had a Christmas concert to attend right after our meeting. What would the third-graders think if they saw me with dirty, matted, snarly hair?

Face-to-face meetings each month will take a little longer, which is why I like to stay away from them. They seem to generate a lot of chitchat, and folks seem to spend more time straying from the topic. We're women, we can't help it. Many a club has folded because the social chatter at the monthly meetings took more time than the stock talk. If you do meet face-to-face, keep it a policy to get all of the investment-related business out of the way first, then the socializing can begin. The "meeting" part of our twice-a-year face-to-face get-togethers takes at least three hours.

None of this has to be decided upon until your next meeting, but discussing it is a good thing. Before you leave, have your next meeting time and place decided upon. This is the only thing that you need to have done when you leave. Who is coming to the next meeting, where should you have it, and who is bringing the treats? (Priorities.)

When you leave this first meeting, it may seem like you didn't get a lot accomplished, but you did. You are all excited and ready to get going! You have met everyone and know what the goals of this club are going to be. This is the most important step. Everything is easy from here. All you should be doing at this First Flock is sharing your excitement about starting an investment club and getting the logistics of running one successfully.

It's like the first day of school, when you never got a homework assignment. No, you were more concerned with who was in your class and whom you sat by than what the subject was. Enjoy your first meeting, and come back again later in the book for some real homework.

Chapter Summary

- O Tell everyone to buy this book.
- O Get a drink and some snacks before hopping aboard; this ship ain't hittin' any land for a while.
- O Discuss amount of dues per month.
- O Discuss how often to invest.
- O Discuss computer availability for each member.
- O Discuss investment philosophies.
- O Find volunteer to research online brokers.
- O Discuss names for the club.
- O Take drink and dessert break. (Dessert has to contain more than 15 grams of fat per serving. This is required.)
- O Discuss operating procedures.
- O Discuss officers.
- O Adjourn.

chick chat

TITLE: **MY VOTE
From: Megan

I am so flustered! I'm online and not getting my usual invitation into the meeting! I am instant-messaging all of you, and it keeps telling me that none of you are signed on. So either I am totally crazy, or you guys changed the time of the meeting. I snuck away from Kevin for a minute to join our online meeting—I want to vote for AOL—is it too late? HEEEEEELP! Ohmygawd, I am sweating! What is happening?

I'll just post anyway while I try to figure out where you guys all are. Interesting news on Coke, eh? (Thought I should at least TRY to get some investment talk in here, to try and calm me down.)

Cheryl, I can't believe it's your due date! Should I send you some castor oil? Let's start naming her/him. Guess the weight, length etc. At some point, however, we must discuss the Ally McBeal thinness/hemline issue. How high can it go and how thin can one get?

IMJstJelusCzIGtABgButt,

Megan

TITLE: **S&P REPORT
From: Cheryl

Yeah! Two centimeters and counting! Here is your S&P 500 report for this week.

America Online (AOL) is up 2.36% vs. S&P up 1.13% (great way to start our newest acquisition while I sit here like a beached whale waiting for mine)

Coke (KO) up 7.95% vs. S&P up 14.98%

Pfizer (PFE) up 12.86% vs. S&P up 14.98%

Chicks' portfolio up 11.11% vs. S&P 15.05% ("I think I can, I think I can!")

Barely Breathing,

Cheryl

TITLE: CHERYL'S PREGNANCY
From: Cheryl

I'm here! I'm at the hospital, and I'm in labor. I brought my laptop to pass the time. (I'm checking stocks when I get a contraction. Helps me *focus* on something else.) Yikes. Gotta go, this is getting harder.

Soon to be mother of TWO,

Cheryl

TITLE: RE: CHERYL'S PREGNANCY
From: Karin

I just happened to be online when Cheryl was in labor. So hysterical. Here was our instant-message session:

Karin: Hey! Where are you?

Cheryl: I'm in the hospital in labor.

Cheryl: Trying to pass time.

Cheryl: This is no fun.

Karin: OHMYGOSH, I am so excited. Bad pains?

Karin: Did you take drugs?

Karin: How close are the contractions?

Karin: How long have you been in labor?

Karin: What's the heart rate? OHMYGOSH, OHMYGOSH. Where ARE YOU???

Karin: Cheeeeeeeeeeerryl?

Cheryl: Karin, this isn't Cheryl anymore, it's Forry. She threw the laptop at me on that last contraction. I'm gonna sign off now, I have to help her.

Cheryl had a baby girl, 7 pounds 4 ounces, at three o'clock today. Olivia. Welcome, baby Olivia!

TITLE: RE: CHERYL'S PREGNANCY
From: Lorene

Happy holidays and WELCOME to the world, little Olivia! Now we all have a wonderful baby Chick to remember this year by. Do you think she's too young to start investing? Like maybe we could buy her some

Disney or something? How about BabyGap? Warner Bros.? Fisher-Price? (I think they're private.) Who owns Similac? Oh wait, you're nursing—ummm—Gerber? Playtex? Ah, never mind.

Smooches to the baby Chick,

Lorene

8

You've Got Mail

Some of us are becoming the men we wanted to marry.
— GLORIA STEINEM

ou've met. You've decided some things. You have enthusiasm and curiosity and you're ready to take the next step. It's time to get to the Internet! Doesn't that sound fun? No? But you only have a month until your next meeting. Come on, Chicky, let's go! (I'm sure that this is old hat for a lot of you out there, but I'm just as sure that there's someone in your club who still has never heard of the World Wide Web, so bear with her and us. And there may actually be something in here that you don't know yet.)

Oh dear, computers and the Internet have you in a tizzy? No no . . . relax, it will be a rebirth. There is a whole big world out there. I will serve as your Lamaze instructor. Breathe one, two, three, four. Your Web baby will healthy and beautiful. Trust me, I know this. (After four C-sections, I finally figured that it doesn't matter how you get there or how long it takes, it's the end result that counts. Some of us need a little forceps help in everything we do.) It's important to just get to the Internet—any way, anyhow. In this chapter I will take you step by step through the process of getting to the Internet. Puuuuuuuuuuuuuush.

Being online is not required to invest or learn about investing, but it's a time-saver. It's fast and it's smart. It makes communicating both in and out of an investment club so much easier. How many times have you been on the two-minute telephone call that ends up taking an hour? If you get online, you can send an e-mail in about the same time it takes you to flip from Oprah to Rosie. The Chicks all got online because it was the only way we could communicate with each other. We live all over the country and continue to move around. There was no way we could be in a face-to-face investment club unless our daddies owned FlyforLess Airlines. Maybe in my next life.

Even if you are living a couple of miles apart, don't forget about those jam-packed calendars that barely allow you enough time to put gas in the car. Who has an extra three hours a month for an investment club meeting? Not I, said the hen. The best part about being online is that you can hold your monthly meetings over the computer lines. This means you don't have to put on any makeup, squeeze into your Levi's, or even get out of bed. Now that's my kind of investment club. By the way, you can get out of bed right about now, but not before you take a good hard look at those jammies you're wearing. Yikes! Feel free to check out the Chicks sleepwear on our website. (Your neighbors asked me drop the hint.)

Karin, Karin, Karin. Thank you very much for getting me those new Chick pajamas for Christmas, but remember, not everyone is as proficient in this computer language as you are. You can't just throw out terms like e-mail and expect that everyone will understand. It was the hardest thing in the beginning when you were trying to teach me. All those words you kept saying. Now explain things better to the girls reading this.

Yes, Mother, dear. Did I say e-mail? Sorry. I promise to explain what each of those Internet-related terms mean, but only the ones you need to know. There are so many terms that are never going to make it into my day-to-day vocabulary, so why should I pass them on? (Besides, I will always and forever think of Java as coffee and not a computer language.) I won't confuse you with any unnecessary jargon.

You probably already know about e-mail, but I'll tell you anyway, only because a promise is a promise. E-mail is mail—notes, letters, cards, or even pictures or videos—that you send or receive over your phone line and read on your computer screen. (You can also hook up to a cable service, but more on that later. Right now, we're going to keep things simple.) You receive them only a few seconds after the sender has sent them.

It's so amazing, so simple, so fun . . . and how it all happens still baffles me. But it's not important to figure out *how* it all works. What is important is to just get online, send your first e-mail, and get Chicky with it.

By saying or using the terms "getting online" I mean having a computer and getting hooked up to the Internet. It is the *only* way our club would have survived.

When people ask me what the key ingredient to our club's success has been, I tell them the truth—our IQ. (Why do I get so many blank and disbelieving stares when I say this? Is it not possible that we all have extremely high IQs? Leave me alone, people.)

To us, IQ stands for Internet Queens. If only I could say it was something different, like we are all magna cum laude Ivy League graduates, or that we only allow Mensa members, or we inherited tons of money from our relatives aboard the *Titanic* . . . but none of those would have kept us going, either. The only reason we have been this successful is that we are all online. The point is, we're living proof that you don't need to have an intelligence quotient higher than your bowling score in order to be a successful investor. And you don't have to be a geek to make your computer the key tool in your investment success.

Getting online has so many advantages for an investment club (not to mention the gazillion other personal benefits) that if you're serious about saving time and making some money, this is your best bet. Here are the benefits:

1. Immediate access to a company's financial statements instead of having to write to the company's investor relations department and wait for a reply.
2. Access to press releases and articles on any company you're interesting in investing in.
3. You can create a message board where your club members can post information which is consolidated in one place.
4. You are able to hold your meetings on the Internet, which allows each member to attend without ever leaving home.
5. You can buy your stocks through an Internet broker at a deep discount.

6. You can track your group portfolio and have all the facts and figures available to everyone twenty-four hours a day.

Benefits of Being Online

Immediate Access to a Company's Financial Statements

Each quarter (four times a year), a public company is required to report their earnings to the SEC (Securities and Exchange Commission). These are made public to the individual. BTI, Before the Internet, the only people who had immediate access to these financial statements were the big brokerage houses. You were at their mercy if you wanted any information on a company's sales, debts, assets, et cetera. But now, ATI, After the Internet, this information is available to you whenever you want it, out there in cyberspace. There are many places on the Internet that contain this information—all for an immediate free click of your finger. A few of the Chicks' favorite websites are www.marketguide.com, www.msninvestor.com, and www.fool.com. (And, of course, now we all use our www.chickslayingnesteggs.com.)

Immediate Access to News on a Company

If there is an article on your company, or a news release about one of your portfolio holdings, you can find it on the Internet. It's like going to the public library and asking your librarian to bring you all the documents written about General Motors in the last six months. She will tell you to come back next week, when she will have a stack ready for you. If you are online and want to research General Motors, you simply search for General Motors articles or news releases, and you will have your results in a matter of minutes.

Message Boards

This is just about the most exciting thing I have ever found on the Internet. (Next to Amazon.com, which is an online shopping bonanza for me.) Message boards are to your club like a diary is to a teen girl, each day having a different topic. Our Chicks Laying Nest Eggs message board's main theme is our club's activity. We talk about things like where our next face-to-face meeting should be, what is happening with our different companies, what new companies we should look at, who owes monthly dues, and what is our favorite kind of mascara. Sometimes we even use our message board to vote for a new company. It does not always happen that every girl can make a meeting, so the board holds their proxy. If you get right down to it, a message board is like a big bulletin board where we can all post (that's why we call each message a "post") or pin up messages for everyone else in the group to read, comment on, argue with, or otherwise respond to.

For example, if you have a message board on your refrigerator and you posted a note that read like this:

Dad—Take Georgia to the groomers for a shampoo. She's out of dog food, too. Thanks!
Kim

When you came home after running some errands, there was a reply to your message:

Kim—I bought you the car for a reason. You do it.
Dad

Family Fenders—I bought the dog food (as usual) and made an appointment for Georgia on Tuesday. I expect you'll have dinner ready when I get home.
Surprise me, Mom

That's how the ongoing conversation works. Now apply that principle to your investment club.

I have included some of the very valuable information from our message board between chapters. Mind you, it isn't always stock-related, but it is investment club–related. It is like our own little soap opera, available when we want to read it. Susie reads it at three A.M., Kristin reads at five P.M., and Julie reads it at seven A.M. We communicate with one another on our message board. Imagine being at a face-to-face meeting and having to listen to everyone talk about the companies they are following. It's nine P.M. and you're tired. You are in no mood to listen to Lynn talk about Pfizer's gross margins, the new drug they are putting on the market, or to all of their news releases of the past month. You are falling asleep. You still have to wrap your niece's birthday gift before you see her in the morning. You want to go home. With a message board, Lynn gives her sporadic reports on Pfizer when she gets them, and the other members are able to read them at their leisure.

Sometimes the small talk at face-to-face meetings can be too much. Come on, we're women. It's expected. But it can get annoying if everyone goes off topic often, and you want to get the meeting over in a timely fashion for once. We do include "girl talk" on our message board (some of us are chattier than others), but no one is forced to read it.

There are many other message boards on the Internet. They run the gamut, from a diary on a specific company to an odd hobby. For example, Nokia investors should keep up with the Nokia message board, where they post only about that company and its goings-on. You can find specific boards on companies on the various websites: www.aol/finance.com, www.fool.com, www.yahoo/finance. There are message boards for the beginning investor or for the financial whiz. Across the Internet there are message boards for those who are quitting smoking or for those interested in the craft of scrapbooking.

Message boards are like going to a worldwide conference on whatever you're interested in and hanging out with people with exactly your interests. Message boards contain a cross section of people contributing information. You have the sixty-five-year-old grandmother in Yuma, Arizona, and the eighteen-year-old at Buffalo State College, both giving their opinion on Southwest Airlines and its service. Obsessives and customers aren't the only ones who weigh in on these boards. Many employees and even some top-level executives like to pop in and out to keep readers informed about what's really (or what they want you to think is really) going on in the company. I'd say this is better than listening to any financial adviser sitting behind a desk. (Sorry, Steven.)

Hold Monthly Meetings on the Computer

This is explained in further detail in the next chapter. We have our meetings one night a month for about a half hour. Our attendance is excellent, which you can't often say for face-to-face investment clubs. (Not to mention I don't have to get in my freezing-cold car in the middle of winter and drive twenty minutes to someone's house, sit there while she tries to get her kids to bed, struggle through a meeting where only half the members have braved the storm, and then go out to the car, which now won't start.) This reason alone should be enough to get you online.

One of the problems with face-to-face investment clubs is that they either turn into a social outing where nothing gets accomplished or end up being a boring lecture. Neither one of those sounded interesting to the Chicks. If Linda decides to go on and on about her Christmas vacation in her message board post, I don't have to read it. I can skip right over the part where little Ashley meets Mickey Mouse. But how do you politely tell her to shut up when you are sitting right next to her? When you're online, nobody has to know how rude you really are.

Our monthly meetings truly don't take very much time. We have our set agenda, stick to it, and save all the small talk for the message board. Some months we get so much accomplished on the message board that we actually cancel a meeting without missing an ounce of information.

Can I interject something? You say we save all the small talk for the message boards. Excuse me? Is it not I who always has to crack the whip and tell us to get a move on during a meeting? Karin, isn't it you who is constantly spitting out hockey scores in the middle of the meeting? "Phil has the puck. He shoots! He scores! They win in overtime!" Our meetings would take twenty minutes if YOU would stick to the agenda and quit watching your TV.

No, Julie, you can't interject.

Buying Stock from an Online Discount Broker

A discount broker allows you and your club to purchase a stock over the Internet for a cheap-cheap-chirp-chirp fee. They run anywhere from zilcho to $25. (This is the actual transaction fee, not the cost of the stock.) You can purchase a stock and pay that little for the middle man? How can that happen? Only on the Internet. More on discount brokers later in the book.

Tracking Your Portfolio

One of the things that can be a little frustrating for an investment club is keeping track of what you own, how much of it you own, and its daily value. In offline investment clubs, usually just the treasurer holds all of this information. If you wanted to know how your portfolio is doing, you'd have to call the treasurer, interrupt her dinner, and get her to find it for you. Then, after her tedious work, it would all change the next day when the market opens. Ugh. Who knows how many times the treasurer is asked to do this each month; after a while, you feel like you've become a nuisance, so you just stop calling. (Or she has caller ID and stops answering.)

When you get online, there are many places that you can track your portfolio. These places tell you how many shares of each stock you own, what you bought it for, how much it is worth today, what your percentage of change is, and how all this compares to the S&P 500. (This is all available at www.chickslayingnesteggs.com.) I hate to admit this, but computers are better at tracking financials than are most human beings. (Keep in mind that the human programmed the computer, so we can take some credit.) When you put your portfolio online, you get up-to-the-minute changes and how they affect your returns. These can be cross-referenced with your online broker so it is very difficult to have any accounting mistakes. Your broker also has a portfolio value at the end of the day. Do you have an online broker yet? Tsk-tsk. You're on my list.

Have I won you over? Does it make sense to get to the Internet? Come on, Mrs. Flintstone, come out of the Stone Age. It's time. Our dinosaurs don't bite. Wiiiiiiiiiiiiiiiilllll-maaaaaaaaaah!!!!!

How Should You Get There?

Phone Lines, Cable Lines, and Bottom Lines

There are three ways to get online—through your telephone lines, your cable lines, or satellite transmission (those little Frisbee-looking things attached to the outside of your house). Right now, this is the order of their popularity too, but cable is quickly catching up to the phone. I'll give you all three scenarios and their costs, then you decide for yourself. You are Woman now, remember?

If you are going to get to the Internet through your phone line, you will need a computer. Egad, I said it, the "C" word. Breathe. Inhale, exhale, inhale, exhale. It'll be fine . . . a seven-pound bouncing baby computer.

Some of the Chicks have desktop computers, which are bigger and sit and *stay* on your desk. They are a little bit cheaper than laptop computers. Laptops, or notebook computers, you can pack up and take with you. Most of us have laptops because the desk is either covered with laundry or doubling as an island in the kitchen.

Almost any new computer you will get today is Internet-ready. You just plug it in, click on an Internet service provider, and away you go. What on earth is an Internet service provider? Maybe this will help—it's also known as an ISP. Make sense yet? Relax, I'll explain in a couple of paragraphs. No need to take notes; you'll find these terms at the end of the book in the glossary (page 263).

Part of getting our club going was explaining all this to my sixty-something-year-old mother. We needed her, or we wouldn't have bothered. She had never even been on a computer, so we had to start from scratch. Now she handles all of our stock buying and selling . . . online! She was fluent (with what she had to be fluent with) in only a month! Bring it on.

What Kind of Computer Should You Get?

(Stay with me here just a bit longer.)

There may already be an Internet-ready computer somewhere in your house. Do you have teenagers? Then you may be able to just add an

Internet and an e-mail account for yourself onto the family computer. The problem that the Chicks have found is that this whole thing is like a bag of Oreo cookies—you can't be satisfied with just one. If you get really involved—and you will—you're going to want your own computer, your own online accounts, and your own time and space. Since we all know we'll never get all that, let's just settle for the computer.

Whatever computer you buy will be obsolete the day you buy it. What that means is that your boyfriend or your husband or your teenager will look at it and say, "Yeah, that was cool . . . back in the day." You do not need the coolest computer. Buy last year's technology—or something less than the hottest thing in the store or on the website—and you'll have something that should last you for years.

What we're doing doesn't take a lot of computing horsepower. E-mail, Web surfing, word processing: these things don't demand much of the machine. There's one thing that you should spend money on—your monitor (the TV screen, for you complete innocents). Do your eyes a favor and get the biggest and brightest screen you can afford. When you're buying your computer, ask what software is included (or "bundled") with the computer. Think of the added extras when you buy a car. You could buy your new minivan stripped down to the basics, but for a tacked-on fee, you could get an automatic transmission. Or, for an additional $300, you could get power steering. How about the whole power package—power steering, power windows, and power brakes for $800! You go, girl! Then, for a just a few more added-on bucks, you could have the whole entertainment package: CD player, thirteen-inch installed TV, Sony Playstation, DVD player, and Surround Sound. That would be nice. You decide what you will need.

With your computer, you're going to need a word processor, an Internet navigator program (i.e., Netscape or Internet Explorer), and an e-mail program. A word processor will allow you to type up letters or create invitations. It isn't absolutely needed, but on most computers, it is standard. The Internet navigator program will help you explore the internet. And with your new computer, you will want to be able to send and receive e-mail. Those are the basics. Once you get accustomed to using those things, you can decide if you want your computer to play videos, balance your checkbook, store your digital photo album, or do any of the thousands of other tricks that it's capable of doing.

Software is a terrific bargain when it comes along with your computer; it gets horribly expensive (and confusing) if you have to pay retail at the computer store.

Finally, it doesn't matter whether you have a Mac (an Apple) or a PC (an IBM PC compatible, a.k.a. Wintel or Windows computer). The great thing about the Internet is that e-mail doesn't care what kind of computer sent it or got it—text files are always readable. And the Internet doesn't care what kind of computer you use to do your research—it delivers the same information to everyone in readable, usable form.

I personally own a couple of Dell PCs. I shouldn't be pushing Dell, but I just did. I've had the most success buying from them and using their computers, not to mention the ease of their setup, and their customer service is superb. I have done business with some other computer manufacturers and haven't had such a swell experience. Okay, I don't really own two (tail now between legs), I have three. You won't find a Dell in any store. It is only a mail-order company, which, as a bonus, eliminates driving to the store and talking about computers with that guy who has a pierced tongue. Ouch.

Dell's 800 number is: 800-WWW-DELL, (800-999-3355 or 800-578-3355). I recommend Dell to my friends. Not all of them listen. Here's what some of them have bought; these are, in our collective opinion, very good companies:

Compaq: 800-888-9909
Apple: 800-MY-APPLE
Gateway (mail-order only): 800-846-4208 or 800-GATEWAY

When buying your computer, here is all you have to say: "Hi, my name is Wilma, and I want to buy a laptop (or a desktop). I want it mostly for home use. I want to be able to get on the Internet with ease and I want to be able to do that e-mail thing. I want it for a few other things too, like balancing the checkbook, typing up some letters, and inputting my address book. I want it to be cheap, as in not cost me much, I just lost everything but the kitchen sink buying lottery tickets and I don't have much left over for a computer, but I should get a computer and start investing. What money do I have left to invest? Just never you mind. Even my kids are better at this computer stuff than I am, they have computers at their school, you know, and I just feel it's about time I learned what was going on with that. What kind of computer do you recommend I get?"

You see, buying a computer is simple.

When you buy a computer with a built-in modem (which will most likely be recommended to you once you mention that you want to get to the Internet), you will be using a phone line from inside your house to get connected to the Internet. A modem is the thing that actually dials a telephone number from inside the computer, then communicates with the computer on the other end of the line. If you don't have two phone lines, it can sometimes be a pain in the rear when you need to talk on the telephone and be on the Internet at the same time. Two phone lines are crucial if you have kids who want to check their e-mail right after school at the exact same time you are waiting for your husband to call on his way home from work so you can tell him to pick up dinner again.

The computer still serves many purposes when it isn't surfing the Internet, but it might help to get two phone lines because you know how your mother hates busy signals.

Internet Service Providers

I'll make this short and simple. Basically, an ISP is a company that can get your computer from sitting on your desk like a hunk of cheese to moving and shaking on the Internet. (There is a disco at the end of this chapter, kind of like the monster at the end of the book. Read on, Pebbles.) An ISP is the middleman, the bridge from your computer to the Internet. There are good middlemen and there are average middlemen. They will all get you there, but some are faster than others. It's like taking a Greyhound bus from New York to L.A. or letting your hair down and cruisin' in the fast lane in a Lamborghini. Some bridges take the more scenic route, but in the end, they'll all get you there. The more expensive the toll, the more goodies they'll provide for the trip. Isn't that how it always is? Whatever happened to the People's Express airline, anyway?

Route #1: The Phone Line

There is one Internet service provider that is the leader and has become a household name. America Online, or AOL. At the moment it uses your telephone line to get you to the Internet. (This is all subject to change, as they are merging with Time Warner, and cable access is in their future.) When I first got online, I didn't go with AOL and I wish now that I had. I thought I'd save a few bucks and go with the local guy. It ended up costing me a lot more time whenever I would get online and do anything. No one has ever said I was the brightest Chick in the coop.

AOL is simplest for beginners, and if you have a question, it seems like everyone and their brother is on it. Wait, he is! Your brother is online right now. Instant-message him and tell him I said hi! Oh sorry . . . we aren't that far yet. I'll tell him you said hello and that you would like it if he would have Thanksgiving at home next year. His kids are brats.

AOL is the most popular ISP in America, with millions (I don't want to say exactly how many millions, because by the time you read this, it will be twice that) of subscribers, including my mother. The bonus with AOL is, they have local telephone numbers everywhere, so you can hop online even when you're in Webster, Wisconsin. (Note: If you're reading from Maine, you guys have to do something about that private phone company system you got going there. AOL ends up costing me tons when I go to visit my good friend Megan.)

Now there are other Internet service providers in your area; they have names like Mindspring, Erols, Juno, and MSN. There are tons, too many for anyone to research, and too many for me to mention. AOL is number one, and the one that the Chicks started with. You don't all have to be on the same ISP to communicate, you just have to agree on where you'll meet on the Internet, and where you'll have your message board.

ROUTE #1 TOTAL TRIP BILL

(all figures approximate, like the weight on your driver's license)

Computer	$600–$2,000
Installing another phone line	$75.00
AOL (or other ISP) per month, unlimited use	$21.95
Second phone line per month	$15.00

Don't forget that there are always coupons in your newspaper for installing a second phone line for free, or at least at a discount!

Thank you, Mother. (She's a coupon monger. Always looking for a bargain, that Jeanette. Too bad I didn't inherit that trait.)

The phone companies also offer another option. Can you believe they offer an alternative to themselves? Who hit them in the head? Their other service is called a digital subscriber line (DSL). This is five times faster than a regular phone line for only twice the price per month ($40–$180). It was their answer to the super-fast cable lines.

Route #2: The Super-Fast Cable Lines (Able to Leap Tall Buildings in a Single Bound)

Another way to go online is through your local cable company. Cable is like getting to the Internet via a Concorde jet. Many of the cable operators now offer Internet service through companies like @Home and RoadRunner. This option is looking better every day and doesn't have to involve the costly investment of a computer. Although if you already own a newer computer (or are buying a computer that is newer than three years old), it is probably cable-ready. My Dells are. Yes, it is true, I use both America Online and @Home as Internet service providers. I'm living proof that no one can eat just one potato chip.

When you go this route, you're accessing the Internet through the cable lines. The cable company will hook up a cable modem to your computer that runs through their cable lines. Installation fees for cable modems are about $99 (figured in below). You can still watch TV while using your computer, and your daughter can talk on the phone to Jimmy for the eighth time today. Everyone is happy. (If this isn't a teenager's heaven, the television, the phone, *and* being online, what is? It's a wonder they have any time left over to ignore us.) This is still pretty new, but it's very exciting. Not all the cable companies offer it yet, but more and more are.

Call your local cable company and ask if they offer cable Internet access. Wait, what am I thinking: This is a "please show me how to do it" book. Dial the phone, and say this:

"Hi, this Betty, and I'm a customer of your cable company. What? You want my phone number? Why? I just wanted to ask a question. Fine. Bedrock-1234. Well, I was just wondering if your cable company offers Internet service? You do? Great. How much is it going to cost initially and how much per month? Do you have to lay any new cable lines or anything? Should I use my own computer or do you have computers that I can use? How fast can you install, because I have my first investment club meeting next week. Really? Cool. I'll be here waiting with bells on."

Within days, you will be surfing the Web. Oops, another idiom. The Web. Stay tuned . . . definition to follow.

ROUTE #2 TOTAL TRIP BILL
(all figures approximate, like your golf handicap)

Computer	$600–$2,000
Installation fee	$99.95
@Home per month (added to existing cable bill)	$39.95

Route #3: Beam Me Up, Scottie . . . The Satellite Dish

I am sitting in New York City right now, in a hotel that offers WebTV. WebTV gives you Internet access through a satellite dish. I have never used it before in my entire life. What are the chances of me being at this point in the book and being presented with WebTV at the same time? Someone is watching over me.

First of all, it is so cool. You use this little portable keyboard just like the remote control. I am sitting on the hotel bed reading my e-mail up on the TV. There are no wires or anything, just a keyboard in my hands. Freedom.

If you are looking to get to the Internet, surf around, and only send e-mails, this is the way to go. There is no hefty computer expense and you don't even have to find a desk or table, much less any room for it. You use your existing television with a keyboard about the size of a, well, a keyboard.

WebTV also uses your existing phone lines. The satellite dish dials up your Internet service provider for you but uses the call waiting function on your telephone to let other calls get through while you are surfing the Web. The speed of WebTV will be as fast as your phone line service allows, so there would be no speed difference between WebTV and dial-up access. The drawback to WebTV is that you can't print any of the stuff you see on your screen. If you find a great article in Forbes Magazine Online, you either have to read it on your screen or take a picture of it, get it developed, enlarge it, and *then* bring it to bed. Also, you can't do anything else that a computer can, like write letters, download documents, or install software (games included). Download is when someone sends you a picture of your cousin Rachel in an e-mail. You must download it to look at it. When you download, you are gathering particles of information from cyberspace and installing them on your computer. When they come back together on your computer, voilà— Rachel! The sender's computer has uploaded them for you to download. With WebTV, you don't have the hard drive (brain) of a computer that stores all the pertinent particles to download, because you don't have a computer. You would have to go without seeing the picture of Rachel, and anything else that needed to be downloaded, saved, or printed.

You can get WebTV at 800-GO-WebTV.

ROUTE #3 TOTAL TRIP BILL

(all figures approximate, like your high school grade point average)

Installation fee	$99.95–$199.95
WebTV per month	$21.95
Call waiting per month	$6.95

	Cable	Phone	DSL Line	WebTV
Computer cost	$600–$2,000	$600–$2,000	$600–$2,000	—
Installation fee	$0–$99.95	$75.00	$0–$75.00	$99–$199*
Monthly service	$39.95	$21.95	$39–$189*	$21.95

	Cable	Phone	DSL Line	WebTV
Monthly fee for additional phone line	—	$20.00	—	$6.95
Total monthly charges	$39.95	$41.95	$39–$189	$28.90

*depending on your area

The World Wide Web

Woo-hoo! You're almost there. You have the hardware (again, that's your computer) and have chosen your ISP, but what's next? We're off to see the wizard, the wonderful wizard of . . . sheez, pardon me, we're off to the Web, the World Wide Web.

The Internet consists of websites. Put together a lot of websites from around the world and you have the World Wide Web. Websites all have addresses like www.chickslayingnesteggs.com, or www.dell.com, or www.yahoo.com. Each website contains whatever kind of information its owner chooses to put out there. To get to a website, type in its address in the blank provided by your Internet service provider. There is so much on the Web that I could go on forever, but you'd fall asleep and never get to the disco. (Yes, I said disco. Just wait. It's a surprise.) The Internet is just something you have to play with, or "surf," for a while and see what types of things interest you. You can do anything from getting a college degree, buying a new car, listening to a radio station across the country, watching a video, or planning a trip to Wall Drug in South Dakota. Don't forget to pick up that bumper sticker. It'll look great on your new little Bug. Please no! Not the Bug. Keep her clean.

Websites come in handy for an investment club when you want to research the stock market and companies you want to invest in. This has opened a whole new world for personal investors. You no longer need to wait for an investment adviser to tell you which companies are the best to invest in, then pray he knows what he's talking about. You can find the good businesses all on your own and get their financial statements at the same time Wall Street does. There are a ton of financial websites with daily updates and articles on every business on the stock market. Since the Chicks have already weeded through some bad ones, I'll give you the Web addresses for the crème de la crème later in the book.

Are you still with me? Pat yourself on the back, take a break, put the book down, and go kiss your kids. Don't they grow way too fast? I was just thinking that my baby is already two years old, and by the time you read this, she'll be three. From my fingers to your eyes, my baby has aged a year. (long pause)

Sorry, what was I saying? Oh yes, the World Wide Web. It really is that easy, almost as easy as changing a diaper, and much more pleasant. Well, that's a great example. Okay, how's this: it's as fun and easy as putting on your dancing shoes and boogying the night away with John "I wanna seduce you on the dance floor" Travolta. That's what I said, baby, Johnny Travolta. You guessed it, how perceptive of you. You have just entered the Funky Chicky Discotheque, shimmering ball and all.

Soundstage Direction (Brothers Gibb music plays loudly)
    Ah, ha, ha, ha, stayin' alive. Stayin' alive.
    Dance yourself into the kitchen, grab a glass of water, and come on back.

Chapter Summary

0 Getting to the Internet makes sense because you can:
    1. Access a company's SEC filings
    2. Access immediate news releases and articles
    3. Create message boards
    4. Have monthly meetings online
    5. Use discount brokers
    6. Track your portfolio
0 Decide if you want to go phone, cable, or satellite.
0 Be an IQ.
0 Get your hardware (the computer).
0 Make the call, Chicky!
0 World Wide Web needs a Wizard.
0 What shall you wear to the disco? Don't forget your headband.

chick chat

TITLE: DAYTIME EMMYS
From: Karin

I just got done watching the daytime Emmys. How silly am I . . . but it's addicting. I mean, Rosie, Oprah, and Erica Kane all in the same room. Too much. Anyway, somewhere in the middle of the show, they were announcing someone REALLY important—you know, like the president of the Academy or something. I should have been paying attention, but I was too busy ironing. (I wasn't really ironing, I was dishing up ice cream, but ironing just sounds better.) So, by the time I settle in with my Cookies and Cream, I see everyone in the audience standing up and applauding this man. Get this: THE MAN IS MY NEIGHBOR! The man who talks with Phil about hockey and with the kids about what fish they're catching; the man who invites us out on his boat. I am this close (put finger and thumb real short distance apart) to the Academy.

How long do you think it will take me to get my soap opera career off the ground now?? Gotta run . . . I need to borrow some sugar.

Logan

TITLE: **CISCO IN VEGAS
From: Lynn

Is anyone thinking about our next purchase? (Karin, don't worry about it, I know you're busy flying back and forth trying to become a daytime soap star.) Anyway, I am thinking that we should buy Cisco. Have you seen their ads? Technology goes mainstream. I didn't know that the whole Internet runs on Cisco. (In my simple language.) I am running the numbers and am going to do a little presentation on them in Vegas. So excited to see all of you girls there!

By the way, even though we are an investment club, we do get to do a little gambling, don't we? We don't have to tell. Remember our motto, "What is said and done at investment club meetings, stays at investment club meetings." Smooches,

Lynnie

TITLE: RE: **CISCO IN VEGAS
From: Julie

I am not going to Vegas if I can't play some craps. I'll listen to your thing on Cisco, and I'm still voting for the Gap, but I can be bought.

Julie

TITLE: VEGAS
From: Jana

Hey, I was just curious . . . if we are going to Vegas, does anyone know if Wayne Newton is playing anywhere? I remember when we were kids I got kicked out of Circus Circus for playing the slot machines. When I went outside, I saw a billboard saying that Wayne Newton was playing somewhere. I swore to myself that I would come back to Vegas someday as an adult, play the slot machines, and go see Wayne Newton.

TITLE: VEGAS
From: Jeanette

Who's Wayne Newton?

TITLE: **WAYNE NEWTON AND S&P REPORT
From: Cheryl

First let me express my shock that you don't know who Wayne Newton is, Netty! He's MR. LAS VEGAS and has been around for quite some time!

When I was five years old, my parents took me to see him at the Circle Star Theatre (was that the billboard, Jana?). He was singing the song "Red Roses for a Blue Lady" and walked out into the audience, grabbed my hand, and took me up onstage! I remember being absolutely mortified! (I was so shy then.)

As for the S&P Report, ba-da-bing-ba-da-boom . . . we're beating the S&P! We're up 55.84% compared to the market's 28.27%. Here is how all of our stuff is doing:

AOL up 104.43% vs. 9.97% (market during same time period)
KO up 2.19% vs. 25.03%
PFE up 29.11% vs. 25.03%

Cheryl

TITLE: RE: **WAYNE NEWTON AND S&P REPORT
From: Karin

"I remember being absolutely mortified. I was so shy then."

Don't let Cheryl fool you—it was the biggest day of her life. That feeling she got onstage, well, she absolutely craves it. I, too, happen to have a funny story about Wayne Newton.

I remember going to Cheryl's wedding rehearsal dinner a few years back where I saw, to my surprise, this pair of child's go-go boots on the buffet table. What were these, I asked? Well, Cheryl's mother proudly explained, "We've saved them all these years . . . those were the boots Cheryl wore when she went onstage in Vegas with Wayne Newton."

Don't believe the shy and mortified crap.

Karin

TITLE: RE: **WAYNE NEWTON AND S&P REPORT
From: Cheryl

I wish I had more time to defend my shy self here, but between these two children under the age of two, I'm swamped. I'm even skipping the S&P report this week. We're holding our own. Go AOL. I'm afraid I can't bring the boots to Vegas to show you—my mom covets them—but I was a pretty hot number back when I was five. I do have a new pair that I own now (my thirty-four-year-old version). I'll bring them. Do you think there is a birdcage I can climb into in Vegas?

Cheryl

Stock Market Main Course

Why don't you write books people can read?
— NORA JOYCE TO HER HUSBAND, JAMES

Did you enjoy the appetizers? Need a napkin? You have a little something there on your upper lip. Over to the left. Yeah, right there. You got it. Now, all that stuff in the previous chapters about calling your girlfriends, tiptoeing around Mars, meeting the Chicks, and getting to the Internet was just a small snacky-poo—an hors d'oeuvre. (I think I pronounced that word "horse-duver" for years.) You ready now for your main course? I will be serving a filet of beef (with the fat cut off) and au gratin potatoes. I'm going to warn you right now, it's a lot of food, but don't worry, you're ready.

In this chapter I'm going to tell you why you should invest in stocks instead of mutual funds, treasuries, or bonds. I'm going to teach you what a stock is and where you can buy and sell it. By the time you're done with this chapter, you'll never again wonder what the NASDAQ is, or try and figure out if the Dow Jones Industrial Average has something to do with baseball. You will understand what folks mean when they start talking about bull or bear markets. The next few pages are going to give you all the basics you'll ever need, so pull your chair up to the table, say grace, and let's get cooking.

90

Why Invest in the Stock Market?

This one is plain and simple. Over the last millennium that people have been investing in the stock market, the S&P 500 (the market) has had an average return of 11 percent. There is no place else in the world where you can put your money and get that kind of consistent return.

Karin, Karin, Karin . . . stop. Explain the word "return." You had no idea that a return could be anything but the reason you recycle your Diet Coke cans for five cents until you joined the Chicks. Now you throw that term around like an old pro. Explain, please.

Ooops, sorry. Return. Return the ball, Martina, it's not in my court! Well, she said I was an old pro, and I love tennis—oh never mind, bad joke. Wall Street uses the word return in another way. Instead of saying, "What was your profit off your investments last year?" they say, "What was your return, or rate of return?"

Return is your profit over a time period. This number is expressed as a percentage. If I invested $1,000 in a company by buying its stock, and at the end of the year that stock was worth $1,100, that would be a 10 percent return. How'd I do that? (To be honest, the first time I typed this, I put in that it was an 11 percent return. I mean, it looks like an 11 percent return. This is the reason I am not doing our club's accounting.) I think we will go over a few number problems just for *you* to get the hang of it. Go wipe the dust off your calculator and let's do some rate-of-return problems.

Problem #1

How do you calculate the above problem, because it sure as heck looks like 11 percent to me.

Answer: Take the total worth of a stock today minus the price you paid for it ($1,100 − $1,000 = $100). Then divide that number by the price you paid for it ($100 ÷ $1,000 = .10). To change a decimal to a percentage, you multiply by 100 (.10 × 100 = 10 percent). Voilà . . . your answer is 10 percent. I swear I could do this without a calculator if my brain didn't occasionally cramp up on me.

Problem #2

If Sandi bought stock in Home Depot (HD) at the beginning of the year for $52 a share, and today she is going to sell it for $63 a share, what would her return be?

A. 81 percent
B. 21 percent
C. I dunno

Answer: Take the price the stock is trading at today minus the price you paid for it ($63 − $52 = $11). Then divide that number by the price you paid for it ($11 ÷ $52 = .21). Then change the decimal to a percentage by multiplying by 100 (.21 × 100 = 21). DING DING DING . . . the answer is B, 21 percent.

Problem #3

Suzanne, my literary agent, owns a couple of stocks that she bought right after she made a ton of money off me by selling my book. She owns equal amounts of Home Depot, Nokia, and Microsoft. Here is what her portfolio looked like at the beginning of the year, and what it looked like at the end of the year:

	Beginning of Year	End of Year
Home Depot (HD)	52	63
Nokia (NOK)	68	120
Microsoft (MSFT)	91	101

What was her portfolio's return for the year?

A. 211 percent
B. 35 percent
C. I don't care and I can't find a calculator

Answer: Let's do the math (52 + 68 + 91 = 211). This is what her stock prices were at the beginning of the year. At the end of the year they were worth (63 + 120 + 101 = 284). Then we subtract the beginning of the year from the end of the year (284 − 211 = 73). Then divide this answer by the beginning-of-the-year totals to get the decimal percentage change (73 ÷ 211 = .3459). Multiply this by 100 to get it in percentage form (.3459 × 100 = 34.59 percent). Rounded up, that's 35 percent! Way to go, Suzanne! A Chick through and through.

One last example and then we'll move on.

Problem #4

If a train is traveling east at 68 mph and didn't see the oncoming train on its track going 42 mph, where will the survivors be buried and at what time?

I absolutely hate word problems, not to mention I absolutely *hate* math, but if you can get through this, you too can use the word "return" with confidence.

The Real Problem #4

Suzanne's husband, Tom, won the lottery ten years ago and now writes books for a hobby. He put all of his winnings into the stock market and hasn't checked on them since. He needs some help because he is going to sell it all but needs to know his capital gain percentage for his latest horror story. His books are very good. He bought these four stocks:

	Amount Invested	Amount Worth Today
Coke (KO)	$2,500	$15,258.98
AT&T (T)	$2,500	$4,187.85
Philip Morris (MO)	$2,500	$4,200.44
General Electric (GE)	$2,500	$24,273.26
Total	**$10,000**	**$47,920.53**

What is his total percentage gain? (This is not including any dividends that the companies might have paid. Dividends are the little bonus checks they send you for owning their stock. Tom spent all of that on typing paper.)

You got it, right? You are a pro. Steffi, let me introduce you to my friend

Andre. Andre, this is Steffi. Well, if you didn't get it, the answer is 379.21 percent. Go back and try again before you peek at the solution. Here is the answer: $47,920.53 − $10,000 = $37,920.53. Divide that by $10,000: 3.792053. Change to a percentage by multiplying by 100: 379.21 percent.

Equities

For goodness' sake, Karin, another word you throw out there just to see if anyone blinks. What the heck are equities?

Well, give me a minute, I just started!

The first time I heard the word equity I was sitting across the desk from Banker Guy with Bad Hair. Phil and I were selling our first house. He asked how much equity we had in our home. "I'm not sure," I replied. What was he saying? How much equity? Equity, equity, equity . . . AaaaGggHHhhh!! "I'll have to get back to you on that, I'll check when I get home," I said. I had no idea what he was talking about.

"Equity" means the value of your property less debt. Simple as that. "How much equity do we have in our home" means the same as "How much money do we have invested in our home and what is its value? How much would you walk away with if you sold it?" That is equity.

Why would I bring up the Bad-Hair Banker Guy story? Because people also use "equities" when referring to your investment portfolio (especially men, who, once they find out you are investing on your own, will want to see how much you really know about what you're doing—so be prepared). When they say, "What equities do you own?," use my rule of thumb and just exchange "equities" for "investments." Even though it doesn't mean exactly the same thing, it works. Just pretend that your Bad-Hair Banker Guy said, "What investments do you own?" and answer accordingly.

If you want to be exact, equities are the value of your shares, or the value of your investments. Please tell me I was not the only one who didn't know this.

The second question Bad-Hair Banker Guys usually ask is "Have you diversified your equities?" To diversify means to expand or branch out;

diversifying your investments simply means you own stocks from more than just one company or industry. For example, if you were to expand your portfolio, you could own stocks in clothing retail, technology, pharmaceutical, the Internet, or any other business that you could find a stock for. We'll talk more about diversification and portfolio management later, but I just wanted to give you the ammunition in case anyone does try to intimidate you with all the fancy jargon. Remember: rate of return means profits, and equities mean investments.

Karin, could we get back to why the stock market is the best place for your money?

Why certainly, let's do that, but first let's look at some alternatives to the stock market to get a feel for what else is out there.

Mutuals, Treasuries, and Bonds . . . Oh My!

Now that you know how to figure the return on your equities—by the way, your new vocabulary is impressive—where should you invest your money? Mutual funds, bonds, or U.S. Treasuries? Can you say lions, tigers, and bears? Oh my! Let's take a look at their history before you decide.

What Are Treasuries?

There are two types of treasuries, Treasury notes and T-bills, and I hate to bore you, but we have to explore them a little. These are what the pros call "fixed-income securities." What that means is that the United States government is borrowing money from you and promising to pay it back sometime in the future with interest. They are both issued through the Department of the Treasury (hence, Treasury securities) and are backed by the full faith and credit of our government. Stop giggling. You loan them money via a Treasury that you buy from them, and a guaranteed amount (see where the "fixed" comes from) is paid back to you when you sell it. Profits from these securities are exempt from any state and local taxes, as they should be when you lend money to Uncle Sam.

Treasury Bills—Also known as T-bills. T-bills are short-term, highly liquid investments from the U.S. government. You purchase this type of security and sell it back when it matures, anywhere from three months to a year. They are sold at a discount and return to their full face value at maturity.

Treasury Note—These are the same as above but have a longer maturity term. When you buy this type of security, you are paid a fixed rate of interest every six months, and you get the full face value of the note when it matures. Maturity ranges from two to ten years.

They sound great, don't they? Uncle Sam paying *you* interest. There is a catch, though. Think about it, our stock market has returned an average of 11 percent per year, and U.S. Treasuries have returned an average of 3.3 percent per year. That statistic alone should be enough reason to steer clear of Treasuries. Eleven percent kicks butt. But to add salt to the wound, over this same period, inflation has grown at 3.3 percent. Now, let's think about this. If you invest in U.S. Treasuries, you get an average return of 3.3 percent, equal to the increase of your cost of living due to inflation. Nothing gained. I'm going to rule that one out as a future investment, and so should you when you are thinking long-term.

Corporate Bonds

If we look at corporate bonds, they, too, lose out to the stock market. A corporate bond is a long-term promissory note between you and an issuer (a corporation). They agree to pay you the face value of the bond over so many years. Let's say you bought a bond for $100 and CorporationChic agreed to pay you $115 at the end of three years. It is guaranteed when the bond matures, and you can receive sporadic interest payments over time.

Over their history, bonds have returned an average of 4.5 percent per year. The stock market has returned 6.5 percent more per year than a bond. (11 percent − 4.5 percent = 6.5 percent . . . see, the math is getting easier.) No-brainer. If I were to put all my money into the S&P 500 Index fund (remember, this is the fund that gets you a small piece of all five hundred companies and mimics the S&P 500), I'd consistently be beating both bonds and U.S. Treasuries, year after year. Let me see, lions, tigers, and bears, or the yellow brick road? The stock market is where I want to put my money to have it make me the most money. Now let's look at the most popular investment vehicle of the twentieth century—the mutual fund.

Mutual Funds

I cannot count on all my fingers and toes the number of times I have heard "I only invest in the safe stuff, the mutual funds. I wouldn't want to play the stock market. Too risky for me."

It makes me want to throw up.

Five years ago, I was saying the same thing. What I didn't understand is, you don't *play* the stock market, you invest in it. Sounds stupid, doesn't it? But it's a distinction that too many people don't make. Investing in the stock market is more like putting money away in a savings account called the Pepsi-Cola Company, or Home Depot, than it is like betting the bank on whether red or black comes up on the roulette wheel. But to many people, the market still seems like too much of a gamble. The thing is, if you pay attention, do a little homework, and stick around for a while, the only sure way to lose is to miss out on all the fun.

Sure, there are companies that are risky, and there are people who prefer to gamble with the risky stocks, but we won't be touching them with any ten-foot poles. We don't have time for that, and we wouldn't want to put our money in that much jeopardy. We have enough other things going on in our lives causing anxiety attacks. Our investing philosophy (and believe me, you're going to hear all about it) is long-term, low risk, and allows us to play with our families instead of our portfolios.

Fee-fee-fee-fum: I Smell the Blood of a Fund-ish-man

The mutual fund industry is built on the premise that you *should* be afraid of the market, that it's too big, too complicated, and too risky for an amateur like you. Mutual fund managers (or their ads) have brainwashed us into thinking that the stock market, invested in alone, without their help, is going to confuse us and eventually break us.

Baloney.

They need us to invest our money with them because that is how they make a living: by selling us their product and charging us fees. There are fees charged to manage your portfolio, fees charged when you buy a fund, and fees charged when you sell a fund. They are called expense fees, front-end load fees, or back-end load fees. On top of all those fees, you are automatically charged a 12b1 fee, anywhere from .5 percent to 2 percent annually, just to run the fund. If you hand a $1,000 check over to a financial adviser, don't assume that you are investing $1,000. You aren't.

All that would be fine, and that's what I told myself for years, if they were getting a better return than the S&P. But like I said, 90 percent of all mutual funds *underperform* the S&P! Do you think the coach of a professional football team will continue to have a job year after year if his team misses the play-offs? Would an actress continue to get work if she kept flubbing her lines? (*Baywatch* is a whole different story.) Yet mutual fund companies continue to skew the numbers in their favor (freedom of speech lives on television), consistently underperform the market's average, and instill a fear in us that to be safe, we need to invest in mutual funds. Their message: the stock market is risky, and mutual funds are the smart, safe way to go.

There's a reason it's so hard for mutual funds to beat the market, and it's something you'll never see in one of their wonderful television commercials: mutual funds are made up of stocks. Each fund by law must be made up of no more than 5 percent of any one stock. So that means a fund has to have at least twenty different companies in it (20 × 5 percent = 100 percent). That is required.

Let's look a little closer at what this means. If we were setting up a mutual fund company, we could probably find the biggest twenty companies in the world and put them into a mutual fund and call it The Twenty Biggest Companies in the World Fund, but once we sold all the shares in this fund, what would we have left to sell? If you have no product, you don't make a commission. We'd have to make up another mutual fund, say one called Ten Good Businesses and Ten Risky Businesses Without a Tom Cruise in Sight Fund. More fees to charge, and the mortgage in Tahoe can be paid. How about this one: *Ten Lottery Tickets, Nine Small Businesses, Eight Good Companies, Seven U.S. Treasuries, Six Corporate Bonds, and Five Golden Rings.* Cha-ching, we got ourselves a new car and a partridge in a pear tree. That picture's getting real clear now, isn't it? (Stop singing now.)

The simple fact of the matter is that there are over nine thousand different funds ready to be sold to you. There can't be enough great companies out there to support this many funds, right? Stop the insanity!

You don't have to take the bad with the good. You don't have to buy the lottery tickets when you only want the golden rings. You can weed through all the companies quite quickly and buy only the cream of the crop without a mutual fund manager and *with no fees!* Individual investors, folks like us, are not subject to the same restrictions that fund managers are. Our portfolio can be made up of as many or as few stocks as we want. You could have all golden rings if you wanted. You see, some freedoms work in our favor.

Why are there all these funds, and why is everybody giving them their money? A great philosopher, John Locke (I know he is related to me somehow, even though I can't seem to find any written documentation of it; Locke was my maiden name, so I just know I have to be, I mean, how could I not be, don't you see a resemblance in thought process?) once said, "New opinions are always suspected, and usually opposed, without any other reason but because they are not already common."

Hence my theory about the case of the mutual fund. Everyone has them. They are popular. So you try to introduce something different, like investing in the stock market on your own, and you're going to get a few disapproving looks, if not some resistance. People would prefer to stick with what is common. "Follow the pack and be safe" kind of thinking. Ask yourself, though, why were Pokémon cards so huge? Because everyone had them. They aren't necessarily the smartest investment, or even a very fun toy. The same goes for Beanie Babies, Tickle Me Elmos, and Cabbage Patch Kids. Everyone wanted them because everyone had them. No one really knew what the huge attraction was, they just had to have them.

I can think of several ideas in history where people were slow to change or believe a new idea. The world is flat, man will not walk on the moon, and we will not have a personal computer in our home. It's time you broke the mutual fund mold. Be a leader. Be smart. Be a Chick.

Why and How a Company Sells Stock

Let's say the Chicks started a business called Henny Penny's. We sell things from toothpaste to coveralls for Farmer Joe. Business is good in Ames, Iowa, so we open another Henny Penny's in Waterloo. You can't keep the customers away. Within a few years we have eight stores across the country and are ready to expand some more, but we need cash. We decide to look for private investors. We find someone, a venture capitalist, who has some extra money lying around and likes our company. He will invest in us in exchange for part ownership of our company.

We agree that he can own 20 percent of Henny Penny's, and we divide up the company into a thousand (a random made-up number) shares. We sell him two hundred shares for an undisclosed amount because we are a private company and don't have to tell no one nothin', and the Chicks keep eight hundred shares. His shares are called preferred stock, which is what private investors own. (Sometimes the public is let in at this juncture, but not often.)

After three more years, business is booming. We can't even keep our Chick weather vanes in stock. We decide to expand further, but we need more money. We will take our company to the people and go public. We find ourselves a brokerage house, Barney and Sons, who will help to issue our common stock, which the public can buy.

We want to raise $3 million. Someone at Barney and Sons would divide the $3 million needed by the number of shares to be sold. He could decide to sell three million shares at a dollar each, or three hundred thousand shares at $10 each. Either way, Henny Penny's will get its $3 million, so it doesn't matter which option is chosen. Say he chooses the $10 price. Barney and Sons would set a date for Henny

Penny's common stock to be sold on the market. It is called their initial public offering, or IPO. At the end of the day, Henny Penny's has their $3 million, and the public owns three hundred thousand shares of stock. Now let's just hope the Chicks continue to succeed so at the end of the year each share is worth at least $12. (Chicks *have* to beat the market.)

The Stock Exchanges

When Barney and Sons goes to sell shares of Henny Penny's stock, they have to do it on a stock exchange. This is the place where cash is *exchanged* for stocks. Compare it to a swap meet. (One of my favorite swap meets is in Los Angeles at the Rose Bowl. Whoa, baby, you can exchange your cash for luggage, antique furniture, and faux Gucci watches.) But if you want to exchange your money for a stock, you have to do it on a stock exchange.

The different U.S. stock exchanges are the New York Stock Exchange (NYSE), the American Stock Exchange (AMEX), and the National Association of Securities Dealers Automated Quotation (NASDAQ). Each of the exchanges has requirements your company has to meet before you can sell your stock at their swap meet. The main requirement has to do with their market capitalization.

Market Cap

First, market cap is short for market capitalization, and easier to say, too. To figure the market cap of a company, you take the number of shares out in the public (outstanding), or owned by the public, and multiply it by its trading price that day. On day one of Henny Penny's going public, it had three hundred thousand shares outstanding. Now multiply that number by its trading price of $10. Henny Penny's market cap is $3 million! Let's do a couple of market-cap multiplication problems:

1. Imagine that Coca-Cola Company has 2.5 billion shares outstanding and is trading at $47 per share.

$$2.5 \text{ billion} \times \$47 = \$117.5 \text{ billion}$$

That means Coke's market cap is $117.5 billion. (Needless to say, these aren't the exact numbers.)

2. Imagine that The Gap has 870 million shares outstanding and is trading at $37 per share.

$$870 \text{ million} \times \$37 = \$32 \text{ billion}$$

That means its market cap is $32 billion.

One more problem.

3. If, at the end of the year, Henny Penny's shares are trading at $12, what would its market cap be?

Bravo . . . $3.6 million. 3 million × $12 = $3.6 million.

Get it? Got it? Good.

And just for you extra-credit hounds:

4. If the train had stopped within three feet of the oncoming train traveling at 42 mph, would it have halted on the north or south side of the border?

Have you ever heard someone say, "Most of my investments are in large caps"? For years, all I could ever reply was, "Wow, you must have a really big head." Behold the new me, and now, the new you. Companies are grouped into micro-cap, small-cap, mid-cap, or large-cap, depending on their market capitalization. Everywhere I turn, there is a different classification chart, and this is probably because the big companies keep getting bigger, or because Internet companies have thrown the whole charting thing out of whack. It doesn't really matter whose chart you use, as long as you know the basic order. The large-cap stocks, also known as the blue-chip stocks, are companies with at least a $5 billion market cap; mid-cap would be $500 million to $5 billion; small-cap, $150 million to $500 million; and micro-cap, below $150 million. Henny Penny's is still a micro-cap, but give us time, the sky is not falling.

Market Cap at Each Exchange

Now, back to our three different exchanges. The New York Stock Exchange (NYSE) is the biggest and the oldest of the three exchanges, and it's located in . . . duh, New York. It's on Wall Street in Manhattan. To make the NYSE, you have to have at least 1.1 million shares of your company outstanding and a market cap of at least $18 million. Henny Penny's is not listed here. Some of the companies that are listed on the NYSE are Wal-Mart (WM), America Online (AOL), Home Depot (HD), and General Motors (GM). Companies are identified on the NYSE by ticker symbols (the letter combination used to represent them). The NYSE tickers contain one to three letters.

The second biggest of the exchanges is the NASDAQ, which isn't located in a city, so you can't physically go watch the wild and crazy guys in suits running around with pieces of paper flying out of their hands. All the stocks listed on the NASDAQ are traded over a network of computers. Buying and selling is just a mouse click away. Most of the stocks listed on the NASDAQ are technology-oriented, like Microsoft (MSFT), Cisco (CSCO), Yahoo (YHOO), and Amazon (AMZN). NASDAQ ticker symbols contain four letters to identify the company. To be listed on the NASDAQ, you must have a market cap of $75 million. If your market cap dips below $50 million, you can be delisted. But wait—if you can't meet that requirement, the NASDAQ gives you another option. If you have at least four hundred shareholders, outstanding stock worth at least $1 million, assets totaling at least $6 million and $1 million in pretax income, they'll let you in. (You can reread that if you want to, but you don't really need to know it.)

The third and the smallest of the swap meets is the American Stock Exchange (AMEX or ASE). To be listed on the American Stock Exchange, you need to have at least 250,000 shares outstanding and a market cap of at least $3 million.

Indexes

The only way I can think to explain indexes is by using an old wives' tale. You aren't going to find this comparison in any Wall Street book, and I

guarantee you, they will think I'm a crazy woman if you tell them. Pretend you are pregnant. I said *pretend!* For months, you are dying to know
what the gender of your baby is, but you don't want to find out for sure
because you'd rather guess for nine months and be surprised. Instead,
you try every old wives' tale in the book to try and determine the gender. Are you carrying high or low? Are you out front or pregnant all the
way around? If you pee in some Drano and it turns blue, it's a boy; pink,
a girl. Maybe you would string a ring over your belly, or swing a needle
from a thread over your wrist. In the same pregnancy, using all of those
tests, I had four boys, four girls, and an alien. So what if it's silly; it's fun
to indulge during a baby shower so you don't have to talk to your second
cousin from Kansas City.

Anyway, the most popular of the old wives' tales is the heart rate. If
the heart rate is above 140, it's a girl, and below 140, a boy. I'm not saying this is fact, so don't go painting the nursery, but it's one of the tales.
One-forty is the benchmark. The Heart Rate 140 would be the standard
index. It's the one everyone knows and uses. Every pregnant woman
compares their baby's heart rate to the 140 Rule. It's the accepted and
most popular "Guesstimating the Sex of Your Baby" Index. It's the S&P
500 of the pregnancy market.

S&P 500

The S&P 500 Index gives us the same benchmark for the stock market:
something to track everything else against. Remember, the S&P is the
most popular of the indexes because it combines the top five hundred
companies in the United States and averages their daily weighted
worth. The stock market has many different indexes for guesstimating
the gender of your baby—I mean many indexes for tracking different
industries.

The Dow

The Dow is made up of the thirty largest-cap companies in the U.S. It's
very similar to the S&P, only instead of five hundred companies, it contains only thirty companies, such as Sears, McDonald's, and IBM. The
average worth of these companies is called the Dow Jones Industrial

Average (DJIA). I have to add that there are a few other confusing things weighed into the average of these companies, but for simplicity's sake, think of the DJIA as averaging the market cap of each of the thirty companies every minute of every business day. You'll find it on your cable finance channel in the little ticker box in the bottom corner. Both the Dow and S&P averages are reported live in that box daily. It doesn't matter which one you want to call the market, it's up to each individual: the Dow Drano Test, or the S&P Heart Rate. Or you can report on both. Twins!

The Russell 2000 and So On . . .

The index that tracks the smaller companies is called the Russell 2000. It averages, yep, you guessed, two thousand of the small-cap companies across the U.S. Then there is the Wilshire 5000. It averages, get this, six thousand U.S. companies of any size. Do you think Mr. Wilshire had few too many cocktails? There are so many indexes out there to compare your portfolio against, each one measuring a different sector.

You can use whatever index you want, but it's best to compare apples to apples. You shouldn't compare a stock portfolio of large caps to the Russell 2000. On the other hand, tracking an index is helpful; for example, if the NASDAQ 100 (Index tracking top 100 stocks of the NASDAQ) has had a better return the last few years than the Dow, you might want to consider adding one of those stocks to your portfolio.

Here is the average annual performance of these five indexes as of December 2000:

Index	Tracks	1-Year 1999–2000	5-Year 1995–2000	10-Year 1990–2000
S&P 500	500 Large U.S. companies	10.33%	16.42%	14.84%
The Dow	30 Large U.S. companies	6.18%	16.08%	15.14%
NASDAQ 100	100 Stocks from the NASDAQ	39.29%	18.62%	20.78%
Russell 2000	2,000 Small U.S. companies	4.20%	8.80%	13.85%

At the end of each day, you will hear your newscaster announce that the Dow and the S&P were either up or down (and they don't always do the same thing). You might want to stick around and watch, so you'll have to skip taking your makeup off until after the news is over. Again, the number reported is just the average daily fluctuation of that index. You are a genius.

Bull or Bear?

One last market vocabulary lesson, and then I'm going to bed. You might have heard people talking about a bull or bear market. A what? Bull or bear? What do they mean by that, and why use the beastly animals?

Picture a bull in a fight with another bull. Which way are his horns going? Exactly. He is thrusting them upward. And how about a bear in battle, what is he doing with his paws? He is batting them downward. Aha, a bull market is one that goes *up*, and a bear market is one that goes *down*. You know it had to be a cave*man* who came up with those terms. A woman would have come up with names like a manic market when it's up, or a PMS market when it's down.

Matter of fact, let's just stick with that. Heck with the bull and the bear, we will call it a manic or PMS market. Wall Street usually uses these terms when talking about the market over a long period. There were a few PMS years followed by five manic ones. Okay, okay, the caveman would say there were a few bear years followed by five bull. Or they might say the future looks bullish. But listen up, Chickies; we say the future looks manic. They say Black Tuesday, we say Manic Monday. You say tomato . . .

Hey, my news is on right now, and I want to see what kind of a market day I had, manic or PMS, so would you mind if I went and watched it? I'm afraid my jokes may get worse if I continue; this happens when I get tired. Thanks. I'll continue in the morning.

Good night.

P.S. It was manic.

This chapter deserves a detailed summary—it was a lot of food, and I'm afraid if someone mentions the words "mutual fund" to you, it will all come back up. Get some water and Pepto-Bismol, sit down, and relax; it's all tied up in a neat little package below:

Chapter Summary

○ Stock market returned an 11 percent average over its history.

○ Return = interest over set time period.

○ Equities = investments.

○ Treasuries, bonds, and mutual funds . . . take a sip of the Pepto right now.

○ Ninety percent of mutual funds do not beat the market.

○ Invest in stocks: this is my final answer.

○ John Locke is related to Karin Locke Housley (this is the only reason I would quote a *male* philosopher in a woman's investment book: he's my uncle, and I *will* find proof someday).

○ Preferred stock is for private investors.

○ Common stock is for public investors.

○ IPO—initial public offering—first day the stock goes on the market.

○ Stock is sold on an exchange: NYSE, AMEX, or the NASDAQ.

○ Market caps: micro, small, mid, large (a.k.a. blue-chip).

○ Indexes are used to track a section of the market.

○ Bull—manic; bear—PMS.

---

chick chat

TITLE: PHIL'S ACCOMPLISHMENTS
From: Karin

Hey guys! I was going to copy and paste a couple of articles here from the newspaper, but I think that might be infringing on some copyright laws. I just wanted to tell you that last night Phil became the all-time American point leader in the National Hockey League. That's like for ALL of the NHL's history. You are catching me in one of my proud moments, when I actually forget about my soap opera career. It's times like this that you want to say Wayne who? (That's Gretzky, Cheryl, not Newton.) Seriously, though, Phil's so dang humble that someone has to post about this moment. Seems like he just started yesterday, and it's been eighteen years! I had all the kids there, and we of course beamed. (If only I could have bought stock in him. Oh wait, do four kids count as dividends?)

Karin

TITLE: **MEETING MINUTES
From: Megan

Way to go, PHIL! YIPPPPEEEEEE from the Kaminski clan! I'm doing the minutes this month 'cause Jana was so sick in Vegas that I took over. Is a tipsy Megan better than a feverish Jana? You be the judge. Also, I want to apologize for getting the meeting minutes to you a couple of days late—but it was worth it. It was Kevin's first game back in the lineup after the broken face . . . and guess what? He scored a natural hat trick! Yippee! It was pretty awesome—it's not exactly Phil's accomplishment, but hey . . .

AsProudOfMyHsbndAsKrnIsHrs,
Megan

Oh wait, I almost forgot to post the summary of the Vegas meeting. Must have been all that time I put into thinking of that one-word sentence.

Vegas Meeting Summary

○ Jeanette gives a Treasury report, and Cheryl gives the S&P report.
○ Chinese food is then passed around.
○ Discussion about our Coca-Cola stock lagging behind the market. Lynn wants to sell. Lynn goes to the bathroom. In her absence, we quickly vote to keep Coke. Lynn comes back, she is informed about our decision and continues to state the reasons why we should sell Coke. We let her go on for a while. We get her off the subject and onto Cisco. She gives a Cisco report. Julie adds to it. Lynn makes a

motion for us to buy Cisco. Julie seconds. We buy Cisco. Lynn is happy. She forgets about the Coke.

0 Did you get that? We voted to BUY Cisco!

0 We discuss our operating procedures again. Cheryl talks about her mother's investment club and their procedures. We adopt some of their rules. Motions are made and seconded by I can't remember who. But they were, really they were. We need to adopt some meeting rules. This wingin' it (get it?) is for the birds, not CHICKS. Put on the agenda for next meeting and post your thoughts to the message board.

0 Discussion ensues about ten women in one house, and how is it that nine are menstruating at the same time.

0 Company reports on Coke, Pfizer, and AOL. Nicely done, Chick Megan (me), Chick Jeanette, and Chick Lorene.

0 Discuss how to get news releases from the wire services.

0 Lorene paints nails.

0 Gifts handed out by Karin, wine and Chinese food spill on carpet, Jana has a fever and barely speaks, and Julie wants to play craps.

End of face-to-face meeting

10

Banking on a Philosophy

Life is either a daring adventure, or nothing.
— HELEN KELLER

B efore we got together for our first meeting in Minnesota, we were mostly Virgin Investor Chicks (great name for a club). We had no idea where to start the purchasing process. How do you pick a stock? Where do you begin to find a "good" company? What were going to be the club's criteria for picking a stock?

We knew how to pick some things, say, hairdressers. You know you don't select a hairdresser unless he or she meets a few qualifications— i.e., has done at least one person you know, charges a reasonable price, is no more than thirty miles from your front door, and your girlfriend's hair doesn't look like she just got out of bed (unless she's going for that female rock-star look). Okay, but how could criteria for a hairdresser help us weed out the great stocks from the mediocre or risky stocks? Where could we start looking for the good ones? Within thirty miles?

At one of our earliest meetings, we decided to look at a few of the different investment philosophies that were developed by masters of the field—Warren Buffett, Peter Lynch, and Tom and David Gardner (The Motley Fool). Each one has his own investment philosophy and criteria. By the end of the chapter, you will get the same overview of some great investment approaches that we developed in our first meetings. They will prepare you to weed through some real stocks, tossing aside the bad and keeping the good.

Sister Chick Susie reported on Warren Buffett and his investment approach at one of our meetings:

Warren Buffett

Born December 25, 1946, in Pascagoula, Mississippi, Mr. Buffett achieved notoriety with his second (released) album in 1973, which featured a song called "Why Don't We Get Drunk." But it took the Top Ten song "Margaritaville" to turn him into a pop star—

Oops. That was Jimmy Buffett . . . cult icon.

Chick Susie is not usually this humorous, she must be sipping one of her Kahlua and milk drinks. On to the real stuff, Suse.

WARREN BUFFETT'S PHILOSOPHY
By Chick Susie

Warren Buffett is arguably the greatest investor of all time. If you had invested $10,000 in Berkshire Hathaway (a stock fund that he owns, runs, and makes available for purchase to the public) when he took over in 1965, you would have about $22 million today. That's over 25 percent per year! He's proof that it's possible to consistently outperform the market. Sure, you're thinking, his stock-picking prowess made him a billionaire, but how can that help a Chick, and what does it really mean to me?

I guess the club could just invest in Berkshire Hathaway, make it simple, let Warren do the stock picking for us, and buy a small piece of his prowess. If we decide to buy shares of his Berkshire Hathaway; what are they going for today—um, $60,000 a share? Holy high stakes, Batgirl! I think we opt for plan B.

Well, what do you know, Warren offers a plan B—a Berkshire Hath-away B stock. (He split up his Berkshire fund into smaller parts so it could be affordable to the public again.) It trades in the neighborhood of $2,000 per *affordable* share. Hmm, that isn't all that appealing either.

Maybe we should invest in the companies that Warren invests in, get an idea what Warren's next stock pick for his Berkshire is going to be, and scoop up that stock. Man, this is not possible either. Why? Because the SEC (Securities and Exchange Commission) allows a one-year confi-dentiality period for large investors who buy less than 5 percent of a pub-lic company. Don't ask me why, that wasn't my assignment. That means we won't know until the year's up what companies Warren is investing in or buying. By then, it's old news for our inquiring minds.

With all these options depleted, let's just try and learn to think like Warren Buffett, get into his head and learn his investing style. It will help us to form our own style or philosophy, and once we do, we can look at some of his companies and evaluate them based on our own criteria.

Compared to Peter Lynch, it's difficult to learn from Buffett. Lynch writes books designed to help you invest, whereas Buffett keeps his invest-ing techniques to himself. Sly dog. Typical male. Hoarder of prowess. He authors only his annual reports, which are quite interesting, available on the Internet, but too much for the beginning investor to start with. Don't attempt to look at one until you have the whole investing thing down for at least a year. When you read it then, you will be shocked by what you know and understand.

Several authors have tried to explain his formula for success, and part of my assignment was to read these, so here is my bibliography—of course, out of place (don't tell Sister Theresa, my ninth-grade English teacher).

The Warren Buffett Way and *The Warren Buffett Portfolio,* by Robert Hag-
    strom
Buffett Step By Step, by Richard Simmons
Buffettology, by Mary Buffett

And this is what I've learned so far:

1. Buffett is a long-term investor. He has said that you should invest in companies that you would feel comfortable with even if the markets closed for a few years and you couldn't sell.
2. Buffett views investing as buying a piece of a business, rather than buying shares of stock.
3. Buffett focuses on well-known companies with strong growth prospects and often with a strong international presence.
4. Buffett looks at the following factors and considers them important: return on equity; changes in operating margins, debt levels, and capital expenditure needs; and cash flow. (Author's note: these are explained in the next chapter.)
5. Buffett prefers to hold a few great stocks rather than many good stocks. He thinks most investors misunderstand the nature of risk and the need for diversification.

It sounds pretty simple to me, but isn't there enough of his prowess to go around?

Some of the companies that Warren owns stock in and made part of his stellar returns for Berkshire Hathaway are:

○ GEICO (discounted car insurance which I have carried for years)
○ American Express (I never leave home without it)
○ Coca-Cola (I'd like to buy the world one)
○ Walt Disney (I have almost every video)
○ Sears
○ Dean Witter
○ Discover
○ McDonald's
○ Gannett
○ The Washington Post Company

From one stock-picking guru to another: Peter Lynch. Chick Cheryl adores him, so she got the honor of reporting on him. Take it away, Cheryl!

PETER LYNCH . . . A ROOSTER WHO THINKS LIKE A CHICK!

BY CHICK CHERYL

Okay gals, I was assigned to research Peter Lynch. We've all probably at least heard of him, but some still may be asking, just *who* is he? I bet you've seen him before without even knowing it. He's that Andy Warhol–looking guy who does the print and television ads for Fidelity Investments.

Peter Lynch is arguably one of the most famous and most successful mutual fund managers *ever*. During his tenure as manager of Fidelity's famous Magellan Fund, some of his stock gains were worthy of *The Guinness Book of World Records* (no kidding!).

All that fame and fortune aside, any man who can make comparisons between stock picking and pie baking, or the stock market and dieting, is a man who can get my attention . . . and thank God, because he definitely has many things to say worth hearing!

When I was first asked to research Peter Lynch, I wasn't quite sure what we might have to gain. After all, this was the Master of the Mutual Fund Biz, and we've already decided that we came together because we wanted *nothing* to do with the fund biz. But I continued to read the philosophies of this man and found out what a champion of the individual (i.e., amateur) stock picker he was. He claims that the "stock stars" (of which he was one) of the 1980s unfortunately created an exaggerated reverence for the professional skills of Wall Street. Like pie baking, he says, stock picking has become a dying art because people don't want to do the work—simply because they haven't been taught how. Why bake from scratch when you can just pop a box in the microwave? *Taste,* my friends! (Note to self: get that cobbler recipe from Mom!)

Not only does Lynch prefer stocks (or stock mutual funds) to just about any other investment vehicle over time, he also believes that an amateur investor who devotes a small amount of time to researching companies in an industry she knows a little bit about can outperform *95 percent* of the paid experts who manage the mutual funds, plus *have fun doing it!* Now, that's cooking!

He does admit, however, there is no simple "recipe" for stock picking. It's both an art and a science . . . too much of either is a dangerous thing. After all, if the future were told by balance sheets alone, mathematicians and accountants would be the richest people in the world. In fact, I found it encouraging that even Peter Lynch kept reiterating that no advanced math is required to be an excellent stock picker. And even though computers are the lifeline of us Chicks, Lynch is computer illiterate, and Warren Buffett uses his only to play bridge. There is hope for all of us!

Lynch claims that his greatest source of investment ideas comes from the shopping mall. Boy, do I like this one. I can jump in the car, spend three hours at the mall, and tell my husband I'm doing important research for the financial viability of our future. Quite often, Lynch states, if you like the store, chances are you'll love the stock. (By the way, he offers a little tip: in double-decker malls, the most popular stores are usually found upstairs. I did not know that.)

Similarities of taste in both food and fashion might make for a dull culture but can make owners of these retail and restaurant chains quite wealthy (and thus, their stockholders). He urges us to become aware of early business successes that are occurring in our own neighborhood. Do our own research. Don't simply read a company's quarterly and annual reports; stay abreast of what the competition is doing. For example, say you own Chrysler—is someone coming out with a better minivan? Get out and test-drive the new competition! (You may end up investing in a great new stock *and* find yourself driving off in a great new car! Not a bad thing.)

"What helped me the most is *logic,*" says Lynch about his years at Fidelity, "because it taught me to identify the inherent illogic of Wall Street." Chicks should be great at this, because everyone knows women are always logical—right? (It's okay to smack your husband if he happens to be laughing right now.) Lynch states that Wall Street thinks much like the ancient Greeks did, sitting around debating how many teeth a horse has when the right answer would be . . . go check a horse!

Lynch says that if we are alert shoppers, we have a chance to get the message about retailers earlier than Wall Street does, and to make *back* all the money we ever spend on merchandise *by buying undervalued stocks.*

Talk about a rebate! That last part is the key. Lynch notes there will always be "missed opportunities," but thankfully, the market is merciful and will always give us a second chance. There is a 100 percent correlation between what happens to a company and what happens to their stock; however, they don't always move in sync. That is the opportunity he is looking for—a stock at a sale price. In hindsight, he says, it's always best to focus on the company, not on the stock.

When it comes to research, he says we should think of ourselves as "investigative reporters": to read relevant public documents, talk to intermediaries, and then talk to the companies themselves. Most important, keep notes on the "stories" heard. For example, say the *National Enquirer* assigned me to study and report on Tom Cruise. (An assignment I would just die to have! It's okay, my husband can research Elle Macpherson while I'm checking out Tom.) First, I would read all I could about him in *The Star* and *People* magazine. Next, I would talk to people who know him or have had Tom "sightings." And last (be still my beating heart), I would try to talk to Tom himself. Fortunately for us investors, talking to a company directly will be much easier than trying to get a movie star on the line. They have to tell us all about themselves in their annual reports and quarterly filings, and most corporations even have an office dedicated to talking to investors. See how easy this is?

Another important point he makes is that once you've bought a stock, your work is far from done. A long-term strategy of buy and hold is not the same thing as buy and forget. Every six months you should do a routine checkup on every stock you own. This is an especially important reminder for us long-term investors. Even with blue chips, big names, and Fortune 500 companies, buy-and-forget strategies can be unproductive and downright dangerous. What this proves is that it's not enough to keep up with your stock's price—you bought it because you liked the company story, so you better stay current on what that is.

So what does this mean for the Chicks' holdings? When reviewing our stocks, we should try and answer two basic questions: Is the stock still attractively priced relative to earnings? And what is happening in the company to make the earnings go up? With the second question, one of three conclusions can be reached:

1. The story has gotten better, in which case you might want to *increase* your investment.

2. The story has gotten worse, in which case you can *decrease* your investment.

3. The story is unchanged, in which case you can either stick with your investment or put the money into another company with more exciting prospects. However, we must be careful here; Lynch warns that it is all too easy to fall victim to the common practice of "pulling out the flowers to water the weeds." (This happens to be Lynch's favorite expression, and Warren Buffett even asked for his permission to use it in his annual report.)

At year's end, he says, a stock picker should always perform a review, company by company. For each holding, we should be able to find a reason we believe the next year will be better than the last. If you can't do this, then ask yourself why you want to continue owning it. A stock's story keeps changing, for either better or worse, and you have to follow these changes and act accordingly.

Since we were talking about the mall, one thing to note is that in both retail and restaurant chains, the growth that propels earnings and stock price is *expansion*. Each has about fifteen to twenty years of fast growth ahead as it expands. Another beauty is that there usually is no competition to worry about from abroad. Success is defined by those companies with capable management, adequate financing, and a methodical approach to expansion (slow and steady). Problems always arise when there's a rush to glory. (Remember the turtle and the hare?) Lynch suggests that we follow these industries, as we already do, by looking at their growth rate, debt, same-store sales, and inventories.

Here's another Peter Lynch pearl of wisdom. There's no shame in losing money on a stock; everybody does it (misery loves company). It *is* shameful, however, to hold on or, worse, buy *more* when the fundamentals are deteriorating. "Never bet on a comeback while they're playing taps!" On the flip side, never question your greed after recording huge gains in a stock. Instead, question the company's saturation. A terrific illustration of this is to imagine ABC canceling Oprah's show because she had won too many daytime Emmys. Stick with it, it's a proven winner!

I may have belabored the point about buying what you know, but Lynch just makes it sound so simple. Go hang out at the mall, see what stores and products are doing well, and bingo—box office success. There must be a bit more to it, and there is, but this is a wonderful place to start. To ensure that you're adhering to the simplistic approach, Peter suggests not buying anything that you can't illustrate with a crayon. At Fidelity, they would have weekly meetings to discuss their prospective stock purchases and holdings. Each person would be allowed three minutes to tell the story of the stock they'd been covering. In reality, Lynch says, ninety seconds was always more than enough to provide adequate information on whether to buy or sell. The key, he says—and this is a great one, (I just love simple talk)—is to try and explain your stock's story in language simple enough for a fifth-grader to understand and quick enough so he won't get bored.

Again, Lynch provides us with some wonderful analogies that any Chick can relate to—especially you cold-weather Chicks. Lynch compares the stock market to the freezing temperatures in Minnesota. Do subzero temps surprise you in the winter? No. (Tick you off, maybe.) Do you assume they're the beginning of an ice age? Of course not! Well, the market works the same way. Dips in stock prices are a recurring event which you just have to deal with. So put on your parka and start shopping! But be careful, he warns, owning stocks is like having children— don't own more than you can handle.

If I had to put Lynch's entire philosophy into one sentence, it would be "Invest in what you know." We are all experts in our own little world. We each know what we like and what we don't like. How does that work for me? Well, I'm a mother of a two-year-old and an eleven-month-old; I think I'm keeping the Huggies company alive with just my children! Kimberly-Clark might be worth a peek (NYSE: KMB). Or how about the fact that I'm so excited to have a baby girl that I've already started buying her Barbies even though she hasn't yet had her first birthday? Maybe I should give Mattel a look (NYSE: MAT). Every Sunday after church, our family's big treat is to go to our local Starbucks (NASDAQ: SBUX) for a mocha. (Did I mention we stood in line behind Brooke Shields last week? Didn't notice how many sugars she uses, but boy is that girl big . . . ahem, tall!)

THE MOTLEY FOOL'S RULE MAKER (A.K.A. TOM GARDNER'S PHILOSOPHY)
By Chick Karin

A couple of years ago, I had the good fortune to have dinner with Tom Gardner at a hockey game. We ate while watching the game, so I'm calling it dinner. It was then that I changed my dream from interviewing Tom Cruise (be still my beating heart) to getting inside Tom Gardner's brain. I have never met a smarter man when it comes to combining common sense and investing in the stock market. (Mr. Gardner, get your head in the door, I haven't met Lynch or Buffett yet.)

Tom and his brother, David, own and run the Motley Fool website (www.fool.com), host a nationally syndicated radio show, and have written many financial best-sellers. Tom's online Rule Maker portfolio has consistently outperformed the market, year after year, over the last three years. The Motley Fool Rule Maker philosophy is one of the easiest and least time-consuming of all the stock-picking philosophies in the bookstore. Matter of fact, after you read this book, it wouldn't be a bad idea to go buy *The Motley Fool's Rule Breakers, Rule Makers,* by the Gardner brothers. The Chicks incorporated a lot of their criteria when formulating our stock-picking approach, and reading their book will reinforce what you are reading here.

Like Buffett, Gardner believes that an investor's attitude is important, that you have to approach the purchase of a stock as if you're literally buying a piece of the business (and you are, even if it is a tiny little piece). And, like Lynch, he believes that you should always buy what you know, but he takes it a step further and recommends that you *research* what you know.

But those are just underlying factors in Tom's Rule Makers portfolio criteria. For starters, a Rule Maker must be the most well-known brand in its market, the leader in its field, *the* name in that business. For example, in soft drinks, Coca-Cola; in computer software, Microsoft; in entertainment, Disney; and in clothing, the Gap. To be a Rule Maker, you must be the big cheese in your business to even get looked at, and then you have to meet seven further criteria. But before we get to those, I have some bad news for you. To find your own set of Rule Makers—to work Tom's criteria—you have to do the numbers.

By numbers I mean that you have to figure out what the numbers on your Rule Maker candidate's quarterly report tell you. A quarterly report is what a company is required to submit to the Securities and Exchange Commission (SEC). It documents the company's cash flow for the last quarter and consists of a balance sheet and an income statement. Corporations listed on the exchanges must file this report four times a year. You can get a copy of these reports on the Internet or directly from the company you're investigating. (More on this later.)

If you want to find your own Rule Making stocks, every time a quarterly report comes out, get the report you need (from the company's investor relations department or from the Internet), find the numbers you need, and evaluate them according to a set of benchmarks. You can put any company—the one you work for, a Buffet or Lynch company, or the company off Highway 95—to the test with the numbered checklist you'll find below.

Don't panic! It's an easy checklist. The numbers you need are easily found on the balance sheet and income statements of a company's quarterly earnings report. I know, I know, this all sounds difficult, from locating the company's quarterly earnings report to evaluating things like cash flow, but after a while you will find yourself saying, "Hey, did you know that Coke's numbers are out today?" (If you call them numbers, you'll sound like you know what you're talking about—and soon enough, you will!) We're going to go into the rules of Rule Making companies in a little more depth than we have Buffett and Lynch's criteria, because this is a great way to introduce you to the numbers, and to show you that it's much, much easier than you ever imagined it could be.

Seven Criteria of a Rule Maker

1. **Repeat purchase of low-priced products:** This is good common sense. Would you rather own stock in a company with a product that people had a daily need for, or a company that sold only large one-time purchases? For example, if you are an automobile manufacturer, how often are you going to get the customer to buy one of your products? Once every two years, if you're lucky. I'm betting you won't see that customer again for at least another two years when she drives out of the lot in her new VW Bug. This company would get to make a profit off that Chick only once every three years. Now, how often do you think she buys a Diet Coke? At least once a day, maybe more. That means Coca-Cola makes a profit at least 365 times a year off just one person! I'd rather be Coca-Cola than a car manufacturer, and I'd also rather invest in Coca-Cola than a car manufacturer.

   Rule Makers are companies that have repeat purchases often. Examples of those would be drug companies, soft drink companies, oil companies, and clothing companies. (There are more.) These companies make a profit more often because their product is purchased more often. Even in consumers' worst financial times, they will find extra cash to purchase the needed items. You can't live without heat, and I won't live without my Diet Coke, but I could go without a new car.

2. **Gross margins:** *What* did I say? Gross what? Margarines?

   Relax. Breathe. Gross margins are a reflection of how expensive it is to make a product compared to the price it can be sold for. A gross margin is a number that tells us how much profit the company makes off each product sold. To make it into Rule Maker status, a company must have gross margins of least 60 percent.

   A product that is sold for a smidgen more than it costs to make it would have a *low* gross margin. An example of this might be a Saturn car (but hey, they come with those driver-side vanity mirrors). A car costs a lot in relation to a pack of gum, but car companies don't make a huge profit on each car they sell because if their product cost much more, people wouldn't be able to afford them.

A company that could achieve high gross margins would be one that doesn't have to spend a lot making its product. An example of this, again, is Coca-Cola. It doesn't cost a lot to add a little sugar and fizz to water, but they can sell it for almost twice what it costs to make. Same goes for the drug companies. How much do you think it costs to make a little aspirin? Or how much can it cost the cigarette manufacturers to roll a little tobacco over and over again? They seem to charge you an arm and a leg. (That would be a high gross margin.)

To figure out the gross margins of a company, you need to go to its income statement. Take the total sales and subtract the cost of goods sold (this number is also called the gross profit). Then divide the gross profit by the total sales to get your number. As an equation, it looks like this:

$$\frac{\text{Total Sales} - \text{Cost of Goods Sold}}{\text{Total Sales}} = \text{Gross Margins}$$

Let's do two examples.

If it cost 40 cents to make a can of Coke, and it sells for $1.00 in the vending machine, what would Coca-Cola's per-can gross margin be?

$$\frac{\$1.00 - .40}{\$1.00} = .60$$

Remember, to change a decimal to a percentage, you multiply it by 100. So .60 × 100 equals 60 percent. In our example, Coca-Cola's gross margins would be 60%!

Example two. If one of those new little VW Bugs sells for $23,000 but it costs Volkswagen $20,000 to make one, what is Volkswagen's gross margin on the car?

$$\frac{\$23,000 - \$20,000}{\$23,000} = .13$$

Volkswagen would have a 13 percent gross margin.

Looking at these numbers, you can see that Coca-Cola is, by this measure, a Rule Maker, while Volkswagen is disqualified.

3. **Net margins:** Another very important benchmark that needs to be met in order to become a Rule Maker is to have net margins that are greater than 10 percent. Net margins tell us how much profit a company is making after you subtract all of its expenses; you don't want a company spending *all* of its profits. If you make a 60-cent profit on every can of Coke and spend 59 cents of it telling the public why they should buy it with advertising, you'd make one penny on each can. Your net margin would be one penny, or 0.1 percent. You can't run a business making one penny on every dollar. And you certainly can't be a Rule Maker with those net margins. Rule Makers have to have some cashola left over. To figure a company's net margins, we take its earnings after expenses and divide by sales. The equation looks like this:

$$\frac{\text{Net Income}}{\text{Sales}}$$

In order to make Rule Maker status, the result must be greater than 10 percent.

4. **Sales growth:** This one is easy. To become a Rule Maker, the sales growth must exceed 10 percent per year. This isn't the easiest of feats to achieve when you are investing in brand-name companies that have been around for years, that have taken time to become *the* name in their field. It's easier for small start-up companies to achieve faster growth because they haven't saturated the market yet. The world is theirs. But if you're a Wal-Mart, what land is left for you to build on? There is already a Wal-Mart in almost every city—how can it continue to grow? Where there's a Wal-Mart, there's a way. Have they infiltrated the whole world? No. Then there is still room for expansion and growth. Maybe they have to come up with a new product or expand their Internet presence. Rule Makers must keep their wheels turning in the sales growth department and never let their guard down.

Let's do a sales growth calculation:

Henny Penny's total sales, year one: $25,000
Henny Penny's total sales, year two: $50,000
Henny Penny's total sales, year ten: $1,000,000

The sales growth from years one to two is figured like this:

Subtract year one from year two:
$50,000 − $25,000 = $25,000

Divide the difference by the first year:
25,000 ÷ 25,000 = 1.00
Change to a percentage. Multiply by 100:
1.00 × 100 = 100 percent

Henny Penny's year-one sales growth was 100 percent!

The sales growth of Henny Penny's over its ten-year history would be:

A) 500 percent
B) 3900 percent
C) The train was traveling east at 48 mph.

If you answered B, you were correct. Here is the math:

$1,000,000 − $25,000 = $975,000
(Sales the tenth year − sales the first year)

$975,000 ÷ $25,000 = 39
(Divided by the first-year sales)
39 × 100 = 3900 percent
(Multiply by 100 to get a percentage)

5. **Cash to long-term debt ratio:** This is my favorite one. Rule Maker companies should be cash hogs. The richer the better, and the best are

filthy rich. They should have of all their debts taken care of and be ready to use all that extra cash to *grow*. In order to make it to Rule Maker status in the cash to debt ratio, they must have $1^1/_2$ times as much cash as they do debt. You will find the cash and the long-term debt on the balance sheet. Look for those exact words on the balance sheet: long-term debt. Short-term debt means nothing in this equation, as it will be repaid in the short term, like the next few months; it's only the long-term debt we need to compute. Long-term debt is like mortgages on buildings the companies own, or large outstanding loans.

Here is the formula:

$$\frac{Cash*}{Long\text{-}Term\ Debt} = \text{should be more than 1.5 to qualify as Rule Maker}$$

6. **The Foolish Flow Ratio:** This one is a bit trickier, so I'll give you the equation first, then explain.

$$\frac{Current\ Assets - All\ Cash*}{Current\ Liabilities - Short\text{-}Term\ Debt} = \text{The Foolish Flow Ratio}$$

The current assets, the cash, the current liabilities, and the short-term debt are all found on a company's balance sheet. Rule Makers should have a Flow Ratio below 1.0. The top part of the equation is current assets minus cash. Why do we take the cash out? If we remove the cash from the current assets, what is actually left is the merchandise they haven't yet sold. This includes products that are left lying around in the back warehouse. They choose to call them assets. But are they really? I don't think having ten thousand pairs of shoes sitting in the back room would be called assets. Who is going to buy last year's clunky heels? We need to take the cash out of the equation so we know how many unsold goods they have lying around. (They should really be called liabilities, but I don't want to

---

*All cash means anything that can be converted to cash quickly. This figure would include marketable securities, short-term investments, and cash equivalents.

get into that.) Take the cash out of the equation, and you have the rest of their current assets. This number should be *low* to qualify as a Rule Maker. They shouldn't have a lot of unsold inventory in the back room. So think of current assets minus cash (the top part of the equation) as the inventory that they expect to sell within the next year—or at least they hope to sell within a year. The greatest Rule Makers move their product out as soon as it comes in.

The bottom number, current liabilities minus short-term debt, is the costs that have to be paid in the next year. Rule Makers should hold off as long as possible on paying current liabilities (these are different from long-term debt), which allows them to keep the cash in their own pocket. They can earn more money on it this way. We subtract the short-term debt out of the current liabilities, as it carries an interest rate payable along with the amount. This would be known as a "bad liability," so we take it out. So the current assets (minus cash, of course) should be *smaller* than the current liabilities minus short-term debt. Divided out, a small number on top of the equation and a large number on the bottom will give us a small Flow Ratio. But if the top is larger, that spells trouble. A low Flow Ratio means the company has its inventory under control and has mastered the current liabilities balancing act. Read this paragraph hundreds of times—it is the most important thing to understand. I'll do an example.

Henny Penny's has current assets of $500,000. It has cash on hand worth $400,000. Its current liabilities are to the seamstress for making the new coveralls and to pay rent on the building. The current liabilities total $150,000. We have no short-term debt. Here's how to figure the Flow Ratio:

$$\frac{\$500,000 - \$400,000}{\$150,000} = .667$$

.667 is lower than 1.0, so Henny Penny's makes the Rule Maker cut. Did you have any doubts?

7. **Familiarity and interest:** This is similar to Lynch's "If you can draw it with a crayon and explain it in less than three minutes" phi-

losophy. Only, Mr. Gardner adds, is it a company that you know and are fond of? Are you familiar enough with it, is it a product that you'd find in your home, and do you like the overall product or service? You wouldn't want to invest in a company that makes automobile carburetors, unless, of course, that is your forte. If you know who the top dog is in the carburetor manufacturers, then go for it. I, on the other hand, prefer to research companies like Martha Stewart Omnimedia, Amazon.com, and UPS. It's who I am, home ec is my middle name, I love shopping online (Amazon), and guess who ships my packages? UPS. That is familiarity and interest in a nutshell.

And that is the Motley Fool's (Tom Gardner's) Rule Maker philosophy in an eggshell.

Most Admired

All right, you've just had a crash course in three investing philosophies that helped shape the Chicks' philosophy. Where do we come in, and what can you do? We came in with our eyes open, and so should you. What we learned from looking at all these ideas is that it's not that hard to come up with great investment strategies. They're out there, right in front of you, every day of the week. All you have to do is keep your eyes—and your mind—open.

When I first starting looking into investment techniques, I came across *Fortune* magazine and its Most Admired Companies list. *Fortune* surveyed thousands of businesspeople from around the country to compile their list. The magazine caught my eye, so I bought it. What I found was amazing. Combined, the top ten companies have beaten the S&P 500 every year except one since 1994. This Most Admired Companies portfolio, compiled by the people, available to the people for free (almost), was able to do what 90 percent of the mutual funds couldn't! I was dumbfounded.

I also thought, What a great place for an investment club to start!

Immediately, I got the idea that the Chicks should take look at these companies. If everyone else loves them, and combined they are beating the market, there must be some gems in there. And then the laziness in me said, "Why don't the Chicks just buy all ten, be done with it, and we'd beat the market?" Nah, what did Helen Keller say at the beginning of this chapter—"Life is either a daring adventure, or nothing"? I'm going with Helen on this one. I wanted to know *why* I was buying, and I wanted to find the best of the best. But it is a great place for an investment club to start.

The 1999 Most Admired Companies were:

1. General Electric
2. Microsoft
3. Coca-Cola
4. Intel
5. Hewlett Packard
6. Southwest Airlines
7. Berkshire Hathaway (there's our Mr. Buffett again)
8. Walt Disney
9. Johnson & Johnson
10. Merck

Right away, I noticed that every one of these companies have repeat purchasing of low-cost products—one of Tom Gardner's Rule Maker qualifications. Jump on the Internet and look around, and you'll realize that they all also fit a number of Mr. Buffett's and Mr. Lynch's criteria. Interesting, eh?

I know that was a huge crash course in investment philosophies, but it was my attempt at summarizing a lot of knowledge into a small space. This is enough to get you started, whet your appetite (what do you mean you're full?), and start you thinking about what your club's philosophy should look like. This was how the Chicks started, and boy, I can't tell you how smart we are now.

Karin, we are not that smart, we are still learning.

Speak for yourselves.

Chapter Summary

○ "Life is either a daring adventure, or nothing."
○ Warren Buffett—owns and runs Berkshire Hathaway.
○ Peter Lynch—buy what you know.
○ Motley Fool's Rule Maker:
  Research what you know.
  Repeat purchase of low-priced product.
  Gross margins greater than 60 percent.
  Net margins greater than 10 percent.
  Sales growth greater than 10 percent.
  $1\frac{1}{2}$ times cash to long-term.
  Foolish Flow Ratio less than 1.0.
○ *Fortune* magazine's ten Most Admired Companies.

chick chat

TITLE: GUESS WHO'S GOT AN EGG IN THE NEST?
From: Chick Karin

That's all I'm gonna say.

Karin, lovin' freshly baked buns in the oven

TITLE: RE: GUESS WHO'S GOT AN EGG IN THE NEST?
From: Chick Megan

I'm so embarrassed. You saw my gut and you could tell I was pregnant. The only problem is . . . I'm NOT! It's not me!

It is NOT me, but I'm going to try the high-protein-low-carb diet now, so you can stop spreading such things about me.

Does anyone have Suzanne Somers's phone number?

Megan
Is it you, Karin?

TITLE: RE: GUESS WHO'S GOT AN EGG IN THE NEST?
From: Chick Lorene

It's not me.

Four is enough here.

Lorene

TITLE: RE: GUESS WHO'S GOT AN EGG IN THE NEST?
From: Chick Julie

I'm too old, but Karin, isn't four enough over there too? Stop the insanity.

Julie

TITLE: RE: GUESS WHO'S GOT AN EGG IN THE NEST?
From: Chick Kristin

I'd like to be married first. Poses a problem. Not me.

Kristin

TITLE: RE: GUESS WHO'S GOT AN EGG IN THE NEST?
From: Chick Lynn

Six kids here is plenty too, but I do have the Suzanne Somers book if you want it, Megan . . . though if you get any skinnier, I'm going to insist that you eat some of this chocolate staring me in the face. It's that time again, so I KNOW it's not me.

Smooches, Lynn

TITLE: **S&P REPORT
From: Chick Cheryl

I'm still nursing, please DON'T be me! I'll give you the S&P report in the meantime. The whole market went down a little from the last posted report; our portfolio is up 52.91% compared to the market's 18.13%.

AOL up 177.42% vs. 11.66%
CSCO down .63% vs. 1.52%
KO up 5.61% vs. 26.95%
PFE up 41.28% vs. 26.95%

TITLE: RE: GUESS WHO'S GOT AN EGG IN THE NEST?
From: Chick Jana

No wonder I was sick in Vegas! It's ME! The Growing Chick. Jana (going back to bed for another nap, but I thought I better post before my mother did: she can NEVER keep a secret!)

11

The Chicks' Dozen

I hear and I forget. I see and I remember.
I do and I understand.

— CONFUCIUS

You made it! Can you even? You made it through all those philosophies, and your brain isn't a scrambled mess! They actually made sense! Well, maybe the second time through. Did you ever in your life think that you'd even know who Lynch and Buffett were, much less understand them? Bravo! See, you *can* do it, and it's not that hard-boiled. Where do you go from here?

If you are going to invest in the stock market, you must come up with your own personal philosophy, for yourself and for your club. If you remember what I said in the beginning, the single most important step after choosing the right members for your club is to <u>pick and stick with a philosophy</u>. This goes for the individual, too. This is the "Pick an Egg and Crack 'Er Open" step.

What investment approaches made sense to you and did you believe in? Weed through them in your head. What criteria did you like or dislike?

I am going to propose that you start with the Chicks' Dozen as your club's working philosophy. I say this only because there are over a million different investment approaches out there, and you could spend more time researching them than you would actually learn by practicing one. The best way to learn—yes, my sixth-grade math teacher said it too—is by doing. But don't worry, you're not carving this thing in stone.

There is nothing written that says that you can't change your criteria as you go along; the Chicks did, and you probably will too as you learn more about the market and about yourself as an investor. Learn as you go and tweak when necessary. Start with the Chicks' take on things, and modify after some practice.

It's like a beginning golfer. Until you get the golf swing down, you don't want an expert coming in and changing it. Learn how to swing first, then modify. But remember, the most important step at this juncture is to *have* a philosophy.

I may as well jump into what the Chicks' Dozen philosophy is all about, and then I'll go through a few of the companies that have survived our twelve-step checklist. I'll take you through each criterion and apply it to our company. (So silly that each of our stocks needs to go through a twelve-step program before becoming Chick-owned, when I think it's the Chick who needs the twelve-stepper after she finally completes her research. You should see us the week leading up to a stock purchase—wine in one hand, calculator in the other.)

Chicks' Dozen

I'll go over them one by one, and then you can dog-ear this chapter and use it as your manual in your stock-picking prowess.

 1. **Buy what you know:** This goes back to the Lynch idea—open your refrigerator, what do you see? Who made the steak sauce? Heinz. Whose product is the soft drink? Coca-Cola. Wassssuuup with the beer? Anheuser-Busch. Got Gatorade? Quaker Oats. Go to the pantry—who makes those Fritos? Frito-Lay. Graham crackers? Nabisco. In the medicine cabinet, who made the Q-Tips? Johnson & Johnson. In your purse, whose cell phone is that? Nokia. Go to the mall; which store is the busiest—Abercrombie and Fitch? Hop on your computer, your Dell computer, and go to the Internet; what is your favorite site, Amazon or Yahoo? Who provides your car insurance? Geico. Start by looking at companies that are familiar to you, that you know and love, and buy what you *know*.

2. **K.I.S.S. (Keep It Simple, Sister):** Lynch would say, "Can you draw it with a crayon?" Do you understand the industry that this product is part of? Food, clothing, and car insurance are pretty easy to understand, but cell phones might be a bit more difficult. Trying to understand bandwidth or the language of the airwaves requires a bit more research. I wouldn't know a thing about mechanical hydraulics, if there is such a thing, so my trying to explain that company to a fifth-grader may not make sense. Our companies must be easy enough for us to understand. When you can understand a company and its industry, it is much clearer to see if its product or service is going to be in demand in the coming years, or if consumer appeal will dwindle.

3. **Industry:** If you can understand an industry, what do you feel the growth, or potential for growth, will be over the next decade? Do you think that it will have quite a few years of breakthrough growth or average growth? Is your company on the cutting edge of something, like a new technology? A Chick looks for a company in an industry whose growth looks to be greater than average. (This calls for some female foresight.)

4. **Leader in its field:** Is the company a leader in its field? Would everyone recognize the name if you said it? If I said General Motors, would you say cars? If I said America Online, would you say Internet? If I said Keebler, would you say cookies? Yes, yes, and yes. Those are all leaders in their field. When you look for companies, look for the top dog. Chicks don't want to invest in small start-ups. They're too risky. We want the top dogs in the field because they are established and proven. This is how you look for the top brands. Say the first thing that comes to your mind. Kids' clothes? GapKids. Chocolate? Hershey's. Say the word computer, and what comes to mind? Dell? Apple? Compaq? They all work. What is your favorite restaurant—Outback Steakhouse? McDonald's? Enough, you get the picture. Erectile dysfunction? Pfizer. Okay, that's really enough.

5. **Repeat profitability:** We would like to invest in a company that has its customers coming back quite often throughout the year. We want our companies to market a product or service that is needed or used often by the consumer. Repeat profitability. As Chicks, we

look for these companies, the benefactors of a repeat profit. Drug companies, clothing manufacturers, financial services, soft drink companies, telecommunications, and utility companies are good places to start. The makers of television sets, automobiles, or airplanes aren't going to enjoy the same daily profit luxury from each consumer. (As I write this book, Coca-Cola is making a ton off me, especially if they really do make 60 cents on every can.) How many times do you log on to your Internet service provider? How often do you use your cell phone? Repeat consistent use is our middle name.

6. **Gross margins:** We want gross margins of at least 50 percent. Do you remember how to do gross margarines? Do you remember what gross margins are? Dig deep. How old are you? Perfect, then you're fine. Senility doesn't set in until at least seventy. You have not forgotten, but just saying the words "gross" and "margin" can cause dementia. It's like your husband's selective hearing; women are professionals at selective dementia. Gross margins figure the relationship between how much a company sells a product for (sales) compared to what it cost them to make it (cost of goods sold). They are the percentage of gross profit (sales minus cost of goods sold) relative to revenue. After you subtract how much it costs to make a product from what you charge for the product, put it in relation to what your sales are. I am going to use my cleaning woman as an example. (Tricia, I hope you don't mind, but you do the best laundry north of Texas.) When Tricia gave me her original bid to clean my house, she said that it would cost me $60 a week including supplies. Sounded reasonable to me, so I hired her. (I actually thought this was a bargain, since it included changing the sheets on all five beds in the house.) The first day Tricia arrived, it took her ten hours to clean my house. Hmm, I thought, she isn't making that much money. Ten hours for only sixty dollars. But wait, Tricia is no dumb businesswoman. The next week she came, it took her six hours. The week after that, four, and now it only takes her two hours, and it still costs me $60. You see what she did? She quoted me $60 for the house, and I agreed. She lost money in the

beginning because she needed to get my house in order. It didn't take her long to decrease her cost of the service (her time lessened). She didn't have to do the windows every time, she didn't have to organize the closets every time, and she didn't have to wipe down all the baseboards every time. This extra time was part of her cost of starting up business at my house. Her company, Tricia's Cleaning Service, was able to become more efficient at her service, hence decreasing her time spent at my house and increasing her gross margins. This will happen in most new businesses. Until you get under way and figure out how to become more efficient and decrease your costs of your goods or service, your gross margins will be low. I'll show you the numbers (this is found on a company's income statement). I'll show you where to find a real company's income statement at the end of this chapter.

$$\frac{\text{Sales} - \text{Cost of Goods Sold}}{\text{Sales}} = \text{Gross Margins}$$

This is also sometimes written as:

$$\frac{\text{Revenues} - \text{Cost of Sales}}{\text{Revenues}} = \text{Gross Margins}$$

FYI, when you take the sales of a company and subtract what is costs to make that product (sales — cost of goods sold), this is called your gross profit. I don't want to confuse you, but on some companies' income statements, they do the subtraction for you, and it is labeled gross profit. It saves one calculator step. This is a good thing.

If we were to figure Tricia's gross margins, they would look like this:

First week:
$$\frac{\$60 \text{ (sales)} - (\$20 \text{ (supplies)} + \$80 \text{ (man hours)})(\text{cost of sales})}{\$60}$$

$$\frac{\$60 - \$100}{\$60} = \frac{-40}{60}$$

$$= -66 \text{ percent Gross Margins . . . tsk-tsk}$$

Present:
$$\frac{\$60 \text{ (sales)} - (\$5 \text{ (supplies)} + \$16 \text{ (man hours)})(\text{cost of sales})}{\$60}$$

$$\frac{60 - 21}{60} = \frac{39}{60}$$

$$= .65$$

.65 × 100 = 65 percent Gross Margins

Way to go, Tricia! Wait a second, should I be cheering for this?

7. **Net margins:** We want net profit to be at least 8 percent. To become a Chicks' Dozen stock, the net margins should be at least 8 percent. That means we want a company to be making at least 8 cents on every dollar. After they have deducted all of their expenses for researching, creating, advertising, marketing, and paying the head honcho, we want them to be making 8 cents on every dollar. This number is also on the income statement. (Later, in chapter 14, we'll get you there. Breathe.) To figure out net margins, you simply divide the net income by the sales. Like this:

$$\frac{\text{Net Income}}{\text{Sales}} = \text{Net Margins (also called Profit Margins)}$$

If I were to use Tricia's Cleaning Service as an example again, we would need to get her net income. I am going to make it up, because my dear sweet Tricia is very private. (For public companies, this number is available on the income statement, but private companies keep this information, well, private.) I am going to figure it over a one-year period for Tricia's Cleaning Service.

First, I would add together all of her expenses—the gas she uses to get to all her clients' houses ($1,000), the insurance for her car ($400), what she pays her baby-sitter to watch her kids ($500), what she pays her sister to help sometimes ($8,000), what she pays herself ($14,000), the cost of the flyers she put in the mailboxes ($40), all those cleaning supplies ($1,050), and what she pays Uncle Sam ($850). Those all total $28,840. Those were her expenses, and remember, I made them up to illustrate for you.

Let's say that all the money she takes in during the year from clients is $31,200.

To figure the net income, you take the income and subtract all the costs. This would be called the net income. (In order to remember the difference between net and gross, I think of a basketball hoop—it's gross when it goes into the hoop, and swoosh, deduction, all net when it comes out.)

$$\$31,200 - 28,840 = \$2,360$$

To figure the net margins, divide that number (our net income) by the sales.

$$\frac{\$2,360}{\$31,200} = .0756$$

$$.0756 \times 100 = 7.56 \text{ percent}$$

Tricia's net margins are 7.56 percent. She makes seven and a half cents on every dollar. Not bad, Chick Tricia.

If I took this one step further—and if I were Chick Tricia I just might—how do you think you would increase net margins? If you were Coca-Cola, how do you think you could increase net margins when you've become about as efficient as you can possibly be? Did someone say increase the price? Yep. Increase the price.

It would be so easy for Tricia to tell me that instead of $60 a week, she needs to charge $65 a week. She now has me addicted to her service (her brand), and I wouldn't even think of going elsewhere or trusting anyone else. By increasing her income, the top line of the equation, she would increase her net margins. I don't even want to remember how many times Coke has done this to me, and here I stay. Can you say repeat profit?

By the way, Tricia, feel free, you deserve it.

8. **Lots of cash:** We want cash hogs! We want the Bill Gateses of the business world. We want the Budweiser of beers. We want the Rockefeller of companies. We want money to be coming out of our company's ears. We want it growing on every tree in their lot. We want—well, you get the picture. Remember, the more money a com-

pany has, the more it can do. It's just like when you play Monopoly: the more cash you have, the more property you can buy, or the more houses or hotels you can build on your property. Cash gives you freedom. Like I need to tell you this. Don't forget when getting your cash figure to add in the marketable securities, short-term investments, and cash equivalents. These are current assets that can all be converted to cash very quickly, so we consider them part of the cash figure. These numbers are found on the company's balance sheet. It's a simple calculation. Take the amount of cash and divide it by its long-term debt.

$$\frac{\text{Cash*}}{\text{Long-Term Debt}} = \text{we want greater than 1.0}$$

We just want our company to have *more* cash than it has long-term debt; the richer the better.

9. **Flow Ratio:** We want a Flow Ratio below 1.50. I will give you the fraction before I ramble.

$$\frac{\text{Current Assets} - \text{Cash*}}{\text{Current Liabilities} - \text{Short-Term Debt}} = \frac{\text{Flow Ratio (we want}}{\text{under 1.50)}}$$

We incorporated this calculation from the Motley Fool. I don't remember seeing a philosophy that incorporated this figure, and it's one of the most important, so I'll give them credit. (There is a ratio called a company's ratio, but to figure it, they don't take the cash out of the current assets for their top number—this is the most important distinction, and it makes all the difference in the world.) Whoa, I'll slow down. Remember what the Flow Ratio means? It is the fraction that measures how well your company is managing the cash flow in their business. Let me refresh you: you don't want your company to have a lot of unsold merchandise lying around in warehouses (this would be our top number after the cash is taken out). The bottom number, the current liabilities, is what we need to pay out in the next year. (Remember to subtract out the short-term debt,

---

*Includes marketable securities and short-term investments.

as it is not profitable for a company to pay interest on money it owes.) Why would you want to compare the stuff lying in the warehouse to how much cash needs to go out in the next twelve months? Because you want to see what kind of discipline your company has. Are they making more shoes than are in demand? Do they have a ton of last year's analog cell phones taking up space in the back room? Are they managing their short-term/current liabilities in a timely fashion? Are they selling their product as fast as they make it or has demand fallen and can't get up? Are they paying off their bills at the last possible moment?

It takes a very special company, and smart businesspeople, to master this balancing act. If they have it mastered, their Flow Ratio will be below 1.50. This is a good business. The Chicks aren't as stringent as the Motley Fool in our "Flowie" number prerequisite (they like it be lower than 1.00). When we don't have such strict guidelines, it allows more companies to meet our qualifications, and then we can use a little of our women's intuition to choose between them. (Though most of the time the company with the better numbers wins, but this at least allows for some room.) To figure the Flowie you need to get to the company's balance sheet. Take the (current assets − cash) and divide by the (current liabilities − short-term debt). This number will be your Flow Ratio.

$$\frac{\text{Current Assets} - \text{Cash*}}{\text{Current Liabilities} - \text{Short-Term Debt}} = \text{Flow Ratio (we want under 1.50)}$$

10. **Increasing growth:** Now we just need to find some numbers to help check out the history of the company. Is growth really going in a positive direction? We need to track what the past sales growth has been up to this point in time. To add numbers to your belief in the growth of the company, you can find them on the income statement. All you have to do is take the revenues from the most recent quarter and compare them to the revenues of three months ago. Is

---

*Includes marketable securities and short-term investments.

the number larger or smaller? If it is larger, then sales have increased. If it is smaller, then they have decreased.

If sales have decreased, ask yourself why. For example, let's say you are researching the Gap, and their fourth-quarter numbers ending in December had sales equaling ten million (these are made-up numbers). The next quarter, ending in March, had sales equaling eight million. Why would sales have decreased? Why wouldn't they have sold as much merchandise in the first quarter as they did in the last quarter? Can you say Christmas? Some companies have direct relationships with the calendar year, so it is best to check the months involved and what type of company you own. A company that sells pens, pencils, paper, and notebooks is going to have higher sales in its back-to-school months than, say, in May. Ask yourself the reason behind a company's sales increase or decrease before you move on to the next point.

To figure out the exact percentage of increase or decrease, go to your company's income statement and look for revenues or sales. Write down the number; then go to the income statement of the *last* quarter for your company and get revenues (or sales). Subtract the last quarter from this quarter—that is X—then divide X by the recent quarter's revenues; this answer is Y. Multiply Y by 100 and you get a percentage. Here is the formula:

$$\text{sales this quarter} - \text{sales last quarter} = X$$
$$X \div \text{sales last quarter} = Y$$
$$Y \times 100 = \underline{\hspace{1cm}} \text{ percent}$$

I'll use JCPenney (JCP) as an example:

$$\$7,969,000 - \$7,033,000 = \$936,000$$
$$\$936,000 \div \$7,033,000 = .13$$
$$.13 \times 100 = 13 \text{ percent}$$
JCPenney had an increase in sales of 13 percent.

Now I'll use Henny Penny's as an example. (The Chicks run a dang good business, especially when I make it up.)

$$\$500,000 - \$400,000 = \$100,000$$
$$\$100,000 \div \$400,000 = .25$$
$$.25 \times 100 = 25 \text{ percent}$$

Henny Penny's had a sales increase of 25 percent. Yeehaa!

The Chicks don't have a required percentage increase, but we do like to figure out what the number would be, as it helps in picking a stock. A company with a 40 percent consistent increase in sales would be more attractive than one with 8 percent growth. But you have to weigh all the Dozen.

11. **Strong management and operating history:** Because the Chicks, like Warren Buffett, believe we are buying a piece of the company and not just the stock, we want to know everything about it—from who's running it to what his or her place is in the company's history. If some man asked for your daughter's hand in marriage (does anyone do this anymore?), wouldn't you want to know everything about him, from his occupation to his family history? You don't want to be sending your daughter off with some loser! You want to know where he came from, what he thinks their future looks like, were his parents good people, or has he been charged with a felony. Will he make a good husband and father? You don't just get a son-in-law; your daughter will be embarking on a new way of life. There is a lot more invested than what is on the surface. That is why the Chicks need to know "the goods" on a company's management. Are they honest, respectable people? Are they trustworthy? Would they be my friends? Do I like his morals? Has he been married before? I mean, has he run any other companies? How did he do there? These are all important questions to ask when buying a piece of a company. We appreciate a management's candor with shareholders, the media, and the public. We also like companies in which management invests personal assets back into the company. This means they believe in their company. If you worked at McDonald's but always ate at Burger King, that would tell a lot more than any sales numbers. As Chicks, we also need to review and understand the company from a historical perspective.

If you decided that you wanted a little plastic surgery (it's only you and me here, so no one has to know), how would you research your doctor? You would snoop around. Ask a few friends. Interview the doctor; look at his medical degree. Ask to see pictures of other patients. You would start asking people if they had heard of his work (you are doing this for a friend, of course) and maybe ask to visit some other patients he has performed miracles on. You'd also want to know the history of his practice. How long has he been in your city? How long has he been operating, and have any lawsuits ever been filed against him? You might call the Better Business Bureau or maybe even conduct a legal search. This is your body we're talking about here, so I'm willing to bet that you'll do some real concentrated research on this doctor before he brings a scalpel near you, and rightly so. Similarly, when putting your hard-earned money into a company, you should do the same thing. If the company has had peaks and valleys all throughout its operating history, or has impending lawsuits, I'd steer clear, because there are many more stable and successful companies out there.

12. **Buy on sale:** Is there one stock that is a better deal than another right now? The Chicks debated whether or not this should be one of our criteria. We don't want to ever time the market—to watch hourly to see when a stock is on sale. That requires keeping track of the market too closely . . . and that isn't Chicky. We want to buy a good company when we have the money, not just because it's on sale. So why add this point—just to make a dozen? No, no, let's say you are trying on a pair of Nine West shoes and a pair of Steve Madden shoes. They are identical, you know and love both brands, it's an eeny-meeny-miney-mo kind of decision, until you find out one pair is on sale, this week only. Ta-da . . . the decision is made for you. This happened to us when we bought one of our companies. Both companies were almost identical in all eleven of the Chicks' Dozen categories, and we were stuck. Voilà, one was on sale. By sale, I mean when their stock price dips over the past couple of weeks. I don't want to give you a precise formula, because there isn't one. But check the price of the stock's fifty-two-week average.

Is the price today way above, or is it below? This isn't an exact science, but it gives you something to go on when it comes down to a breaking a tie. We're women, we have that intuition, and here is where it comes in handy. It's hard to pass up a sale on a good shoe.

By now you are probably saying, "That's it? That's all they use to pick their stocks, and they're beating the market with that tiny amount of knowledge?" Yep. We're amazed too. We can't believe it's so simple, but it is. Adding anything else mucks it up. Too many cooks in the kitchen. People have asked me what our company's price to earnings ratio (P/E) is, or its return on investments (ROI), or its debt equity. I say, "I don't know." And I think, I don't really care. I don't actually say that, because then I'd have to sit down, explain that I am a Chick, that I believe in investing in good strong companies, that I believe in the Chicks' Dozen philosophy, and I'm doing just fine on my own. I don't have the time; nor do I need to defend what I believe. It works. It's like trying to defend your religion to someone at the front door. It's my personal choice, end of story.

Wow, I can't believe I just brought up the religion topic in an investment book. I wonder if my editor will take it out, since it's not politically correct. Looks like he didn't. Bob's comin' around.

How to Get a Company's Numbers

All of the numbers that you will need to do the above problems are available on the Internet at www.chickslayingnesteggs.com. You are going to need two things from a business's SEC filings: its income statement and its balance sheet. The health of a business is evident in those two pages. The income statement is a short-term indicator of how a company is doing, and the balance sheet reflects its history.

For example, imagine a graph of the Nielsen ratings for *The Oprah Winfrey Show* over the past ten years. Pretty amazing, huh? That would be a snapshot of her show over ten years. Success is written all over it. Now, if we were to grab a little segment of the show—how about the week that John F. Kennedy Jr.'s plane went missing. All eyes were glued to the television, but not to *Oprah*. They wanted live news. For the days that followed, people were watching the news networks instead of a previously recorded *Oprah*. If you took the graph of *Oprah*'s Nielsen ratings during that week, the show would look like a flop and you'd predict it would go off the air soon. But zoom out over ten years, and you don't even see that one-week blip. The balance sheet is the ten-year history, and the income statement is the snippet.

How to Get the Balance Sheet and Income Statement

When you get to chickslayingnesteggs.com, click on the words "company research." A new screen will appear. Type in the name or ticker symbol of your company. Then click on SEC filings. A bunch of weird-looking numbers come up: 10Q, 10K, et cetera. Click on the 10Q, or the latest quarter for your company. (That is what companies call their quarterly reports—10Qs.) When the 10Q comes up, you can then click on the balance sheet, and there is your information. You can go back to that same spot again, and click on the income statement. It's that simple.

You can also call the investor relations office of any company you're interested in.

For a refresher, here are the numbers you will need to calculate the Chicks' Dozen and where to find them.

Income Statement	Balance Sheet
Sales (Revenue)	Cash
Cost of Goods Sold (Cost of Sales)	Long-term Debt
Net Income	Current Assets
	Current Liabilities

Chapter Summary

Chicks' Dozen:

1. **Buy what you know:** We prefer products or services that we use in our daily lives.
2. **K.I.S.S. (Keep It Simple, Sister):** The product or service is something simple that we can understand and explain to a fifth-grader.

3. **Industry:** Do you feel this industry is one that will get great growth over the next decade? Or is it an industry that has exhausted most of its growth opportunity?

4. **Leader in its field, top dog of the brand:** We want to invest in companies that have high visibility and brand awareness in the worldwide marketplace.

5. **Repeat profitability:** The Coke or the car—which do you buy more often?

6. **Gross margins:** We want gross margins of at least 50 percent.

7. **Net margins:** We want net profit to be at least 8 percent.

8. **Lots of cash:** We'd prefer companies to have little or no debt, but to have at least as much cash as they do long-term debt.

9. **Flow Ratio:** We want a Flow Ratio below 1.50.

10. **Growth and potential for growth to increase.**

11. **Strong management and operating history:** We want a management team that's experienced, smart, rational, and believes in the company. Also, review and understand the company from an historical perspective.

12. **Buy on sale:** Is there one stock that is a better deal than another right now?

---

chick chat

TITLE: SETUPS

From: Karin

I'm so sorry, but I had to post this frivolous item. I was searching for resorts in northern Minnesota to hold our family reunion this summer, and I came across something that I totally forgot about. While browsing the resort, I couldn't help but notice the sign for Ernie's Pizza Place. It looked like this:

Pizza
12″ Cheese $11.95
16″ Cheese $14.95

Additional Toppings $1.50
Tap Beer Frosted Mug $1.50
Bottle $2.00
Pitcher Beer $5.50
Setups $1.75

Setups? I haven't heard that word in so long that I had completely forgotten it was even a word. Just wondering if I'm bonkers, but do any
of you know what setups are?

Karin

TITLE: RE: SETUPS
From: Megan
Setups—paper plates, cups, napkins and utensils?

IMSoCurious,

Megan

TITLE: RE: SETUPS
From: Jana
Okay, I know my mom, Julie, Lynnie, and probably Kristin know what
setups are, so that leaves Susie, Lorene, Megan, and Cheryl? Since Megan
already took a stab at it—close but no cigar, Meg—we're down to Susie,
Lorene, and Cheryl.

I, too, haven't heard that word since I moved from Minnesota.

Jana

TITLE: RE: SETUPS
From: Kristin

Ladies—

I hate to admit this, being a Wisconsin girl and all, but I have no idea what setups are. Are they the little cardboard cutouts onto which you put drinks? If not, then I'll go with all of the accessories needed for drinks—ice, glasses, umbrellas, etc.

Kristin

TITLE: RE: SETUPS
From: Megan

Setups: when your husband, who knows you are on a diet, leaves king-size Kit Kat bars in the basement by the freezer. He then questions you about the missing ones later. When you deny deny deny, he pulls wrappers out of his pocket that you thought were deeply hidden in the trash.

OR

When you were late on your mortgage payment and your husband asks you if you sent it in on time this month. "Of course I did," you say. He promptly responds, "Really? They just phoned."

Voilà! Setups!
IThnkIMVrySmrt,
Megan

TITLE: RE: SETUPS
From: Lorene

My guess would be that setups are tables, chairs, staging, sound, lighting, etc.—everything that needs to be set up prior to staging an event.

OR

Probably one of those infamous jokes people in northern Minnesota play on those of us not born, raised, or related to someone from them parts. Yah, you betcha.

Lorene

TITLE: RE: SETUPS
From: Susie

I have no idea what setups are, so I'm consulting the dictionary.

Main entry: setup

Function: noun

1. a carriage of the body; erect and soldierly bearing
2. the assembly and arrangement of the tools and apparatus required for the performance of an operation
3. a table setting
4. *glass, ice, and a mixer served to patrons who supply their own liquor*

I looked no further . . . setups.

Please don't ask us any more hard questions. Could we stick to doing a company's numbers? That takes me less time.

Susie

TITLE: **S&P REPORT
From: Cheryl

Thanks, Susie. I almost had to consult my Iowa in-laws to get the answer.

Here's the S&P report:

Whole portfolio up 49.82% vs. the market's 20.95%
AOL up 194.14% (amazing) vs. 14.32%
CSCO up 7.69% vs. 3.94%
KO up 6.39% vs. 29.98% (ouch)
PFE up 10.67% vs 29.98%

chickslaying nesteggs.com

It's a long way down to the place where we started from.
— SARAH MCLACHLAN

You have your computer all set up (yet another definition) and are itching to get to the Web. You know what you need to look for, and you have the Chicks' Dozen sitting right in front of you. Where should you go? Where do you find a company's financial statements? Where can you get stock quotes? Where can you set up an online meeting? Where can your club start a message board and begin your own soap opera? How do you bring all this stuff together? Just type in www.chickslayingnesteggs.com. We have everything you need . . . plus a little fun.

When the Chicks first started, we were getting our stock information from all over the place, which was okay, but sometimes it still felt like we were in a male-dominated, too serious, and definitely too techie world. C'mon, we want to make some money here, but can't we have a little fun at the same time? And can't we have this conversation in ordinary, everyday English? We kept trying to find a place where we felt comfortable, a site that was user-friendly, but all we ever found was an endless supply of stock-picking boys' clubs. There wasn't a sign on the door that said, NO GIRLS ALLOWED, but it didn't say, GIRLS COME ON IN AND JOIN THE PARTY, either. It was like we just didn't exist.

For the longest time, we ended up just posting on our own message board. We would spy on other boards (when you just peek in without commenting, it's called lurking; we lurked till we felt like online stalkers) but never dared to get involved in a conversation for fear of testosterone poisoning. A website was needed for Chicks and Chicks only. One where we could access all the financial information and have a message board. One where we could go and talk about our investments, club business, and life. We checked out some of the other websites geared toward women. They were so cluttered with other female-interest articles, from cooking to parenting, that it took fifteen steps to get to the finance section. We wanted a happenin' female *investment* site: one that would incorporate Chicks philosophy, allow for message boards, help other clubs get set up, and contain all the financial quotes, data, company news releases, and portfolio tracking available. We were in desperate need of a chickslayingnesteggs.com. So we started it: www.chickslayingnesteggs.com. It's a women's investment site and nothing else.

I remember posting on a company's stock board at another investment site to inquire about the company. I wrote:

Hi, my name is Karin. I'm from the Chicks Laying Nest Eggs Investment Club. We're thinking about purchasing Company X for our next stock. Does anyone know where we can find out more information about its CEO? We heard a rumor that he might be stepping aside, and this is important for us to know before we purchase.

We like to do thorough company research before we buy anything. I've searched and searched and can't seem to find anything on him. By the way, has anyone seen the Company X's new cell phones? Amazing. You can download "Sweet Home Alabama" and have the song be your ringer choice.

Within an hour, there was a response to my message post:

Dear Karin,

It's great that you women are considering buying Company X. But why don't you tell us a little bit about your club and what criteria you use for buying a stock. Do you look at the company's price to earnings ratio? Do you take into consideration when it's overvalued or undervalued? Do you "chicks" watch the stock trends? Next time you post to our message board, we would appreciate it if you would stick to talking about the company's stock valuations and not what your cell phone can sing.

Frits H.

No lie. This is what he responded. Due to Frits, I stopped posting on other message boards for about four months. I was scared to death of getting lambasted again. Anyway, the Chicks bought Nokia (the mysterious Company X), and we are trying to teach our cell phones to sing.

Now it's time for you to hear about our website. I'm not going to try and shove it down your throat, because I don't want you to miss out on all those wonderful male-dominated financial websites. But if you want to hang out in a place where you feel comfortable, come on over. The first thing you should do when you get to www.chickslayingnesteggs.com is set up your message board. Just getting this done is a huge first step for your club. Once you have your message board established, you can set your meeting times and places; leave messages for other members about companies you are interested in; ask your other members questions like "Can anyone please help me get the gross margins for Disney? I am having a problem doing the numbers." Or you can post "Would anyone mind if I dropped Target as my company to research? I already did the numbers, and they don't meet standards of the Chicks' Dozen. Do you think I could take a look at 3M?" www.chickslayingnesteggs.com is accessible twenty-four hours a day, so if you are a night owl, like Chick Susie, you can do all of your research and post all your news, views, and messages at three A.M. Chick Lynn does hers from work, and Chick Lorene does it in her pajamas with her morning coffee, right after she gets all of those kids off to school.

Getting Your Club Online

Getting your club's message board up and running is going to change your life! (I just got back from an Anthony Robbins seminar. This is how I talk now.) Being online is going to be your lifeline. It will be the place where you can keep your club's messages and get all your company research. While I think that everyone should be on our website, I admit that there are other alternatives. You can set up message boards on a ton of other sites. The registration process is pretty similar on all of them, so if you've done it once, you're an old pro. But keep reading; it's still entertaining, and you might learn a new tricky, Chicky.

So how do you get there, and what do you do? Type www.chickslayingnesteggs.com in the address line on your browser. This is our URL, which is Internet-speak for address—in other words, anything with a .com, a .net, or .org after it.

Chicks' Internet Essentials

Club Central

Your first stop in the Chicks' website should be Club Central. If you are looking to start a club and need the steps to get started, this is where you want to be: it's vital to your club's existence. You'll find detailed directions on how to get your club message folder opened. You'll also be shown how to create a "My Club" page. This is the "front page" for your club, a place where you can keep your operating instructions and meeting minutes.

Let me explain one thing about the message board. You will need to know what your club name is going to be before you can open a message folder. ("Message board" and "message folder" are interchangeable terms.) You will be directed to an area where you can open a folder. Next you will need to choose or make up a screen name (a screen name is what you would like to be called). You can be anyone you want to be, so be creative. This is how you will be known on the message boards.

When I first registered for a screen name, I thought about MegRyan, GoldieHawn, IM2Sxy4U, and ended up sticking with ChickKarin. Boring, but at least I wasn't lying.

After your message board is set up, post away. Get all of your members to the website and set up shop. Start your business. Get your club movin' and groovin'.

Like anything good in life, the best way to learn is by doing, so don't just sit here reading about it; get up, get your computer going, and get started. You can come back to the book after you've familiarized yourself with a few of our finer features. Call me Bossy. Give yourself an hour a week to play, and then it will become a daily ten-minute routine. Click and you can find stock prices. Click and you can research companies. Click and you can see what we've been up to lately. Click, click, click. Welcome to the Chicks' World of Investment Clubs Online. You're about to change your world. Chicks online and investing!!

Also under Club Central are links that will let you set up an online meeting. Once all of your members have registered, and you know what their screen names are, send them to the Chicks' website and log in (which is what you do when you type in your screen name and password). After everyone has logged in at your meeting time, invite them all into an online meeting by clicking the Chat Room button. One by one, your Chicks of a feather will be flocking together—all your members will be in the same virtual room at the same time. Start the meeting. I recommend that you reserve a peaceful room somewhere in your house and get yourself a beverage. You are going to want to enjoy this with no distractions.

These two things, the message board and the online meetings, will be the oars to keep your club moving, even if you are in the same town. You don't *have* to see these other women every month. Once every three months is sufficient if you are keeping up with your message board. Our club has flourished despite the fact that we see one another only twice a year, and that meeting is mostly about getting away from it all. (Again, it *is* important to tell husbands that it's an investment club semiannual meeting and that it's tax-deductible.)

Club Central is also the place you can track your investment club's portfolio. If I go into detail here, it will look complicated, even though it takes less than five minutes to input what stock you bought, the date you purchased it, and the price you paid for it. The computers out there in cyberspace will do all your calculating. This is only a place for you to keep track of your portfolio, a way of keeping score. It is not your actual portfolio; that is kept at your broker's.

Also inside Club Central are the links to discount brokers, the SS4 partnership form, and the three tax forms. (I'll tell you more about all that later.)

Chicks'-Eye View

This is where you can get a daily dose of what investment topics the Chicks are writing about. Articles range from "Buying What You Know" to "I Don't Know Anything About the Stock Market, and Can't Find a Minute to Learn" to "Does Retin-A Really Clear Up Your Skin and Who Makes It?"

The Meeting Place

This is going to be where your investment club's message board is stored. You will be able to peek in on other clubs' boards to see what they are talking about—if they let you. When you set up your message board and home page, you have the choice of making it private or public. It's up to your club. If it is private, only you and your members will be able to access it.

We have designated a portion of the meeting place to the Chicks Laying Nest Eggs message board. It is the daily goings-on of our club. Yes, we talk about the stocks in our portfolio, but we also gab about everything else that's important to us—Julie's latest golf game, Kristin's first year of marriage, Jeanette's new tax client, Lorene's roller coaster of a life, Cheryl's acting auditions, Susie's hockey team, Lynn's travels, Megan's world, and Jana's two little babies. Oh, and of course, we discuss where our next regular investment dollars are going. Will we purchase another company? Will we invest in an existing company? Why do we like one company better than another? Are we going to sell some of our losers? Should we sell some of our losers? (We're women, and we take a while to sell.) How is our latest Habitat for Humanity Women

Build project going? Where should we hold our next face-to-face meeting? The meeting place is our communication lifeline. Feel free to take a pecky peek. (My husband is addicted. I think he just checks it to see what I'm saying about him. He doesn't really care if we buy more Nokia or sell our Gap. He just wants to know if I truly enjoyed my birthday present, or what I thought of his last family reunion. I can reveal this because he'll never read this far in the book—he's too busy snooping around the website.)

Company Research

Our company research button will let you get your company's snapshot (an overview of the company in a paragraph or two), quotes and data on other companies, charts comparing them all to the market, and all of their balance sheets and income statements. This is the nuts-and-bolts section of the site.

Meet the Chicks

In this area you can see our portfolio and how it is performing against the S&P. No need to look for Cheryl's S&P reports anymore. They are all up-to-the-minute. All the Chicks' biographies are also posted in this part of the site, in case you haven't gotten enough of us yet.

Oh, puh-lease, Karin.

That is www.chickslayingnesteggs.com. It is a lot of letters to type in the first time, but put it in your Favorite Places or bookmark it on your Internet browser, and you won't need to type w-w-w-.-c-h-i-c-k-s-l-a-y-i-n-g-n-e-s-t-e-g-g-s-.-c-o-m every time you want to go to your favorite site.

Once you get familiar with your computer, the Internet, and chickslayingnesteggs.com, go explore some other investment sites. Each of them has a set of research tools. Figure out which ones are the easiest and most understandable for you and add them to your Favorite Places. We believe that we have just about everything you need, but you may think differently. Some of our favorite sites include:

0 www.fool.com
0 quicken.aol.com

0 www.biz.yahoo.com
0 www.bloomberg.com
0 www.cnnfn.com
0 www.marketguide.com
0 www.stockmaster.com
0 cbs.marketwatch.com
0 www.freeedgar.com
0 www.investor.msn.com
0 www.quote.com
0 www.ragingbull.com
0 www.bigcharts.com
0 www.schwab.com

Chapter Summary

0 www.chickslayingnesteggs.com
0 Set up message board.
0 Set up a "My Club" home page.
0 Also at chickslayingnesteggs.com, you can conduct your online meetings, track your portfolio, and access company data. Comes complete with stock quotes and tax forms (ugh).
0 Chicks' private message board to find out what the Chicks are buying or selling and who's pregnant this week?
0 Discount broker links.
0 If you have a question, put it on the "Ask the Chicks" message board.
0 Hope to see you online soon!

chick chat

TITLE: SURPRISE SURPRISE!
From: Kristin

I got engaged! Yep, I'm telling you guys first! Why not share it with the sisters I've never had? Who else would I want to share the most wonderfully romantic, exciting day of my life with?

I walked off the airplane into Pittsburgh today to be greeted by my boyfriend, Tim. He was on one knee, holding two dozen roses and a sign asking, KRISTIN—WILL YOU MARRY ME?

Apparently, I fell into his shoulder, felt him tremble as he placed the beautiful ring (did I say beautiful?) on my finger, and started to cry. I must have taken too long to respond, as the people awaiting their prospective passengers were whispering. When I realized it wasn't just the two of us in our private, loving moment, I responded, "YES! OF COURSE! YES! YES!"

Okay, gotta run . . . I have to go do Coke's numbers, but as you can tell, I kinda have had other things on my mind. You guys are gonna love him.

Still on Cloud Nine,
Kristin

TITLE: SURPRISE SURPRISE!
From: Lynn

Oh my goodness. That is the most wonderful news I think I've heard all week! Congratulations, Kristin! You are one lucky girl to have so much romance. Some of us dreeeeeeaaaaaam of that.

Smooches,
Lynnie

TITLE: SURPRISE SURPRISE!
From: Susie

Congratulation, Kristin! Take another Chick off the market. I hope Tim knows what a great catch he is getting.

Susie

TITLE: **S&P REPORT
From: Cheryl

How exciting, Kristin! We are so happy for you! Enjoy this time alone with your man before a multitude of babies arrives. Not that I'm swamped or anything. Now for the S&P:

Our whole portfolio is up 28.7% compared to the market's 16.03%. The sky is falling, the sky is falling . . .

AOL up 139.18% vs. 13.04%
CSCO up 16.61% vs. 2.77%
GPS up 3.4% vs. 15%
KO up 3.19% vs. 28.52%
PFE up 1.82% vs. 28.52%

Our next meeting is this Sunday at nine P.M., right? And this is a BUY one, huh? We need a winner, Chickies!

13

Crack Open the Chicks' Dozen

Seize the moment. Remember all those women on the
Titanic *who waved off the dessert cart.*
— ERMA BOMBECK

I went to a chili cook-off in Hudson, Wisconsin, last year. People from all over the tristate area brought their chili to the city park to be judged by the best chili judges in the country. I was looking for a new recipe, so I was determined to taste them all. After only an hour of sampling, my tongue was raw. I wasn't halfway through the entries, and I couldn't even look at Aunt Emma's Surprise from Appleton. I could taste no more. I had failed.

I came home and apologized to the kids. I told them that I wouldn't be able to cook them the world's best chili because my tongue wasn't in any shape to find it. I'd brought all the recipes home, but I wasn't sure what was what anymore. Was Morgan from Madison's chili the one with spaghetti-ish flavor, or was that the green pepper base? Was Signey from Somerset the woman who added whole cloves of garlic after simmering them in onion soup? Did I like it? I was so sad, and the kids could see it in my face.

Then my daughter said, "But Mom, why did you go there in the first place? You didn't need to go get all those chili recipes, we like *your* chili. We think *your* chili is the best!"

What was I thinking? My daughter was a genius! I don't make chili every day, I make it once a month, and they love it! It works. It's easy. Even I love it. Why would I try and change something that everyone loves—to maybe find something better? Is it worth trying a new chili recipe every month for a full year to *maybe* find one they like as much? Is it worth all the work and the headaches? No.

Where am I going with this, you ask? Because the Chicks' Dozen investment approach and my chili recipe have an awful lot in common. The Chicks' Dozen works. It's what we know and love. It's simple. Why should we try another formula when it might not work as well—just so we can risk getting confused? The Chicks' Dozen has proven itself over and over since we started our club. Our taste buds are happy. We can pull our chair up to the table and know exactly what to expect. So we are going to stick with it.

Bless us this food which we are about to receive . . .

In this chapter I am going to run a few of the companies in our portfolio through the Chicks' Dozen criteria. I will also show some companies that aren't Chick-owned so you can see how they fare. By the time we're through, you'll understand why we chose some and not others. What I hope is that by the end of the chapter, applying the Chicks' Dozen to a company will seem as easy as opening a can of Hormel. I'll start with some of the Chicks' stocks. I have pulled quarterly statements from the companies and included them so you can see what one looks like. It doesn't matter that they aren't the most current; these are just samples so you can see what information is in these essential documents and how to find what information you actually need when you start pulling up the SEC filings of companies you own or are thinking about buying.

Chicks' Do(zen) America Online (AOL)

1. **Buy what you know:** Hmm, who doesn't know AOL? If I haven't talked about it enough already, look at the ads on your city buses. Check out the TV, your newspaper, or a magazine. Didn't you get a little AOL CD in the mail? AOL is as American as apple pie. Know it? You're breathing it. You've got mail.

2. **K.I.S.S. (Keep It Simple, Sister):** Could I explain AOL to a fifth grader? Are you kidding? They could explain it to me. Matter of fact, here is what my daughter said:

> You wanna know what AOL is? That's easy. It's the place on my computer where I get e-mail and information to do my homework. Sometimes I talk to my friends on there.

3. **Industry:** If the Internet isn't the future, and one of the fastest-growing industries, then this book is mud. Is everyone you know online? If your answer's "nope" now, rest assured that they all will be soon. Where will they turn? AOL? I believe so. AOL has grown a lotta-lotta percent in the past years, and I don't see it slowing down. I'm just wondering why they didn't call themselves World Online.

4. **Leader in its field:** Who are its competitors? Tap, tap, tap. Exactly!

5. **Repeat profitability:** Do you know how many times a day I log in? I'm addicted. You take-away-a-my-AOL-a, and I ruffle you feathers. (Reread that in your best Rocky Balboa voice.) What does this company get out of me a month? Well, there's me and 25 million other AOL subscribers at $21.95 per month. That equals serious cashola. That's per month, every month. You decide—who gets the most repeat purchasers, AOL or Boeing? As we write this, AOL is in the process of becoming AOL Time Warner. To us, this seems like a great thing. The biggest Internet service provider connects up to a company with not only a tremendous set of pipes (Warner's cable companies) but one of the greatest content-generating machines on the planet (Warner books, movies, and television as well as all the magazines in the Time family)—how could this not be the next big thing? But that's the future, and right now we're looking at the present, and the numbers from their most recent SEC filing.

[The financial numbers that I used for the criteria numbered 6 through 10 are found immediately after AOL's Chicks'

Dozen on page 165. You can flip to them as you read and calculate along.)

6. **Gross margins:** We want gross margins to be at least 50 percent.

$$= \frac{1,975 \text{ (Revenues)} - 928 \text{ (Cost of Revenues)}}{1,975 \text{ (Revenues)}}$$

$$= \frac{1,047}{1,975}$$

$$= .5301$$

.5301 × 100 (to change to a percentage)

Gross Margins = 53 percent

7. **Net margins:** We want gross margins to be at least 8 percent.

$$= \frac{345 \text{ (Net Income)}}{1,975 \text{ (Revenues)}}$$

$$= .1747$$

.1747 × 100 (to change to a percentage)

Net Margins = 17 percent

8. **Lots of cash:** We want at least as much cash as we have long-term debt.

$$= \frac{2,039 \text{ (Cash)} + 1,192 \text{ (Short-Term Investments)}}{1,646 \text{ (Long-Term Debt)}}$$

$$\frac{3,231}{1,646} = 1.96 \times \text{cash to Long-Term Debt}$$

9. **Flow Ratio below 1.50:**

$$= \frac{4,346 \text{ (Current Assets)} - 3,231 \text{ (Cash and Short-Term Investments)}}{2,307 \text{ (Current Liabilities)} - 0 \text{ (Short-Term Debt)}}$$

$$= \frac{1,115}{2,307}$$

$$= .48$$

Flow Ratio = .48!!!

10. **Increasing growth:** Revenues September 1999 = 1,477 (found online)

Revenues September 2000 = 1,975

1,975 − 1,477 = 498

498/1,477 = .3371

.3371 × 100 = 34 percent

Percentage Change from 1999 to 2000 is 34 percent! Not bad!

11. **Strong management and operating history:** Steve Case, CEO—is he likable? A little Internet search says he's a pretty closed person, but he wears "loud" Hawaiian shirts; that's bold. He sang in a new-wave rock group back in college; really bold. (Isn't it?) The only "weak" area seen was his inability to be a "fiery, charismatic" leader. These days if you're fiery and charismatic, you have lawsuits coming out of your ears. I see this as an asset for our Stevie. Look, the guy wants to take us places via the Internet that we never imagined. He has so far, and I don't think he's stopping now. Again, look at the numbers: Case in point. Ask yourself, if you could invite any Internet man to your dinner table, who would it be? Whose brain would you want to pick? That's strong management. As for operating history, the company is still relatively new, but if you go on what they've done in such a short time, this history is unbelievably huge. (Steve, wanna come for dinner?)

12. **Buy on sale:** This is a usable criterion only at the time of purchasing a stock. After the fact, it's irrelevant. You bought it, on sale or not. When we bought AOL, we were so hungry to get our hands on it, we didn't care what the price was. When you have to have a Kate Spade, nothing else will do.

What's a Kate Spade, Karin?

A purse designer, Mom.

Below is the SEC filing for AOL. This is where you get the information to plug into the Chicks' Dozen criteria numbers 6 through 10.

PORTIONS OF
SEC FILING FOR AMERICA ONLINE, INC.

BALANCE SHEET
(AMOUNTS IN MILLIONS, UNAUDITED)

Three months ended September 30, 2000

ASSETS

Current assets:

Cash and cash equivalents	$2,039
Short-term investments	1,192
Trade accounts receivable, less allowances of $91 and $83, respectively	451
Other receivables, net	137
Prepaid expenses and other current assets	527
Total current assets	**4,346**
Property and equipment at cost, net	1,026

Other assets:

Investments including available-for-sale securities	4,627
Product development costs, net	202
Goodwill and other intangible assets, net	513
Other assets	239
Total Assets	**$10,953**

LIABILITIES

Current liabilities:

Trade accounts payable	$256
Other accrued expenses and liabilities	773
Deferred revenue	1,083
Accrued personnel costs	119
Deferred network services credit	76
Short-term debt	0
Total current liabilities	**2,307**

Long-term liabilities:

Long-term debt	1,646

INCOME STATEMENT
(AMOUNTS IN MILLIONS, UNAUDITED)

Three months ended September 30, 2000

Revenues:

Subscription services	$1,206
Advertising, commerce and other	649
Enterprise solutions	120
Total revenues	**1,975**

Costs and expenses:

Cost of revenues	928
Sales and marketing	298
Product development	60
General and administrative	183
Amortization of goodwill and other intangible assets	22
Merger charges	6
Total costs and expenses	**1,497**

Income from operations	478
Other income, net	89
Income before provision for income taxes	567
Provision for income taxes	(222)
Net income	**$345**

Chicks' Do(zen) Oracle

1. **Buy what you know:** For me, this is probably the diciest question of the entire Oracle Dozen. Oracle's goods are not something that you would find in your fridge or pantry, but you probably use it somewhere daily without knowing it. Chick Kristin and Chick Jana swear they couldn't live without Oracle in the workplace. (See why I love a

club? Both those Chicks worked at Oracle at one time.) Oracle develops, manufactures, markets, and distributes computer software that helps corporations manage and grow their businesses. And here's something they do that I can relate to. Of late, Oracle's biggest thrust has been helping companies transform themselves into e-businesses—now, this I use. With a few kids tying me to my humble abode, I have to shop online . . . okay, I love to shop online. I shop everywhere from Amazon.com to Gap.com to eBay.com. And, according to my Chickish experts, an awful lot of the places I shop use Oracle software.

2. **K.I.S.S. (Keep It Simple, Sister):** Let's see, I'll have to keep this simple because it's the only way I even understand what it is they do! Oracle provides the software and servers that help businesses run. They have data up the ying-yang for all the world to access. I can understand that. Was that putting it simply? Data up the ying-yang. And I know shopping online couldn't be easier! It saved my life this past Christmas. I think I could teach a fifth-grader to "point and click"—my gosh, I taught my two-year-old that! I just have to keep the credit card up high on the shelf now.

3. **Industry:** If the world is all turning to the Internet, and we have established above with our AOL purchase that we believe it is, then they need someplace to store data. Or they need someplace that already has the data they need. It's a much-needed industry, and one with great growth to come as more people and corporations get online.

4. **Leader in its field:** Yah, you betcha! (My Minnesota accent coming through.) Oracle leads the worldwide market share in databases and application servers and supplies the leading Internet platforms for e-businesses. It is the world's leading supplier of software for information management and the second-largest software company overall. No wonder so many companies turn to them for help with their e-businesses.

5. **Repeat profitability:** Yeah baby . . . just think of newer versions of the software. Companies will have to upgrade, so as not to completely change their existing databases. Cha-ching. Repeat cha-ching.

As far as e-commerce goes, Oracle helps companies (for example: eBAY) hold lots of data by using Oracle databases. They charge these companies what they call a "site license fee." Companies renew their license, and Oracle simply collects the cashola!

Pete and Repeat went down to the lake. Pete fell in. Who was left? Repeat.
Pete and Repeat went down to the lake. Pete fell in. Who was left? Repeat.

Well, you get the Oracle picture.

[The financial numbers that I used for the criteria numbered 6 through 10 are found immediately after Oracles' Chicks' Dozen on page 171. You can flip to them as you read and calculate along.]

6. **Gross margins:** We want them to be at least 50 percent. Oracle kicks some booty in this area; theirs are 70 percent.

$$= \frac{\$2,261,875 \,(\text{Revenues}) - \$673,878 \,(\text{Cost of Revenues*})}{\$2,261,875 \,(\text{Revenues})}$$

$$= \frac{\$1,587,997}{\$2,261,875}$$

$$= .7020$$

$$.7020 \times 100 \,(\text{to change to a percentage})$$

Gross Margins = 70 percent

7. **Net margins:** We want net margins to be at least 8 percent. How much is ole Oracle really making? CEO Larry Ellison should be standing tall. Oracle boasts a net (profit) margin of 22 percent, more

---

*Cost of services.

than double our 8 percent requirement. I just might invite him to my Internet dinner table, too. Pick, pick, pick. For more on Larry, see Strong Management below.

$$= \frac{\$500,677 \text{ (Net Income)}}{\$2,261,875 \text{ (Revenues)}}$$

$$= .2213$$
$$.2213 \times 100 \text{ (to change to a percentage)}$$
$$\text{Net Margins} = 22 \text{ percent}$$

8. **Lots of cash:** We would like our companies to have at least as much cash as they do long-term debt. Oracle shines again with a ratio of 4.38 times cash to long-term debt.

$$\text{Cash* / Long-Term Debt}$$
$$\$4,837,097 \text{ (Cash)} + \$225,475 \text{ (Short-Term Investments)}$$
$$/ \$300,731 \text{ (Long-Term Debt)}$$
$$\$5,062,572 / \$300,731 = 16.83 \times \text{Cash to Long-Term Debt}$$

9. **Flow Ratio below 1.5:** Oracle is definitely running a tight ship with a ratio of .66, well below the 1.50 criterion.

$$= \frac{\text{(Current Assets} - \text{Cash)}}{\text{(Current Liabilities} - \text{Short-Term Debt)}}$$

$$= \$7,258,595 \text{ (Current Assets)} - \$5,062,572$$

$$\frac{\text{(Cash and Short-Term Investments)}}{\$3,307,109 \text{ (Current Liabilities)} \$3,660 - \text{(Short-Term Debt)}}$$

$$= \frac{\$2,196,023}{\$3,303,449}$$

$$= .66$$

---

*Cash plus short-term investments.

10. **Increasing growth:** In this sample last quarter alone, sales have increased 17 percent.

Sales ending August 1999 (Q3) = $2,321,883 (found online)
Sales ending August 2000 = $2,261,875
$2,261,875 − 2,321,883 = −$60,008
−$60,008 / $2,321,883 = −.0258

−.03 (rounding off) × 100 = 3 percent sales decrease from a year ago August

Uh-oh. Looks like we are going to have to keep an eye on Oracle's sales, especially quarter to quarter. We want to make sure that this doesn't continue to slide. (At the time of the Chicks' purchase, this number was going in the positive direction.) As for future growth, I have to repeat a quote from Larry Ellison a few years back: "If the Internet turns out not to be the future of computing, we're toast. But if it is, we're golden." Well, hello Goldie! How many spare minutes do I steal each day to get to the Net? Never enough!

11. **Strong management and operating history:** I heard one day, when Oracle's stock was up just a bit, that CEO Larry had made $1.3 billion. Sheeeeez . . . I'd call that a slight personal stake in the company. He is fiercely competitive (just ask his fellow yacht racers or Bill Gates), and he has a unique ability to motivate employees and partners toward a common vision (or so I've been told). As far as Oracle's operating history, I think I'll let one of Oracle's loan officers answer this one for me. After all, you know what kind of background checks those guys do before they hand over the almighty dollar! Cheryl's husband was on a flight to his home state of Iowa in 1995 and sat next to a guy who worked for a bank that loans Oracle money; they were his number-one account. When asked what he thought, he said, "If you saw their balance sheet, you'd buy as much as you can as often as you can!" Can you ever distrust a guy from Iowa? When Chick Jana worked for Oracle, I, as her computer-illiterate sister, would ask what she was actually doing there. At that point she would say, "Getting rich in my stock options." Since then she has, and continues to let them make her richer. Larry? Will you come to dinner?

12. **Buy on sale:** Again, when we purchased the stock, there was no doubt that we wanted it, on sale or off sale. We just wanted a piece of Larry . . . I mean Oracle.

Below is the SEC filing for Oracle. This is where you get the information to plug into the Chicks' Dozen criteria numbers 6 through 10.

PORTIONS OF
SEC FILING FOR ORACLE CORP
NASDAQ: ORCL

BALANCE SHEET
(AMOUNTS IN THOUSANDS)

Three months ended August 31, 2000

ASSETS

Current Assets:

Cash and cash equivalents	$4,837,097
Short-term cash investments	225,475
Trade receivables, net of allowance for doubtful account of $262,958	1,696,320
Other receivables	162,847
Prepaid and refundable income taxes	213,780
Prepaid expenses and other current assets	123,076
Total current assets	**7,258,595**

Long-term cash investments	70,000
Property, net	936,757
Intangible and other assets	1,247,175
Total assets	**$9,512,527**

LIABILITIES

Current liabilities:

Notes payable and current maturities of long-term debt (a.k.a short-term debt)	$3,660
Accounts payable	253,243

Income taxes payable	517,123
Accrued compensation and related benefits	401,693
Customer advances and unearned revenues	1,269,585
Value-added tax and sales tax payable	83,723
Other accrued liabilities	778,082
Total current liabilities	**3,307,109**
Long-term debt	300,731
Other long-term liabilities	178,128
Deferred income taxes	355,661
Stockholders' equity	5,370,898
Total liabilities and stockholders' equity	**$9,512,527**

INCOME STATEMENT
(AMOUNTS IN THOUSANDS)

Revenues:

Licenses and other	$807,238
Services	1,454,637
Total revenues	**2,261,875**

Operating expenses:

Sales and marketing	572,964
Cost of services	673,878
Research and development	251,027
General and administrative	105,965
Total operating expenses	1,603,834
Operating income	658,041
Net investment gains/(losses) related to marketable securities	15,433
Other income, net	102,769
Income for provision for income taxes	776,243
Provision for income taxes	275,566
Net Income	**$500,677**

Chicks' Do(zen) Gap, Inc.

1. **Buy what you know:** The Gap certainly fits the mold here. My credit card handles it all: Gap, GapKids, BabyGap, GapBody, Old Navy, or Banana Republic. (All those companies, though different storefronts, are owned by the Gap.) From back-to-school shopping to finding pajamas the night before "pajama day" at school, it is the one and only brand that I can count on to appeal to my children. And how can you not envy the impeccably folded clothes? They make it a joy to shop in their stores (stark contrast with my kid's drawers and closets).

2. **K.I.S.S. (Keep It Simple, Sister):** Is there anything simpler than the Gap? It's clothing! We all know clothing! The Gap is an international specialty retailer that operates stores that sell casual apparel, shoes, and other accessories for men, women, and children. Again, clothes for sale around the world. Pretty simple to me.

3. **Industry:** I don't see the retail clothing industry gaining any greater growth in the next ten years than it did in the past ten years, but the Chicks see the Gap as gaining momentum in that particular industry. Its popularity has increased, and it has plenty of room to grow with stores of all Gap names.

4. **Leader in its field:** Where would you buy an eight-year-old boy some decent clothes that he will like? It's not a tough answer: the Gap. In addition to the loyal Gap fans, the Banana Republic also has a large audience appeal. They have a higher-quality, more expensive product, but people buy it. They also have clientele specialists, shopping by phone and Internet e-tailing options. On the opposite end of the spectrum is Old Navy: a cheaper, no-frills version of the Gap. All leaders, all owned by Gap, Inc.

5. **Repeat profitability:** The Gap definitely makes the grade here. For my family, Old Navy is at least a monthly stop-off. Not to mention that every baby gift from this house comes from GapOnline. Of course, I'm on everyone's birth announcement list, and even if I'm not, I can't resist. I love babies.

I'd like to change things up a bit here. We bought the Gap in June of 1999. Shortly after, things started to head in the wrong direction. Gross margins, net margins, and a couple more requirements turned south (in lieu of saying "sour"). Luckily, we have Chick Megan on the job of tracking the company, and she alerted us to the faltering numbers immediately. We haven't decided yet to sell, but Megan is keeping a very close eye on it. Let's look at the Gap's numbers from quarter to quarter over the last year. I will not calculate for you, but get your own Texas Instrument out and try to come up with the same answers.

THE GAP, INC.

(NYSE: GPS)
QUARTERLY BALANCE SHEET

In Millions of U.S. Dollars (except for per share items)	As of 10/28/00	As of 07/29/00	As of 04/29/00	As of 01/29/00	As of 10/30/99
Cash and short-term investments	$352.2	$327.9	$436.2	$450.4	$485.7
Total inventory	2,567.5	2,080.9	1,652.0	1,462.0	1,825.0
Prepaid expenses	475.6	375.0	315.7	285.4	306.6
Total current assets	**3,395.3**	**2,783.7**	**2,403.9**	**2,197.8**	**2,617.3**
Property/plant/equipment, net	3,621.5	3,244.9	2,905.1	2,715.3	2,473.5
Intangibles, net	344.7	345.8	348.6	275.7	254.5
Total assets	**7,361.5**	**6,374.4**	**5,657.6**	**5,188.8**	**5,345.3**
Accounts payable	1,728.5	922.9	728.1	805.9	725.6
Accrued expenses	28.4	617.8	669.5	751.7	720.1
Notes payable/short-term debt	1,482.4	859.4	631.5	169.0	636.5
Total current liabilities	**3,239.3**	**2,400.1**	**2,029.0**	**1,752.9**	**2,223.6**
Long-term debt	1,003.5	1,022.9	769.3	784.9	808.9
Other liabilities	498.5	452.3	431.5	417.9	394.7
Total liabilities	**4,741.3**	**3,875.3**	**3,229.8**	**2,955.7**	**3,427.2**

QUARTERLY INCOME STATEMENT

In Millions of U.S. Dollars (except for per share items)	13 Weeks Ending 10/28/00	13 Weeks Ending 07/29/00	13 Weeks Ending 04/29/00	13 Weeks Ending 01/29/00	13 Weeks Ending 10/30/99
Revenue	3,414.7	2,947.7	2,732.0	3,858.9	3,045.4
Other revenue	—	—	—	—	—
Total revenue	3,414.7	2,947.7	2,732.0	3,858.9	3,045.4
Cost of revenue	2,157.5	1,837.1	1,601.9	2,256.5	1,741.1
Gross profit	1,257.2	1,110.6	1,130.1	1,602.5	1,304.3
Interest expense (income), net operating	20.5	11.7	9.0	13.4	10.6
Other operating expenses	943.3	809.3	750.3	937.3	797.6
Total operating expense	3,121.2	2,658.1	2,361.2	3,207.2	2,549.3
Operating income	293.5	289.6	370.8	651.7	496.1
Income before tax	293.5	289.6	370.8	651.7	496.1
Income tax	107.1	105.7	135.4	237.9	181.1
Income after tax	186.3	183.9	235.5	413.8	315.0
Net income	186.3	183.9	235.5	413.8	315.0

How Gap Fares on the Chicks' Dozen Points 6 through 10 from Quarter to Quarter

Criteria 6 through 10	As of 10/28/00	As of 07/29/00	As of 04/29/00	As of 01/29/00	As of 10/30/99
Gross margins (we want > 50%)	36.8%	37.6%	41.3%	41.5%	42.8%
Net margins (we want > 8%)	5.46%	6.24%	8.62%	10.72%	10.34%
Cash to long-term-debt (> 1.0)	.35	.32	.57	.57	.60
Flow Ratio (<1.5)	1.7	1.6	1.4	1.1	1.3
Sales (should be increasing)	3,414.7	2,947.7	2,732.0	3,858.9	3,045.4

So there you have it, Gap's decreasing numbers. Sales picked up this most recent quarter. If you want to do a little exercise, fill in the quarters that have followed since this book has been published and see if any of the numbers have turned around. Here, I'll get your chart all ready for you.

Criteria 6 through 10	As of 10/28/01	As of 07/29/01	As of 04/29/01	As of 01/29/01	As of 10/30/00
Gross margins (we want >50%)					36.8%
Net margins (we want >8%)					5.46%
Cash to long-term debt (>1.0)					.35
Flow Ratio (<1.5)					1.7
Sales (should be increasing)					3,414.7

10. **Increasing growth:** Growth in fiscal year 1999 included the addition of approximately five hundred new stores, and in 2000, they opened approximately five hundred fifty new stores. Growth, growth, baby. Let's hope their financial statement can grow along with their new store openings.

11. **Strong management and operating history:** Virtually no detail— from window displays to fabric blends—is too minute to escape CEO Millard Drexler's attention. Every week, the fifty-five-year-old strolls anonymously into Gap stores from coast to coast to schmooze with consumers and clerks alike in a constant drive to improve the company's products and services. In his spare time, he reads letters from his customers. (Hey, Millard, did you get my dinner invitation yet?)

Born and raised in New York City, Drexler spent most of his working life in the clothing business. Prior to joining the Gap, he was the CEO of Ann Taylor and spent time at Bloomingdale's and Abraham and Straus. Millard and I went to the same college. He holds an undergraduate degree from the State University of New York at Buffalo and an MBA from Boston University. I forgot to do the Boston part. Smart, smart, Millard.

Over the last ten years, the Gap has continued to demonstrate consistent sales and earnings growth, while their gross and net profit margins are among the best in the industry. Between 1988 and today, the company's total shares outstanding has decreased (which means they are slowly buying back shares of their own company: even *they* know how valuable it is.) Strong management and operating history.

12. **Buy on sale:** Again, you should weigh the stock at the time of purchase. Are you haggling between two really good stocks? Which one is on sale? We loved the Gap, with or without a sale price. We just wanted to buy it, so the "on sale" factor was not figured in, mostly because at the time of the purchase, there was no other competition. When you want those Gap jeans today, you just can't wait until they go on sale (because the ones you want usually don't).

Chicks Do(zen) Estee Lauder (NYSE: EL)

A while ago a man hopped on over to our message board and wrote, "Why don't you guys check out Estee Lauder . . . seems you would most certainly be buying what you know with that stock." I personally was offended. A make-up company? Puh-lease. But, for the heck of it, we ran it through our Chicks' Dozen.

1. **Buy what you know:** Anyone nearing their thirties certainly knows anti-aging creams, moisturizers, and cover-ups. The Estee Lauder Companies, Inc., own almost everything in my makeup bag and then some. Do any of these brand names sound familiar? Estee Lauder, Clinique, Aramis, Prescriptives, Origins, M.A.C., Bobbi Brown Essentials, Tommy Hilfiger, La Mer, Jane, Donna Karan, Aveda, Kate Spade, Stila, Jo Malone and Bumble and Bumble.

2. **K.I.S.S. (Keep It Simple, Sister):** Not only can you explain this company to a fifth-grader, they are probably starting to use some of the above products! I know my daughter has the Origins "Clean Sheets" candle burning in her room right now.

3. **Industry:** Personal and Household Products. I would call it, the Makeup Industry, but I'm not in charge of naming the industries.

This industry is also what they call "Noncyclical." By noncyclical, it means the product isn't purchased more at some time of the year than later. It has equal buying power appeal throughout the year. Is there ever a month of year you can go without mascara? Exactly.

4. **Leader in its field:** You betcha! (I can't shake the *Fargo* lingo.) Its strongest competitor is L'Oreal L.A. (Owner of Lancome, Ralph Lauren, L'Oreal, Maybelline, and Plentitude.) For it to continue to be the leader in its field, it has to grow faster than the others, and it looks like they do this by scooping up more and more companies to add to their bag. They're definitely this Chick's Choice of Cheeks.

5. **Repeat profitability:** Again, who can ever go without mascara or moisturizers? I think I buy one product of theirs a week. (I just can't figure out why people still tell me I look tired.)

Now, starting with Estee Lauder, I'm going to give you a chance to do the numbers all on your own. The answers will follow on the next page, but don't even think about cheating, or I'll make you sneeze while you put on your mascara. Get out your calculators.

I'll give you the financials that I got from www.marketguide.com, and you can fill in the blanks that follow. The step-by-step process is found at www.chickslayingnesteggs.com, so if you get stuck, you can go check the complete process there.

In Millions of U.S. Dollars	As of 09/30/00	As of 06/30/00	As of 03/31/00	As of 12/31/99	As of 09/30/99
Cash & equivalents	233.8	320.3	367.6	347.7	250.2
Short-term investments	0	0	0	0	0
*Cash *and* short-term investments	233.8	320.3	367.6	347.7	250.2
Total receivables, net	725.7	550.2	606.9	686.9	699.0
Total inventory	521.5	546.3	444.9	463.5	510.4
Prepaid expenses	220.7	201.7	188.8	197.0	189.0
*Total current assets	1,701.7	1,618.5	1,608.2	1,695.1	1,648.6

*Long-term debt	418.1	418.4	421.5	422.1	425.1
*Notes payable/ short-term debt	6.6	7.0	7.0	6.8	111.7
*Total current liabilities	929.8	901.8	853.2	951.7	968.2

In Millions of U.S. Dollars	3 Months Ending 09/30/00	3 Months Ending 06/30/00	3 Months Ending 03/31/00	3 Months Ending 12/31/99	3 Months Ending 09/30/99
Revenue	1,177.7	998.9	1,039.1	1,235.1	1,093.7
*Total revenue	1,177.7	998.9	1,039.1	1,235.1	1,093.7
Cost of revenue	263.3	206.5	230.7	283.1	251.8
Gross profit	914.4	792.4	808.4	952.0	841.9
Selling/ general/ administrative expenses (employee benefits)	752.9	690.3	701.3	756.7	697.4
Other operating expenses	8.2	8.3	7.7	9.2	8.0
Total operating expenses	1,024.4	905.1	939.7	1,049.0	957.2
Operating income	153.3	93.8	99.4	186.1	136.5
Interest expense, net nonoperating	(5.1)	(3.2)	(3.3)	(5.2)	(5.4)
Income before tax	148.2	90.6	96.1	180.9	131.1
Income tax	53.4	33.4	35.7	67.0	48.5
Income after tax	94.8	57.2	60.4	113.9	82.6
Net income	94.6	57.2	60.4	113.9	82.6

Estee Lauder Chicks' Dozen Criterion 6–10	As of 09/30/00	As of 06/30/00	As of 03/31/00	As of 12/31/99	As of 09/30/99
Gross margins (> 50%)					
Net margins (> 8%)					
Cash to long term debt (> 1.0)					
Flow Ratio (< 1.5%)					
Sales (we want to increase)					

10. **Increasing growth:** Look at these revenue numbers (in millions):

2000	1999	1998	1997	1996
4,366.8	3,961.5	3,618.0	3,381.6	3,194.5

That would be more than a lash-length increase.

11. **Strong management and operating history:** The company was founded in 1946 in New York City. Members of the Lauder family currently own approximately 58 percent of the company's common stock, but retains 92 percent of the voting power. Their CEO is Fred Langhammer, and Leonard Lauder is the chairman. There are many Lauder family members both on the board and as executives. Estee Lauder sells its products in 120 countries around the world and on the World Wide Web.

12. **Buy on sale:** This is going to be determined at the time you are running it through the Chicks' Dozen. At the time of publishing, it looked like this: 52-week high – 55.87, 52-week low – 33.75, 52-week average – 44.81. The price today is 42.125. That would be a sale! And a little makeup tip from Chick Cheryl before we wrap this one up: She buys a new tube of mascara every three months . . . right about the time she checks in on all of her stocks to see how they fare in the Chicks' Dozen.

Answers to Estee Lauder Chicks' Dozen Numbered Criterion

Estee Lauder Chicks' Dozen Criterion 6–10	As of 09/30/00	As of 06/30/00	As of 03/31/00	As of 12/31/99	As of 09/30/99
Gross margins (> 50%)	78%	79%	78%	77%	77%
Net margins (> 8%)	7.8%	5.7%	5.8%	9.2%	7.6%
Cash to Long-term debt (> 1.0)	.559×	.766×	.872×	.824×	.589×
Flow Ratio (< 1.5)	1.6	1.5	1.5	1.43	0
Sales (we want to increase)*	1,177.7	998.9	1,039.1	1,235.1	1,093.7

*Sales numbers in millions of U.S. dollars.

Chicks Do(zen) Kenneth Cole Productions (NYSE: KCP)

1. **Buy what you know:** Who doesn't know shoes? Who doesn't know Kenneth Cole shoes? If you don't, you're a tad bit outta the loop. (Was that rude? Sorry, but everyone I know has a least one pair of KC's and some of us have more than we can count on both hands.

Chick Lorene even has the handbags to match.) I never thought to run Kenneth Cole through the Chicks' Dozen until Chick Megan ran Steve Madden through the twelve-step criteria. I love Steve Madden shoes as much as I love Kenneth Cole's, but guess who's Chicks' Dozen looked better? Yep, KCP.

2. **K.I.S.S. (Keep It Simple, Sister):** Leather, soles and laces. Comfortable foot-wear with fashion. This is easily explainable to a fifth-grader, although I haven't found any to fit her. Maybe Kenneth has Kids Cole in his pipeline. (Just an idea, Ken!)

3. **Industry:** Apparel and shoes. Even in the summer, I simply have to have a pair of Kenneth Cole sandals. (And, of course, Chick Lorene has to have the purse to match.)

4. **Leader in its field:** Depending on what kind of shoes you are looking for, its number one competitor would be Steve Madden, but stock market sites also list Vans, Reebok, Nike, and Gucci. Personally, Kenneth leads Steve by three in my closet.

5. **Repeat profitability:** Let's see, I have the black suit, the navy suit, jeans and sweater, hunter green suit, little black skirt, little black dress, gray suit, and the list goes on. All my outfits need shoes, and they all must keep up with what's in fashion. No one can own just one pair of black boots (or at least that's what I tell my husband).

Steps 6–10, you're on your own Chicky!!!

Kenneth Cole Chicks Dozen Criterion 6–10	As of 09/30/00	As of 06/30/00	As of 03/31/00	As of 12/31/99	As of 09/30/99
Gross margins (> 50%)					
Net margins (> 8%)					
Cash to long-term debt (> 1.0)					
Flow Ratio (< 1.5)					
Sales (we want to increase)					

(These numbers can also be found at www.marketguide.com.)

Kenneth Cole Productions has already infiltrated the luggage market and men's clothing and is looking to take some market share from the women's clothing sector. I also read that he is planning on creating some merchandise for the home. Watch out, Martha Stewart.

11. **Strong management and operating history:** Kenneth D. Cole is the founder of the company and has been president ever since. He is also on the board of directors of the American Foundation for AIDS Research (AmFAR) and H.E.L.P., a New York agency that provides temporary housing for the homeless. Kenneth doesn't need to walk a mile in someone else's shoes in order to give back to his community. Gotta like that in the man. I'm thinking I'd like to invite him to our Chicks' dinner table, as long as he brings me a few pairs of size 6's in the latest design.

12. **Buy on sale:** This is what was posted on our message board at the time we were considering buying the stock.

52-week high: 50.50
52-week low: 21.75

Anything below their 52-week average of $36.13 would be a shoe sale. The stock closed trading on this specific date at $44. Not on sale, but it doesn't mean it's not a quality stock. Again, it's just a measure if you have two equal companies that are tied in your voting process.

In Millions of U.S. Dollars	As of 09/30/00	As of 06/30/00	As of 03/31/00	As of 12/31/99	As of 09/30/99
*Cash and short-term investments	50.9	43.2	50.2	71.4	36.6
*Total current assets	147.3	135.1	146.6	147.0	123.8
*Notes payable/ short-term debt	—	—	—	—	—
*Total current liabilities	45.7	39.2	39.0	41.0	25.5
*Long-term debt	—	—	—	0.6	—

In Millions of U.S. Dollars	3 Months Ending 09/30/00	3 Months Ending 06/30/00	3 Months Ending 03/31/00	3 Months Ending 12/31/99	3 Months Ending 09/30/99
Revenue	104.2	85.3	90.3	88.2	81.3
Other revenue	6.3	5.3	4.0	5.2	4.2
*Total revenue	110.6	90.6	94.3	93.4	85.6
*Cost of revenue	57.8	50.4	51.1	49.3	46.3
Gross profit	46.4	35.0	39.2	38.9	35.0
Net income	12.9	6.4	7.8	8.6	8.1

10. **Increasing growth:** Let's take a look at their sales growth figures over the last five years (amounts in millions).

1999	1998	1997	1996	1995
310.3	228.1	191.3	151.8	113.8

Looks like that has increased to me. But what about the future?

I decided not to leave you sitting outside the door like my son's smelly shoes and give you the answers to numbers six through ten. All laced up and ready to run.

Kenneth Cole Chicks' Dozen Criteria 6–10	As of 09/30/00	As of 06/30/00	As of 03/31/00	As of 12/31/99	As of 09/30/99
Gross margins (> 50%)	42%	38.6%	41.6%	41.6%	41%
Net margins (> 8%)	11.7%	7%	8.3%	9.2%	9.5%
Cash to long-term debt (>1.0)	No debt	No debt	No debt	119×	No debt
Flow Ratio (< 1.5)	2.1	2.3	2.47	1.84	3.41
Sales (we want to increase)	110.6	90.6	94.3	93.4	85.6

Chicks' Do(zen) General Electric

1. **Buy what you know:** We bring good things to light, or is it life? Either way, it has to ring a bell. Go look in your utility closet. See any lightbulbs with a little circle insignia? GE. GE is a diversified technology, manufacturing, and services company that has a wide range of industries, from broadcasting (NBC: don't you remember all the times David Letterman referred to his bosses at GE? Now Jay Leno has to report to the big bulb) to power plant parts manufacturing (something I'm very interested in: Bleck). The company produces aircraft engines, equipment such as locomotives (when was the last time you used the word "locomotive" in a sentence?), appliances (I personally own a GE microwave, oven, stove, pot-scrubber dishwasher, and refrigerator/freezer), lighting, electric distribution, plastics, and the list keeps going. I don't know if there is an industry they don't have their electric fingers in. Here is a list of how their company breaks down, and what percentage they account for in consolidated sales reports.

Subsidiaries/Affiliates

> GE Aircraft Engines: 10 percent
>
> GE Appliances: 6 percent
>
> GE Industrial Products and Systems: 11 percent
>
> GE Plastics: 7 percent
>
> GE Power Systems: 8 percent
>
> GE Technical Products and Services: 5 percent
>
> General Electric Capital Corporation: 40 percent, and this deserves an explanation: If you need to finance it, charge it, or insure it, General Electric Capital can help. (And you were just asking yourself where the repeat purchase piece of this company was going to rear its head.) The General Electric subsidiary offers personal and business financing worldwide. Industrial financing activities include leasing, lending, and equipment sales and services. GE Capital owns retailer Montgomery Ward.
>
> Montgomery Ward Holding Corp.
>
> National Broadcasting Company, Inc. (NBC)
>
> OEC Medical Systems, Inc.

2. **K.I.S.S. (Keep It Simple, Sister):** To keep it really simple, look around your kitchen. Turn on your television set. Hop in an airplane. GE is almost like a mutual fund due to its diversity and balance. But it's not a mutual fund; it's a stock. It is a company that has its hands in a lot of pots. Yes, it does bring good things to life. (I wonder: If I say that three times, can I get royalties? Either that or jinxed. I'll stop.)

3. **Industry:** Is there an industry that GE isn't involved in? I don't know if the above industries are going to be on the cutting edge in growth, but if you read on, you'll see GE has recently entered the e-tailing world, which could influence their growth and potential for growth.

4. **Leader in its field:**

World's Most Admired Company: *Fortune* (1998, 1999, 2000)

World's Most Respected Company: *Financial Times* (1998, 1999, 2000)

America's Most Admired Company: *Fortune* (1998, 1999, 2000)

America's Greatest Wealth Creator: *Fortune* (1998, 1999, 2000)
First: *BusinessWeek*'s 25 Best Boards of Directors (2000)
First: *Forbes* World Super 50 (1998, 1999, 2000)
First: *Forbes* Super 100 (1998, 1999, 2000)
First: *BusinessWeek* 1000 (1999, 2000)

Need I say any more?

5. **Repeat profitability:** See General Electric Capital under point number 1. I did all the numbers for you. Relax and sip your tea.

6. **Gross margins** = 58.82 percent

7. **Net margins** = 9.60 percent

8. **Cash to long-term debt** = 1.66

9. **Flow Ratio** = 1.14

10. **Increasing growth:** In the last twenty years, GE stock has gone up an average of 25 percent a year. There are not many companies that can boast this over any time period. As a matter of fact, I don't know any. GE share owners have approved four 2-for-1 stock splits since 1983, most recently in 1997. One GE share purchased before 1926 is now worth 1,536 shares. Quarterly dividends have been paid every quarter since 1899 and have increased every year since 1975. Recently GE acquired Honeywell to continue their growth and bring us even more good things.

11. **Strong management and operating history:** I don't know if you can get any stronger management award than *Fortune* magazine's Manager of the Century. Yes, I said century, and GE's CEO Jack Welch was the recipient. John F. Welch (Jack), a native of Salem, Massachusetts, received his B.S. in chemical engineering from the University of Massachusetts in 1957 and his M.S. and Ph.D. in chemical engineering from the University of Illinois. He joined GE in 1960 and became the CEO in 1981. Mr. Welch will be retiring in late 2001, but he's been preparing the company for a smooth and uneventful change of leadership for years. His successor, Jeffrey Immelt, age forty-four, has been with GE for the past eighteen years (all of his working life). Most recently he has been the head of their Medical Systems division.

A lot is happening with e-commerce at GE, though not too long ago it was nonexistent. The explanation is simple: old-school guys were afraid of the computer; reluctant to even have one in their office. Our buddy Jack was right there with 'em. Stubborn. Computer-illiterate. Internet-wary. But when his eyes finally opened, it was electric! Within days, things started happening across all twenty of GE's key businesses. Their plastics company, Polymerland, turned its $10,000-a-week Web business into $2 million a day. The same dynamics were happening at their power plant division.

I'm thinking that before the end of this book, I may have to put the leaf in my dining room table. Tell me it would not be interesting to meet this man. He built a history with a proven successful company, yet stayed open to the new world emerging and jumped in. GE traces its beginnings to Thomas A. Edison, who established the Edison Electric Light Company in 1878. In 1892, a merger of the Edison General Electric Company and the Thomson-Houston Electric Company created General Electric Company. GE is the only company listed in the Dow Jones Industrial Index today that was also included in the original index in 1896. But wait, all work and no play makes Jack a dull boy. So Jack golfs. He is written up in many magazines as one of the top CEO golfers. He is the links rival of Sun Microsystems' CEO, Scott McNealy, and the two battle it out for the Welch Cup every year. Jack, come on over for dinner. Afterward, we can go up the hill and fetch a pail of balls. (We'll leave Scott tumbling after.)

12. **Buy on sale:** For example's sake, I'm going to show you what was posted on our message board the day we considered buying the stock. Here is how it is done:

52-Week High:	$159\frac{1}{2}$
52-Week Low:	$95\frac{3}{4}$

Anything below 127 is a bargain. Stock closed trading today $129\frac{5}{8}$. That's pretty dang close to being on sale. This buy-on-sale factor did come into the picture when analyzing the company. We bought it (and a new set of golf balls with our savings).

As extra credit, use the chart below and do the following companies on your own. All of the answers are found on our website at www.chickslayingnesteggs.com, and your research numbers can either be found at our website or at www.marketguide.com for the best layout.

General Electric (GE)	As of	As of	As of	As of	As of
Gross margins (> 50%)					
Net margins (> 8%)					
Cash to long-term debt (> 1.0)					
Flow Ratio (< 1.5)					
Sales (we want to increase)					

Pfizer (PFE)	As of	As of	As of	As of	As of
Gross margins (> 50%)					
Net margins (> 8%)					
Cash to long-term debt (> 1.0)					
Flow Ratio (< 1.5)					
Sales (we want to increase)					

EMC (EMC)	As of	As of	As of	As of	As of
Gross margins (> 50%)					
Net margins (> 8%)					
Cash to long-term debt (> 1.0)					
Flow Ratio (< 1.5)					
Sales (we want to increase)					

Chapter Summary

When it comes to cracking open the Chicks' Dozen, it really is quite simple. Adapt the philosophy to any and every company out there, decide as a club which criteria mean the most to you, and base your "buy" decision on how the company you've chosen meets the criteria. Keep the philosophy as long as it's working, adding a dash of this or a splash of that. A familiar chili that gives you comfort is better than a fabulous dish that gives you gas. It's a quote to live by. I can't believe I just wrote that.

chick chat

TITLE: MARY LEE HOUSLEY
From: Karin

Just a bit of sad news on this end. This weekend, Phil's parents were supposed to come and visit us. His mom, Mary Lee, has been having problems with her short-term memory lately, but we thought she was just tired. I mean, come on, she is only fifty-nine. But we knew something was REALLY wrong when she kept forgetting about this trip. She was so looking forward to seeing the kids, but she hadn't packed, and she had lost the plane tickets. On Tuesday, she thought it was Sunday and went to church. She keeps getting the days mixed up. She is getting so confused, and more so every day.

Leroy brought her to the doctor this morning and they did an MRI. She has a brain tumor the size of a nectarine. Surgery is next week.

Keep her in your prayers,

Karin

TITLE: **S&P REPORT
From: Cheryl

Oh my gosh. I am so sad. All of us Chicks just had dinner with her in Minnesota! How can this be? This makes the S&P report sound so trivial—and it is, but I'll do it anyway.

Thinking of all the Housleys and praying for Mary Lee.

Cheryl

P.S. Adding our latest company, Nokia, our portfolio is up 30.52% vs. 18.94%.

AOL up 130.60% vs. 15.87%
CSCO up 30.20% vs. 5.35%
GPS down 10.26% vs. 2.35%
KO down 2.9% vs. 31.74%
PFE up 16.31% vs. 31.74%

14

What's It All About, Allie?

Who can turn the world on with her smile?
Who can take a nothing day, and suddenly make
it all seem worthwhile?

— THEME SONG FROM *THE MARY TYLER MOORE SHOW*

o you remember planning your wedding? (If you are a single Chick, just go with me here. It's a good story.) Remember the months, weeks, and hours leading up to the big day? Plan, plan, and then plan some more. Tuxes, dresses, in-laws, flowers, rings, religion, and a cake. You have the date tattooed on your brain. Just get me there! Phew . . . finally, the day arrives. Blurrrrrr. Whirlwind. Emotions run the gamut, up until you collapse in your new husband's arms. Sigh. You did it. Mission accomplished.

You wake up the next day, and there he is. Yep, the same man you had so much fun with the night before. He's *still* there. That's him, all right. Hmm . . . what are you supposed to do with him now? What's the next step in this thing called marriage? Suddenly the planning of the big day seems like a breeze. Is there a magazine you could subscribe to called "Brides Yesterday" or "Wifely Weekly"? Where do you go from here?

I can't help you. I'm so sorry, but you're on your own in the marriage. I have my own to navigate daily. But I *can* help you in the investment club quest. I know what the next step is after the first big meeting. After all of your Chickies have pledged their love to one another (it's a metaphor), I can help you keep the ring on your finger! Call me Dr. Karin. I'm free (kinda). When you wake up in the morning, I'll still be there, but with an agenda in hand.

At this point, you've got some committed members, but what will you choose for your first dance? Where do you meet? Face-to-face? Online? What are you supposed to do at the subsequent meetings? (Every once in a while, I throw in a big word to remind myself that I'm an author.)

In this chapter, we're going to figure out where you'll have your meetings and how to run them, possible assignments for meetings, and what you can do to spice them up. This is the chapter where you apply everything you've learned up to this point. This is what it's all about, Allie.

Where to Meet

If you are all in the same city, you may want to have your meetings face-to-face in the beginning stages. It could save a lot of confusion and create further bonding, but it is not necessary unless you need a night out. If you think you've bonded enough or if you just want to stay home in your pajamas sipping a beverage, your second and subsequent (can I use it three times in a chapter?) get-togethers can be held on the computer.

Remember, all you have to do is go to www.chickslayingnesteggs.com and click on the link that says Chat Room under The Meeting Place.

Once you have navigated the Chicks' website, this will all become routine. A simple click of the mouse and you are in a meeting. Wouldn't Alexander Graham Bell be impressed? I'll show you a sample online meeting later in the chapter.

Before you get to the actual meeting, you need to develop an agenda. Everything that needs to be discussed should be put down on your to-do list (agenda). Post this to your message board one week prior to give everyone time to read it. Because the first meeting involved a lot of getting acquainted and the interested parties voicing their concerns and questions, there weren't a lot of agenda items completed. Don't worry, that's normal. Besides, some of the girls from the first meeting may decide not to join your club. (Can you even?) These are the things that need to be discussed. We went over them in the Flock Frolic chapter (page 53), and you discussed them at the first meeting, but now you can make some real decisions. These things will define your club.

Decision-Making Sample Agenda

Cock-a-doodle-doo . . . meeting starts. Discuss the following:

- Time and dates of meetings
- Amount of money invested per month
- How often to invest
- Computer availability for each member
- An investment philosophy
- Companies to research
- Person to research online brokers
- A name
- Drink and dessert break
- Operating procedures (these may take a couple of meetings)
- Officers
- Partnership bond (details in chapter 16)
- A message folder
- Meeting time for next meeting

Adjourn, and get the Chick outta there.

Our first get-together went smoothly, except we had no idea where to start looking for companies. We wanted a list of halfway decent ones instead of just grabbing in the dark. Below are some of the companies that the Chicks have researched over the years which—at least at one point—did well when pulled through the Chicks' Dozen. It's a starting point, anyway.

Microsoft	Intel
Yahoo	Abercrombie and Fitch
Broadcom	Adobe
Outback Steakhouse	Amgen
Eli Lilly	Starbucks
Papa John's	Hennes & Mauritz
Wrigley	Apple
Biogen	FedEx
General Nutrition Centers	Heineken
Intimate Brands	Schering-Plough
Best Buy	Gateway
Estée Lauder	Sun Microsystems
Anheuser-Busch	Texas Instruments
Wendy's	Wal-Mart
Heineken	McDonald's
Merck	Keebler

The Next Meeting's Sample Agenda

(The sample times are if you are doing a face-to-face meeting, which takes a little longer than an online meeting.)

8:00 P.M.—Cock-a-doodle-doo: Meeting starts.

8:05 P.M.—Minutes accepted from last meeting?

8:10 P.M.—Treasurer's report: Who has paid, who hasn't paid?

8:15 P.M.—Discount broker report.

8:25 P.M.—Discuss www.chickslayingnesteggs.com website. Is everyone able to get around easily? Does anyone need help? If there is still confusion, this might be a good time to gather around a computer and navigate together. The Chicks had to do this. While you're at it, everyone can yell out other favorite investment websites. (My sister directed us to www.drweil.com all the time. If she wasn't on our site, she was into something homeopathic. She called that investing, buying vitamins.)

8:45 P.M.—Chicks' Do(zen) companies: Chicks' Dozen report on companies researched.

9:15 P.M.—Discuss Chicks' Dozen investment approach. Who needs help? Are some things more important than others? Does everyone understand the gross margins, net margins, et cetera?

9:30 P.M.—Vote for a company to buy.

9:45 P.M.—Breathe a sigh of relief! You did it! I hereby announce you Chick and Chick (and Chick and Chick and Chick and so on).

10:00 P.M.—Sleep well.

Below I'll show you an actual online Chicks agenda of one of our meetings. You'll see, it isn't all stock-related. (This was not our first meeting, nor our second or third—we evolved to such tight schedules and mindless chatter.)

Chicks Laying Nest Eggs Agenda

May 2, 9:00 P.M. EST

7:00 P.M. Cock-a-doodle-doo: The meeting begins.

7:02 P.M. Treasurer's report: Chick Jeanette.

7:05 P.M. S&P Report: Chick Cheryl.

7:07 P.M. Discuss giving a percentage of our profits to charity. What percentage? If we make 50 percent, do we give 5 percent; if 40 percent, do we give 4 percent? Take a vote. Do we do this at year's end? How do we do it? Write a personal check or sell some stock? Would we rather consider a cause where we give time?

7:17 P.M. Discuss charities we are interested in, if we voted yes above. This doesn't have to be decided upon tonight, but we could each name one charity to look into for the next month's meeting, or post your charity to the board. Our year ends August 31, so we wouldn't have to decide until then. Table until later, but pick a charity.

7:25 P.M. Flush fund? If we all seem to have some extra cash hanging around and want to throw in an extra $50 or a $100 one month, could we do it and call it a flush fund? It would have to be a unanimous vote at the flush time of the month. What if we voted that we could throw an extra $200 (or a decided-upon amount) in any time during the year, but that is the max? You could either add it to your monthly (like $15 extra each month), or in extra $50 payments sporadically throughout the year, or the whole $200 whenever you wanted. This way, each member can do it on her own when she feels she's "flush." This would help us each put a little more money away. But we would all have to agree to putting the exact same amount in to keep the things even at year's end. Just an idea, but let's vote, yes or no. If yes, what amount?

7:35 P.M. Stock talk (finally). All stock reports on your company should be posted to the board by Friday at five P.M. This is two days before a meeting, so we all have time to read the reports and come to the meeting with some well-thought-out ideas. We will each state which company we want to vote for and why. Get your reports done and posted by Friday. *Muy importante.* This was your assignment: Julie—Microsoft; Jana—Amgen; Lynn—Cisco; Cheryl—AOL; Megan—Amazon; Jeanette—GE; Susie—Gap; Lorene—Pfizer; Kristin—Coke; Karin—Bebe. We will vote in that order.

7:50 P.M. Vote on purchase.

7:55 P.M. Golf tournament in July. The dates are July 30 through August 1 (Friday, Saturday, Sunday). Don't worry about a place to stay; between my mom, Julie, Lynnie, and me, there are plenty of beds. Who thinks they can come?

8:00 P.M. Next meeting, June 7. Adjourn.

Chick Rules (Chicks' Rules of Order)

Every meeting needs to have some order: order in the deep blue sea. Do I stay to the left or right of that red buoy? Do I slow down through a no-wake zone or fly by the seat of my pants? There have to be rules.

In order to navigate rough waters and smoothly run a successful club, you need some guidelines. First, though, may I make a motion that we make no motions? Anybody second it? Is that just not cra-zy? Like loco?

We tried and tried for six months to follow some Robert guy's rules of order. The intro to business must be motioned, the acceptance of our minutes must be motioned, and before we even talk about the next subject, we're supposed to make a motion. We were spending more time trying to figure out what order Robert wanted us to do things than we were actually doing them. Why is Robert ruling a Chick, anyway, when it is Chicks who rule? We decided to create our own order, a New World Order, a Chick Rules of Order for a meeting.

Chick Rules of Order for a Meeting

1. **Cock-a-doodle-doo:** The meeting begins. Call to order—or a simple "Wake up, Chickies, we're starting!"—will suffice.
2. **Follow the agenda:** Most important Chick rule for meetings! This is why I didn't give it a cute name. All meeting agendas should be posted to your message board one week before the meeting. An outline for an agenda can also be found at www.chickslayingnesteggs.com. Members should be allowed to add a discussion item up until the day before the meeting is held. This way, your Head Hen can add the items, post the newly revised agenda to the message board the day of the meeting (with the adjusted time schedule), and there will be no new added topics. New business will be discussed at the next meeting, or on the message board.
3. **Chick Chat:** Since everyone is allowed to add an item up till almost the last minute, there is no need to make motions about topics. You know what is going to be talked about, and everything has a time slot. There should be no exceptions; we have had to table many a discussion because the Chicks' Rules rule. When you follow the agenda during a meeting, go point by point and chatter on each point and *only* that point. The meetings will go very smoothly. No one is confused. After discussion and agreement, summarize in one sentence.
4. **One sentence:** Reword your agenda point in one sentence. Whatever was just discussed in Chick Chat needs to be summarized *clearly.* If it is not correct, and not all members concur, a further dis-

cussion may ensue. (Another big word.) Continue the discussion until one sentence can be formed to your agreement.

5. **Chicken Scratcher (secretary) repeats:** At this point, if everything has come to a lull, the secretary will repeat the idea one last time before she writes it in her tablet.

6. **Agree/disagree:** If you have formulated an idea, and you cannot get the whole group to agree, you may agree to disagree. You can do this by voicing your opinion. How many agree with the action, how many disagree? A simple yee-ha or nay will do. (The Chicks learned this from the horses.) Most points discussed within your club will come to a conclusion, but if not, it is okay to agree to disagree. Let me give you two examples: at the start of each meeting, we always vote on accepting the minutes of the last meeting. It is always agenda point #1. Chick Lorene might ask, "Weren't the minutes supposed to say that AOL merged with Time Warner, not Warner Bros.?" Oh yes, Chick Jana agrees, she made an error in typing up the minutes. Other than that, are the minutes okay? No more discussion, then? Yee-ha. Yee-ha. Yee-ha. Minutes go into our immaculately kept record books. (Thank goodness this is not my job either.) A disagreement may occur—for example, in talking about the flush fund. If there are six members who would like to put in an extra $200 in a year, but four who like the format you have been using ($50 a month), then you agree to disagree and table it until a later date. (The flush fund vote should be unanimous.) The only thing you need an exact head count for is a stock purchase.

7. **Majority rules:** It doesn't matter how many Chicks are in your club, you have to have at least the majority to purchase a stock. There is an addendum to this (I'm full of big words today)—you must have a quorum. A quorum is the minimum number of members to make a meeting valid. A Chicks' quorum, we decided, was to consist of at least half the members. You cannot have four out of ten members at your meeting, and three vote for company A and one for company B and then call it a majority-rules vote. That is called sneaky. A fox in the box. Sylvester after Tweety. You must have at least half the mem-

bers available for your meeting if a no-going-back vote is to take place. (Again, this is the Chicks' way; you can customize.)

Since you've already conducted an in-person meeting, I don't need to go over the logistics of running one. But online meetings could use some detailed explanation.

After you have clicked the Chat Room tab at www.chickslay-ingnesteggs.com, invite all of your other members. They will be in virtual land, and if you haven't checked out the website, this may sound strange; open your mind, it works. You will have Merrie in Illinois, Rosie in South Dakota, Christy in New York, Wendy in Los Angeles, Liza in Hibbing, Mackie in Virginia, and Alison in Mississipi, all on their computers at the same time, in the same virtual room. By room, I mean an open screen with all your members' names there, live, on your computer. Once everyone is in the room, the show can begin!

Here is a log of what one of our online meetings looked like:

Karin: Hey Chickies!

Cheryl: Hey girlie girls! Where am I?

Lorene: One sec, my cell phone is ringing.

Megan: Don't answer it!

Lynn: What is going on? This is our new chat room? I must sip my wine before I get dizzy.

Kristin: Could we get this meeting under way? I have a date.

Jana: You have a date? Kristin has a date?

Kristin: With my fiancé, silly.

Karin: Okay girls, let's get this meeting under way. Can we vote to accept the minutes of the last meeting?

Cheryl: Yee-ha.

Susie: Yee-ha.

Lorene: Yee-ha.

Megan: Yee-ha.

Lynn: Yee-ha.

Jeanette: Yee-ha.

Julie: Yee-ha.

Kristin: Yee-ha. (He's so cute: his name is, Tim remember? Yee-ha, yee-ha!)

Jana: Yee-ha . . . go Kristin!

Karin: Okay, moving on. Could we get the treasurer's report?

Jeanette: Everyone has a copy of the treasurer's report in your e-mail box if you want to look at it right now. Type when you have finished.

Karin: Yee-ha, everyone?

Lorene: ! (I have wet nails, a letter spared is a nail saved.)

Jana: !

Kristin: !

Lynn: !

Cheryl: !

Jeanette: Yee-ha (I'm a stickler for rules).

Megan: ! (Lorene, what color did you paint them?)

Julie: !

Karin: !

Susie: !

Lorene: Vamp from Chanel.

Karin: If we all have read the investment club board, we can save time by not going over each of our company's reports. Let's each tell what company we would like to vote for in our next purchase and why. We will go in this order: Cheryl, Susie, Megan, Jana, Kristin, Lynn, Lorene, and me. (Mom and Julie, we have read your message board post, and we know what you want. Chime in whenever, but you can wait until the vote. Thank you.)

Cheryl: I was thinking I would like to purchase Microsoft. Their numbers were the best of all the companies we looked at. If this is going to be our first real purchase, why not go with a no-brainer and a company that has proven itself?

Susie: I would like to avoid MSFT for personal reasons. First of all, I hate their operating systems, and I'm not a big fan of their management. Sorry. If we look at our Chicks' Dozen, the strong management and operating history point #11, well, they've had some trouble lately. You've read my post pertaining to it—even though they have great numbers, I think we should take into consideration their recent adversity. Just my two cents. Cluck, cluck.

Megan: I think it's obvious after looking at all the posted companies that Microsoft, Qualcomm, Nokia, and Broadcom had the best numbers. Since I love the telecommunications industry, and I feel that BRCM is the freshest of the three, I vote Broadcom.

Jana: Sheez, I was going to say the same thing about Nokia. Even though BRCM and Nokia are similar companies, I think Nokia is a bit more established. Hmm, I'd go either BRCM or NOK. Did you see my link to the picture of CEO Jorma Olilla? He is soooo cute.

Kristin: OHMYGAWD! He's HERE! Tim is here! Put me down for Nokia. I buy a new one every year. (I have a problem keeping track of them.) Their numbers are incredible.

Lynn: I think Kristin is going house-hunting with her beau and is not really into this vote tonight.

Kristin: I'm serious, guys. I was going to vote Nokia even before I saw the picture of Jorma. Did you see their five-year growth? Scrumptious! If you took all three of those companies above that you were talking about, Nokia has the greatest growth. Their numbers meet all our criteria. Nokia even exceeds MSFT and CSCO in some areas. How many of you have Nokia phones? Can I just take a poll here for a moment? (Timmy is just going to have to wait.)

Lorene: I have a Nokia.

Lynn: !

Jana: !

Megan: I have two.

Cheryl: I have none.

Karin: And this little piggy went all the way home (hehe). I have one too.

Susie: Motorola, but I don't like it.

Julie: Yee-ha.

Kristin: Okay, point proven. Isn't this a buy-what-you-know decision? What do we know that's best? We know MSFT, we know CSCO, but I don't know how well we really know BRCM, though it has great numbers. Do we live and breathe it? Tim calls me every day at exactly 12:15 on his lunch break—on my Nokia. (I have it clipped to my pants with a vibrating battery so no one knows why I say, "Do you mind if I step out for a minute?" Don't tell.)

Karin: Well, thank you for sharing, K, but she does have a point; we *all* own them.

Cheryl: Can I change my vote?

Lorene: Can I give my opinion here? Is it my turn yet?

Karin: Order! Order! Order, Chickies!

Julie: Yee.

Karin: Lorene, go ahead. Give your opinion, then we will take our vote as soon as Lorene is finished.

Lorene: Ummmm . . . I like Nokia for the simple fact that I believe the whole world is going wireless. Nokia is the wireless leader. I vote Nokia.

Kristin: I loved Nokia even before I started getting calls on it from that handsome hunk. I really love that their gross margins and profit margins have increased consistently over the past four quarters (and all quarters, for that matter). I love that a humongous chunk of their money goes into research and development.

Jana: Can I add that more than half of Finland (Nokia headquarters) is equipped with cell phones? People use their cell phones instead of bothering to hook up their home phones. This is where I think the world is going. I think this is an industry with some great growth a'comin'. I don't even give out my home phone number anymore, and I've ditched my Palm Pilot for the latest Nokia phone / organizer. I get my e-mail and access the chickslayingnesteggs.com website through my Nokia.

Susie: I am definitely going to have to go to my cell phone store and see what you are talking about. Good-bye, Motorola, hello, Nokia.

Karin: Does anyone have anything else to say about a company?

Megan: I still feel that BRCM is going to emerge as the leader in the telecommunications industry. I could go either way, but just to go on record, I am going to vote Broadcom. (And buy some for myself on the side if we decide not to purchase it as a club, so either way I'm gonna get my way.)

Cheryl: Freak.

Karin: Okay, let's vote.

Megan: Broadcom.

Karin: Nokia.

Lynn: Nokia.

Jana: Nokia.

Lorene: Nokia.

Kristin: He's wearing a pair of Tommy Hilfigers, with this cotton sweater to die for. It matches his baby-blue eyes. Mmmmmmm. Oooh, sorry.

Kristin: Nokia.

Susie: Like I said, good-bye, Motorola . . . hello, Nokia.

Cheryl: Nokia, but Megan, I'm buying some BRCM on the side tomorrow too.

Karin: Okeydoke. Nokia it is! Yeee-haa!

Kristin: Gotta run. Great meeting. I'll fill you in tomorrow on where "the match made in heaven" is going to live. Check the message board.

Jana: I think our little Kristin is in love.

Cheryl: Kinda fun to live vicariously through her, though, ain't it?

Kristin: You know it, baby! I'm still here. Leaving now. Coooooooming Timmyyyyyyyyyy!

Karin: Okay, Chickies, great meeting. Next meeting Sunday the fourth of October . . . 7 P.M. Central. Talk to you then!!

Jana: Kristin, call me as soon as you get home! Bye!

Lorene: Bye.

Julie: Yee.

Susie: Going to cell phone store . . . bye-bye.

Jana: Seeya.

Cheryl: Au Revoir (is that how you spell it?)

Lynn: Adios!

Meeting adjourned.
We bought Nokia.

Special Guest Speakers

You are probably thinking that this is the most ridiculous thing you have ever seen in an Investment Club book. It probably is, but I'm telling you it works! The girls in your club are going to get bored with the routine club meeting. How do I know? I have A.D.D. (Attention Deficit Disorder). I mean, I haven't actually been diagnosed, but if things don't move, I'm done.

Special guest speakers aren't needed in your online meetings, but at your face-to-face ones, it's required. To keep your meetings "the place to be in town," you have to have interesting guest speakers.

Now, I don't mean the loan officer from First Federal. He is not interesting and they are a dime a dozen. I mean interesting, interesting. As in engaging, fascinating, absorbing, and attractive. Woops, not attractive. It was in my thesaurus. Invite anyone whose brain you'd love to pick. An author of a book (I'm available when my kids grow up), a pharmacist, or a magician. Aha, you do think I'm nuts. A pharmacist? Yes, my dearie, a pharmacist. A pharmacist could give you the ins and outs of his industry. Not a lot of us understand it, and you could get his point of view on the new drugs coming out or an "insider" report on each pharmaceutical company.

I was sitting on a plane next to a pharmacist not too long ago and had a long discussion about Zithromax, a Pfizer product. After we landed, I immediately went and looked up Pfizer's numbers and promptly bought some shares. Pharmacists are smart people. But look around you; is there a doctor you know who could give you the latest in laser technology? Is there a computer expert who could come and explain the difference between a Microsoft Windows program and Red Hat's free operating-system software? This kind of investment club speaker is better than any article you can read.

Invite a magician? Wha? This is the Chick in me. I get bored. If I am going to go to a meeting, a face-to-face meeting, it has to be fun. I can't sit for more than twenty minutes knowing that there isn't going to be something fun happening. At one of our meetings, we invited a psychic. True story. Some of us went to the meeting just for the psychic. We knew exactly what we were going to purchase before the meeting, and had been so organized leading up to the meeting, that there really was no reason for us to meet face-to-face. Except for Suzanne the psychic. (Please don't send me any of the religious objections. It was on a whim, and my mother has already reprimanded me. But I love Suzanne.)

Think of someone for your next meeting. Not just Joe next door. Invite someone fun! Invite Candace Cameron of Full House fame! Yeah, she'll do it. She'll do anything. Oh, wait, that's Mikey. But think big in your quest for a guest speaker. You'll be surprised how many people would like to pick *your* brains for any investment ideas. Hey, Candace, will you do our next meeting? Thanks, Chica.

If you can't think of any ideas for a guest speaker, think of a special spot to have your face-to-face meetings. A hotel, a resort, a spa, Las Vegas, Aspen, or Edgar Allan Poe's gravesite (it really is cool). Make it into a field trip or a mini-vacation. Maybe you will want to assign someone to be the travel coordinator. Traveling together is better than any return your portfolio will *ever* get. I'd settle for smaller annual returns, but I won't give up our twice-a-year trips! It makes my year. We have done Vegas, Phoenix, Georgia, New York, and Minnesota a couple of times. We still need to do California, Maine, Missouri, and umm . . . Finland. (They don't know it, but Finland is on the list. We are just waiting for an invite from Mr. Jorma Ollila himself.) As long as you keep the meetings interesting and fun, your club will look forward to them. If they become routine, you will lose the enthusiasm. We have come up with one other way in which to make our meeting fun: a special assignment for each face-to-face encounter. The online meetings in between are routine and now very quick. Our special assignments spice up the same-old-same-old. For one of your subsequent (that's three) meetings, assign each girl a CEO of a company to research and report on. It gives an opportunity to learn other things about a business besides the numbers and how it looks on paper. Humanize your companies.

Or, how about for one assignment, everyone is required to seek out an employee of a company they own or are looking at? Why not ask Laura at the Gap what her benefits are? Ask her if she has ever met CEO Drexler. Does he really stroll through the stores and talk to customers? Is she looking to stay at the Gap long-term or just until her closet is full? What is her discount? Does she get her company's stock at a discount? Could she buy you a pair of jeans at her in-store discount? (I hope Mr. Drexler doesn't read that.) Do their in-mall stores return online purchases? What are the company picnics like?

Interviewing an employee of the company is like inviting the pharmacist to your meeting. Priceless. You get so much information from an employee, and a better understanding of the company, if you talk to an insider.

Another assignment might be to do some charity work. Maybe you can put aside part of your meeting day to go work at a soup kitchen. Maybe you can all wrap presents at the mall. Maybe you can go build a home for Habitat for Humanity. Something. I will go into this further in my last chapter, but I'm going to sneak in one little tip here at the end of this one. For your club to be successful, you have to have heart. It can't be all business. It makes for an incredible bond to do something together for somebody else. Think about it. Not until you get your club up and running, but down the road. Think heart.

Chapter Summary

O After your first meeting, you will have subsequent meetings. There's got to be a morning after.
O Online and face-to-face.
O Online: www.chickslayingnesteggs.com, click Chat Room. (How many times do you think I said www.chickslayingnesteggs.com in this chapter? Right answers get a free trip to Disney World.)
O I'm kidding.
O Chicks' Rules:
    1. Cock-a-doodle doo
    2. Follow agenda.
    3. Chick Chat.
    4. One sentence.
    5. Chicken Scratcher repeats.
    6. Agree/disagree.
    7. Majority rules (quorum required).
O Guest speakers should be special, and if you ever meet the Dixie Chicks, will you put in a good word for me?
O Special assignments: CEO, employees, or charity events.

chick chat

TITLE: MEGAN'S LIFE
From: Megan

Well, I just got home from hockey practice, my latest hobby, and I can barely walk, so I have snuggled up to my computer with a glass of cabernet . . . and caught up on my posts . . . YIPPEE! Nice ending to an exhausting day.

The Kaminskis are happily back in Maine and doing just fine, except for the fact that our truck still hasn't arrived from Vegas, and everything I own is in it. And, while we were in Vegas, our roof back here sprung a leak. It has caused the floor to buckle in several spots in the great room, the drywall is crumbling everywhere, and the carpeting and padding needs to be replaced in the master bedroom. The fact is that after all that has happened in the last two years and what Karin's mother-in-law is going through, none of it matters. Cheryl, I can take over AOL for you and give you a break; this house is no longer stress-central.

IThnkIMBcmngABddhst,

Megan

TITLE: GOLF COURSE
From: Julie

Hey, girls, I need help with my golf course. I'm trying to think of a new name for it. Brockway sounds so, so, so somethin'. Can you help me come up with a new name?

Julie

TITLE: GOLF COURSE
From: Lynn

Speaking of golfing, Julie, I *need* help! I need some golf clubs and I need some place to hit them. What kind should I buy? Ping? Wilson? Taylor Made? BigBerthaShmertha? I think you should call it Brockway Woods.

Lynn

(Megan, I know what you're dealing with there. When our house flooded two years ago, all of our flooring buckled up and started floating. I remember the day I became a Buddhist, though for some reason I keep going to the Lutheran church.)

TITLE: GOLF COURSE
From: Susie

How about Brockway Country Club?

Susie

TITLE: GOLF COURSE
From: Lorene

Brockway Heights? Brockway Oaks? Brockway Pines? Brockway sounds funny now.

Lorene

TITLE: **S&P REPORT
From: Cheryl

I am no good at picking golf course names or golfing (though I can kick Karin's bootie). Here's our S&P Report, and I'm glad you are back in Maine.

Megan

AOL up 245.45% vs. 20.12% (wooooo-hoooooo)
CSCO up 58.69% vs. 9.08%
NOK up 42.10% vs. 3.54% (Can you say Rookie of the Year?)
GPS down 17.05% vs. 5.98%
PFE up 5.77% vs. 36.41%
KO down 10.04% vs. 36.41% (ooof)

On the Dotted Line

You can't hit a home run unless you step up to the plate. You can't catch a fish unless you put your line in the water. You can't reach your goals if you don't try.

— KATHY SELIGMAN

Look how far you've come! You've made huge, huge strides. Now, though, it's time to step up to the plate and form your club for real. It's paperwork time.

This is where a lot of people get hung up because there are so many tough questions like: How do you form a partnership? What makes it legal? Does it cost a lot? Is there some big government office where you need to register your club? Once a partnership is formed, is it really messy to get out? No, no, no, and no. I'm going to tell you how to form a partnership, but it's your choice if you want to don faux leopard hats.

There are three things needed in order to become an "official" investment club. You need to have a set of operating procedures signed and agreed upon by your members; you need to file for an Employer Identification Number (EIN) for our good friends at the IRS; and in some states, you need to file your club's name with the county clerk. (Check with your county clerk, a simple phone call.) There are other ways to form an investment club, but the simplest, and the most favorable come tax time, is the partnership. I am going to address only the partnership.

The easiest way for me to introduce you to the concept of creating your own set of operating procedures is to go over the Chicks' operating procedures. You can take 'em or leave 'em, or make up your own. At our first meeting, we had no idea what we were doing. Cheryl's mom gave us some sample operating procedures from a club she'd belonged to, but our club had been up and running for six months before we actually understood what the rules were all about. The bottom line is that your discount broker will require a signed copy of your club's operating procedures before they will allow you to open an account. So, if you want this club to be anything more than an online tea party, look these over, use them as your original working partnership form, then modify and make them your own as you go. Read on and I'll explain each item after you have a look at them.

Chicks Laying Nest Eggs COOPerating Procedures

1. **Formation of partnership:** Each member of the Chicks Laying Nest Eggs must sign our cooperating procedures.
2. **Name of partnership:** The name of the partnership shall be Chicks Laying Nest Eggs.
3. **Term:** The partnership began on June 1, 1998, and may be dissolved at any time by majority consent.
4. **Purpose:** The purpose of the partnership is to place the assets of said partnership in investments for the benefit of the partners.
5. **Meetings:** There will be ten general online meetings per year. The meetings will be held on the first Sunday night of the month, except for those that fall on a holiday weekend. The meeting will then be held on the second Sunday of the month. There will also be two face-to-face meetings each year.
6. **Attendance:** A member is required to attend at least 75 percent of the meetings, or nine of the twelve meetings. A $25-per-meeting fine will be charged to any member missing more than three meetings, for each time a meeting is missed, unless it is voted on and excused

by the club. If attendance falls below this, and there is no correspondence with said partner, the partner's membership will be evaluated by the club, and her membership could be terminated. It will then be treated as if she had submitted a letter of resignation, as per the withdrawal of partner rules below.

7. **Quorum:** A quorum will require that at least six members be present for a meeting to be permissible.

8. **Officers of the partnership and their responsibilities:** The officers shall consist of: president, from now on called Head Hen; vice president, a.k.a. Second Chick in Charge; secretary, a.k.a. Chicken Scratcher; and treasurer, a.k.a. Egg Carton. The election of new officers shall be at will. There is no set term of office. If someone wants to change positions, or step down, these decisions can be made as they arise.

> **Head Hen:** The Head Hen will conduct meetings starting at nine P.M. Eastern Standard Time. The president will set the agenda for each meeting in advance and have it out to the members the day before the meeting. The president will also be in charge of the twice-yearly face-to-face meetings and their location.
>
> **Second Chick in Charge:** The Second Chick in Charge will conduct the meetings in the absence of the president. She will also be responsible for keeping track of our portfolio and comparing it to the market average (we will use the S&P 500 as our benchmark).
>
> **Chicken Scratcher:** The Chicken Scratcher will copy and paste our online meetings and e-mail them to everyone following the meeting. She will also summarize the meetings and post the minutes to the message board.
>
> **Egg Carton:** The Egg Carton will prepare a monthly financial report and e-mail it to all of the members a day before the online meeting. She will also buy and sell all of our stocks online and prepare the tax return. Be nice to her.

9. **Dues:** Monthly dues will be $50. These must be in the hands of the Egg Carton by the fourth day of every month. A $5 fine will be levied when the payment is late. The Egg Carton will notify all

members via e-mail a week prior to the money's being due. If the full payment is not made by the first of the next month, an additional late fee of $10 brings the total due to $115. If a partner has not paid by the beginning of the third month, it will be made known to all the partners, and her membership can be revoked by a majority vote. It will then be treated as if she had submitted a letter of resignation, as per the withdrawal of partner rules below. No further fines will be charged; however, the club will retain 10 percent of the delinquent member's share value at the time of the sale or buyout, as a penalty for the forced transaction. The delinquent member will be responsible for all fees and expenses pertaining to the sale of any stock or transaction. All unpaid dues and fines will be deducted from share value at the time of final settlement. If payment is made, the total due by the beginning of the third month will be $165.

10. **Philosophy of Chicks:**
    A. Follow the Chicks' Dozen investment criteria for purchasing a stock for our portfolio. Also, follow the Chicks' Rules as pertaining to the order of a meeting.
    B. We can consider selling a stock if it continues to fall out of our Chicks' Dozen, or if we feel our money would be better off somewhere else. Sell votes must be a majority by quorum. Follow Chicks' Sell Philosophy (page 215).
    B. Reinvest all dividends and capital gains.
    C. Travel at least twice a year for face-to-face meetings.
    D. Have fun, keep the tone light.
    E. Perform one Random Act of Kindness per month.

11. **Withdrawal of partner:** A partner wishing to withdraw must submit a letter of resignation to any one of the officers at least forty-eight hours prior to the commencement of a scheduled monthly meeting. She will at this time forfeit her privilege of attending the scheduled monthly meetings. The withdrawing member will be obligated to pay her dues without fine for the three months following her resignation. She will be released from this obligation at such time as a new partner has assumed her financial position or the remaining partners have purchased the share. When stock must be

sold to pay the withdrawing partner, said partner is responsible for all fees and expenses pertaining to the sale of the stock. It shall be sold no later than the Monday following the third scheduled meeting after her resignation was accepted. The withdrawing partner's check will be sent via U.S. registered mail within three working days of the treasurer receiving the transaction funds. The share value will be the current value most recently reported before the settlement takes place minus any outstanding obligations.

If a partner withdraws within the first year of the club's inception, she will only be reimbursed the lesser of either one tenth of the club's worth (or her equal share if fewer members) or of her total dues paid during her time. She will not be entitled to any market gains during the first year.

12. **Valuation:** The current value of the assets of the partnership less the current value of the debts and liabilities of the partnership (hereinafter referred to as "value of the partnership") shall be determined by the close of the market the Friday before the Sunday-night meeting. This value will be determined by the Egg Carton and will be reported in the monthly e-mail the day before the meeting. It will be discussed as the first order of business so the Egg Carton's report can be passed.

13. **Management:** Each partner shall participate in the management and conduct of the affairs of the partnership equally. It will take a majority vote of the membership to buy or sell a stock. If you are not present at the time of the vote, you can vote via a proxy e-mail addressed to all members. The vote should be sent in an e-mail to all members, or posted to the message board. Any member wishing to buy or sell stock between meetings may obtain agreement of two thirds of the membership and will then contact the treasurer to give approval of such transaction. A reasonable attempt shall be made to contact all members via phone, e-mail, and message board, allowing two days for the e-mail to be sent and message board notice to be posted.

14. **Book of accounts:** Records of the transactions of the partnership shall be available and open to examination by any partner at all times.

15. **Money market account:** The partnership shall select an online broker that allows for a money market account with free checking privileges.

16. **Broker account:** None of the partners shall be a broker. The club shall select a discount online broker whose fees are below $25 per trade. Each member will have access to the club's brokerage portfolio, but only the treasurer may have the password to buy and sell stock.

17. **No compensation:** No partner shall be compensated for services rendered to the partnership, except reimbursement for expenses.

18. **Additional partners:** So long as the number of partners does not exceed ten, additional partners may be admitted at any time upon the unanimous consent of the partners in writing or at a meeting.

19. **Death of a partner:** Upon the death of a partner, the club will buy her membership. The partners shall pay the withdrawing partner or her estate, as the case may be, a purchase price equal to 97 percent of her capital account or her capital account less the actual cost of selling the securities, whichever amount is smaller. Settlement shall be paid within two weeks of the valuation date used in determining the purchase price.

In Witness Whereof, the Founding Members have signed and executed these Articles of Association the _____ day of _____, _____, at (City and State).

That's it! Once everybody signs (and attaches their social security number), you're a partnership!

Explanation of Above COOPerating Procedures

1. **Formation of partnership:** After each Chick signs a copy of the operating procedures and attaches her social security number, you have completed the partnership requirements for an investment club. Copy these operating procedures (or create your own), have each member sign, and you are a partnership!

2. **Name of partnership:** Be creative.

3–4. No explanation needed, but you might want to add the word "fun" under #4.

5. **Meetings:** Your club may decide that they want a different night of the week or schedule for your meetings. Put it in writing.

6. **Attendance:** I'm going to let you in a little secret. I wasn't going to publish a book and offer up our *real* attendance requirement. What you read above was our original wording, but it has since been changed. We didn't like it and wanted something a bit more fun. Don't do this unless you have a cohesive bunch, and you might not find that out until you are well into your first year. How do you make attendance fun? Well, after we'd been together for a year, we appointed Chick Megan as the Rotten Egg Patrol. She keeps track of who misses which meeting. At our face-to-face meetings, she gives us a report. (We don't have a big problem with attendance.) Megan then gets to decide what the penalty will be for the absentee—does one absence require that the delinquent Chick buy the first round of drinks, or do two absences require that she walk through the grocery store in her pajamas? These are all up to the Rotten Egg Patrol and subject for discussion; but it makes missing a meeting a little nerve-racking, and our face-to-face meetings a lot more fun. Besides, it was the closest we could get Megan to playing her favorite game, "Captain May I?" Megan has been known to be bought off. I want her job.

7. **Officers:** This too can be tweaked as you go. Our original by-laws said that we would change positions every year, then we changed the wording to say every two years, and now we address the issue at each face-to-face meeting. We are still content with the way things are, though Jana, our Chicken Scratcher, has yet to take the notes two meetings in a row. She always pawns it off to anyone willing. A club does require at least a president, a vice president, a treasurer, and a secretary. You can assign more jobs as you see fit, such as the Egg Beater. Egg Beater Susie reads through our message board posts and pulls anything that might offend. Susie is always politically correct. You could also add an S&P reporter as a job. In our club, our Second Chick in Charge Cheryl takes care of that.

8. **Dues:** We haven't set up a Bounced Egg Patrol as of yet, and nobody has charged me the $5. Phew. Maybe they're just wait-

ing for the book to come out, and then they'll boil me for being late three times. Be reasonable on this one. But when setting monthly dues, you should take a silent ballot vote to decide on the amount. Remember, it should be decided upon from the get-go if this is going to be your think tank and learning club, or your only source for investing. Start as a think tank, then reevaluate in a year. Again, my humble opinion.

9. **Philosophy:** *This is very important.* Make sure everyone agrees on this point before you all sign an agreement. It will guarantee the longevity of your club. Okay, maybe it won't guarantee longevity, but if you want any chance of being a successful club, you have to be in agreement about how you're going to run the club and make your investment decisions.

10. **Withdrawal of partner:** This is wordy, but I'll try to rephrase in English. Let's say someone drops out of your club four months after you have been up and running, and your club's portfolio has made 10 percent during that time. The withdrawing partner should *not* be entitled to her share of the profits. Why? Usually, when someone decides to withdraw, she hasn't gotten "into" the club in the first place and hasn't really done any work or research to get you there. The withdrawing partner in the first year of the club should be refunded either one tenth the club's worth that day, or her original investment, whichever is less. Get it? If each club member put in a total of $200, and today it is worth $240, the withdrawing member would get her $200 back, and no more. But if you had to sell some stock to pay her off, she must pay the fee ($0–$25) that it costs to sell the stock. The best-case scenario is to try and find a replacement for the withdrawing partner. Your members can change the time requirements as they see fit.

11. **Valuation:** This is easy when you're online, but it still is nice to get the monthly e-mail and message board post from the treasurer. Sometimes you get so busy, you forget to check your stocks.

12. **Management:** This just says that each person's vote has equal weight. We will accept a purchase vote via an e-mail to all members, or a post to the message board. We put the sell clause in

there in case of an emergency. We have yet to deem something an emergency.

13. **Book of accounts:** Available online, and we get our monthly report from the EggCarton.

14–16. Self-explanatory.

17. **Additional partners:** You might want to change this wording to better fit your club.

18. **Death of a partner:** We don't even like to think about it, but we have a provision if we need it.

Onward Chickie Soldier!

Chicks' Sell Philosophy

1. We are able to discuss selling a company after we have held it in our portfolio for two years; however, there is no limit to the number of companies our club owns. Each company must be tracked quarterly by a club member. The following illustration shows when each company we own meets this criterion.

2. We are able to discuss selling a company if it has not met the Chicks' Dozen (quantitative and qualitative criteria) for one year; see below for qualitative definition of Chicks' Dozen Disfavor.

    i. Buy what you know: The company has changed its focus or core business to something we don't understand, like, or support.

    ii. K.I.S.S.: Not applicable.

    iii. The industry: Company has experienced a downturn in its industry as a whole; or a company we own has been replaced by a new product or service; or a company we own has fallen behind industry changes at large.

    iv. Leader in its field: The company we own has lost market share. Rival has introduced a new product or service that affects our company's core product(s).

    v. Repeat profitability: Our company is consistently making less money than before.

vi–x. Quantifiable criteria (you know the drill here).

xi. Change in management: The company has suffered key losses in strategic positions, CEO, president, et al., anything that is impactful to a company.

xii. Buy on sale: Not applicable.

3. Vote to sell only at regularly scheduled meetings.

4. Vote has to be a majority.

5. We need to rebalance our portfolio.

6. Because we found a better company to invest in.

7. We screwed up when we originally made the initial purchase decision.

Procedure issue: Any Chick can present any company we own that meets our sell philosophy, but it must be done one week prior to a scheduled meeting. This, similar to our *modus operandi* when purchasing a company, allows us to assimilate the information and make thoughtful decisions.

Employer Identification Number (EIN)

Next, the Employer Identification Number. The reason your club must file for an EIN is that your club needs to file a tax return at the end of the year, and your EIN is how they identify which club you belong to. It is also how your broker will identify you—even if you have a really cute name, they'll go by your number. Tattoo it on your person. You'll be a hit at the beach next summer. "Hey, how are ya? Wanna see my Employer Identification Number? Hold on, it's right here under my sarong. Hey . . . Where are you going?" It didn't work for me either.

You can have your EIN in one day by calling the IRS at 800-829-3676 or 800-829-1040. They will direct you to your state's tax filing headquarters. When you call them, tell them you have your SS4 form in hand and will fax it to them in twenty-four hours, but you'd like to get your EIN immediately. They can give you one in minutes. It would be a good idea to have your SS4 form filled out before calling. You can get it at either your local IRS office or, now that you are online, www.irs.gov or www.chickslayingnesteggs.com. It looks like this:

Form **SS-4**

(Rev. April 2000)

Department of the Treasury
Internal Revenue Service

Application for Employer Identification Number

(For use by employers, corporations, partnerships, trusts, estates, churches, government agencies, certain individuals, and others. See instructions.)

▶ Keep a copy for your records.

EIN

OMB No. 1545-0003

Please type or print clearly.

1 Name of applicant (legal name) (see instructions)

2 Trade name of business (if different from name on line 1) | **3** Executor, trustee, "care of" name

4a Mailing address (street address) (room, apt., or suite no.) | **5a** Business address (if different from address on lines 4a and 4b)

4b City, state, and ZIP code | **5b** City, state, and ZIP code

6 County and state where principal business is located

7 Name of principal officer, general partner, grantor, owner, or trustor—SSN or ITIN may be required (see instructions) ▶

8a Type of entity (Check only one box.) (see instructions)

Caution: If applicant is a limited liability company, see the instructions for line 8a.

☐ Sole proprietor (SSN) _____
☐ Partnership   ☐ Personal service corp.
☐ REMIC   ☐ National Guard
☐ State/local government   ☐ Farmers' cooperative
☐ Church or church-controlled organization
☐ Other nonprofit organization (specify) ▶ _____
☐ Other (specify) ▶

☐ Estate (SSN of decedent) _____
☐ Plan administrator (SSN) _____
☐ Other corporation (specify) ▶ _____
☐ Trust
☐ Federal government/military
_____ (enter GEN if applicable) _____

8b If a corporation, name the state or foreign country (if applicable) where incorporated | State | Foreign country

9 Reason for applying (Check only one box.) (see instructions)
☐ Started new business (specify type) ▶_____
☐ Hired employees (Check the box and see line 12.)
☐ Created a pension plan (specify type) ▶

☐ Banking purpose (specify purpose) ▶ _____
☐ Changed type of organization (specify new type) ▶ _____
☐ Purchased going business
☐ Created a trust (specify type) ▶ _____
☐ Other (specify) ▶

10 Date business started or acquired (month, day, year) (see instructions) | **11** Closing month of accounting year (see instructions)

12 First date wages or annuities were paid or will be paid (month, day, year). **Note:** *If applicant is a withholding agent, enter date income will first be paid to nonresident alien. (month, day, year)* . . . . ▶

13 Highest number of employees expected in the next 12 months. **Note:** *If the applicant does not expect to have any employees during the period, enter -0-. (see instructions)* . . . . . ▶

Nonagricultural	Agricultural	Household

14 Principal activity (see instructions) ▶

15 Is the principal business activity manufacturing? . . . .☐ Yes   ☐ No
If "Yes," principal product and raw material used ▶

16 To whom are most of the products or services sold? Please check one box.   ☐ Business (wholesale)
☐ Public (retail)   ☐ Other (specify) ▶   ☐ N/A

17a Has the applicant ever applied for an employer identification number for this or any other business? . . . . . ☐ Yes   ☐ No
Note: *If "Yes," please complete lines 17b and 17c.*

17b If you checked "Yes" on line 17a, give applicant's legal name and trade name shown on prior application, if different from line 1 or 2 above.
Legal name ▶   Trade name ▶

17c Approximate date when and city and state where the application was filed. Enter previous employer identification number if known.
Approximate date when filed (mo., day, year) | City and state where filed | Previous EIN

Under penalties of perjury, I declare that I have examined this application, and to the best of my knowledge and belief, it is true, correct, and complete. | Business telephone number (include area code)
( )
Fax telephone number (include area code)
( )

Name and title (Please type or print clearly.) ▶

Signature ▶   Date ▶

Note: *Do not write below this line. For official use only.*

Please leave blank ▶	Geo.	Ind.	Class	Size	Reason for applying

For Privacy Act and Paperwork Reduction Act Notice, see page 4.   Cat. No. 16055N   Form **SS-4** (Rev. 4-2000)

File for and get an EIN number somewhere in the first few months of your club's existence. You don't need to have it before your first meeting, but start the process then, and you will have it by your next meeting.

The last of the three things needed to become a partnership is a county-ruled requirement. In some states you are required to file a certificate of copartnership form, which is commonly known as a "Doing Business As," or DBA, form. Call your county clerk and see if you need to register your name with them in order to be a viable partnership. (Minnesota is not one of those states.)

Once you've adopted your operating procedures and gotten your EIN, you've taken one huge step for humankind and one giant leap for your Chick club!

Chapter Summary

○ Write your own operating procedures.
○ Think of a very original name for your club; feel free to include "Chick," if even at the end. Laptop Stockette Chicks, Chicks In Dallas, Synchronized Stock Chickers. It would mean a lot to me. The little things.
○ Sign operating procedures with social security number.
○ File for EIN number—forms at www.chickslayingnesteggs.com.
○ Ask your county clerk if you have to file your club's name.

chick chat

TITLE: LEROY HOUSLEY
From: Karin

I wasn't going to post this, but I have to. My father-in-law is going to kill me, but it is such an unbelievable story.

Mary Lee and Leroy were able to make it up here for one last visit. She is having a hard time getting around and is still confused. The last few months of chemo and radiation have done a number on her. She is napping a lot. But this isn't about her, it's about Leroy.

After we got home from the hockey game, he went out on the deck to enjoy the night air. He was standing there for a couple of minutes when he heard some rustling under the barbecue grill. He walked toward it, only to hear a PSSSSSSSSSST sound and feel something hit his shirt.

HE GOT SPRAYED BY A SKUNK! He is up in the shower right now. My whole house smells like skunk, and the kids have woken up. Taylor threw up, Phil is boiling vinegar on the stove, I have candles burning everywhere, Reide is making a fire in the fireplace, and Wilson is bringing Papa every kind of soap and vinegar.

What next?

Karin

TITLE: SKUNK
From: Susie

Karin, I have been searching the Internet for some home remedies. Try tomato juice, tomato paste, ammonia, or vanilla extract.

If I were you, I'd have him sleep in the garage.

Susie

TITLE: PARIS
From: Lynn

Craig and I are leaving for Paris tomorrow. I will be away from my computer for ten days, as we are going over for a medical conference.

I am so excited! I am going to have to practice up on the little French I know.

Smooches,
Lynnie

TITLE: PARIS
From: Jeanette

Lynn needs your prayers now. On their flight over to Paris, Craig slipped into a coma. Lynn was not able to wake him for the last hour of the flight. When they landed in Paris, they whisked him off to a hospital. Lynn's French is not that great, so it's all confusing and scary. He is still in the hospital. I'll keep you posted when I hear something.

Jeanette

TITLE: PARIS AND S&P
From: Cheryl

Enough already! I'm skipping the S&P report so we can all go hug our families. It is much more important.

Cheryl

16

Broker Be Aware

I base most of my fashion taste on what doesn't itch.
— GILDA RADNER

You have researched companies from Retin-A manufacturers to the makers of your daily vitamin, from Quaker Oats (also the makers of Gatorade) to online grocers. You have learned more about these companies than you thought there was to know. Inside and outside, you dissected and came to a conclusion. You are ready to buy. You want some stock in Henny Penny's department stores because those Chicks really know what they are doing. Your next step? You need to find a broker who can make this purchase for you. Believe it or not, they don't let us common folk walk onto any of the exchanges, open our wallet, and say, "Three shares of GE, please." You need a broker to make your transaction.

In this chapter, you will learn the difference between a full-price broker and a discount broker. I will also give you a list of the largest brokers and where to find them. But wait, what's that noise? Is that your stomach? You have been so engrossed in this book that you forgot to eat? Listen, missy, you can't begin the broker process until you satisfy that stomach. You deserve a break today. Go ahead, McDonald's is always tempting. Splurge. Forget about the fat grams just this once. I'll still be here when you get home.

Welcome back. Now, you've been to McDonald's many times in your life (I'll refrain from saying "hundreds"). What would you do if the girl at the drive-through recommended what she thought you should order? "Hi, my name is Christina, may I take your order, please? But before you begin, may I suggest the Filet-O-Fish? I noticed you are driving a blue Volkswagen, and usually our customers with foreign cars enjoy fish. Plus, they order a Chef Salad. Shall I ring that up for you? A Salad and a Filet? Your order comes to $7.23 [said in a murmur], including a $1.00 commission for my extensive knowledge of *Automobiles and Your Order.* [back to full volume] Please drive through."

What? Since when does Christina tell you what to order? You dang well know what a girl wants: the Quarter-Pounder with cheese meal! Through your trial and error, and years of studying fast-food products, you have become your own expert. Why would you pay for Christina's advice? She doesn't even know you, or your taste buds. Only you know what you want. The thought of it is ludicrous, and thank goodness, because nobody would bother to eat there anymore.

The same goes for hiring a full-price or full-service broker. For example, let's say before you were entranced with this chapter, you were looking at Goldwoman Finches as your brokerage house. It's an all-female investment team. Their motto is "The cock crows but the hen delivers." Their slogan oozes success with attitude. You like that. They are a full-service, all-female brokerage, with Ph.D.s, M.B.A.s, and a dictionary full of big words. Did I mention that club member Leigh Ann's sister is a broker at the firm? Who else do you know in the business? Where would you even start? It's a big broker world out there, and you remain clueless. Going with Goldwoman Finches seems the easiest.

Hold on! You already know what you want! Why do you need another women's investment team to help you decide and buy? You've done the work! You and your club (*your* all-women team) have just spent the last couple of months researching and discussing companies. You've pulled them through the Chicks' Dozen criteria (or your own Chick-made principles), you've read the latest news stories, and you've tested the product (Retin-A is some strong stuff). You've talked about the future of its industry, you've compared it to its competitors, *and* you've gone back to the dermatologist and asked for something milder. Between you and your girlfriends, you are very sure you want to buy Henny Penny's for your first buy. It was unanimous. (Smart move.) You all feel it suits the club the best.

Fact: Christina has been working at McDonald's a lot longer than you. (You've never worked there. You worked at Papa John's 'cause your boyfriend Mark did). **Fiction:** Christina knows what you should order. You may have never worked at McDonald's, but does Christina know what's right for you to order? No, and nor does Goldwoman Finches know what stock is best for you or your club. Only you do, and you've already decided. You want Henny Penny's! Not Chicken Little's, not Crow's Feet, and not even Cockadoodle's Doo. (Does anyone still eat Filet-O-Fishes?)

Why should you pay more to purchase a stock when you already did the work? This is what a full-service/full-price brokerage house offers. Since they are all heavily educated and have been in the business for years, they come to expect higher fees for doing a transaction that doesn't take a lot of brains. They can give you advice, and many do, but at this point, you aren't going to need it. Their advice most likely comes with a hidden-commission agenda. Did you know that Christina gets an extra bonus from Ronald himself for every Filet-O-Fish/Chef Salad combo she sells this month? And to think she said that she was making this recommendation based on some report called *Automobiles and Your Order.* That sure smells like lutefisk to me. Something to think about when looking for a broker.

It's a sad day for the full-price broker. There was a time when he was the only one able to get up-to-the-minute stock quotes. There was a time when he would get the SEC filings before the public. Folks like us used to be forced to wait for the investor relations department of each company to send out their financials if we wanted to check out a company on our own—or else we were at the full-service broker's mercy.

Glory be! The Internet has changed all this: you are able to get the information at the same time as the highly paid broker—for free! Now that you know what to do with the information, and where to find it, you only need someone to make the transaction for you at a reasonable fee.

What is reasonable? The Chicks' rule of feather is: we always want our broker fees to be less than 1.5 percent of our transaction fee. We spend $1,500 every three months, so we want our broker fee to be less than $22.50. Ask Goldwoman Finches how much they would charge you to make a $1,500 purchase. This is very important.

So who will charge you less to buy the stock? Where can you find a broker to make the transaction for you and keep his nose in his own coop? Let the circus begin . . . there are hundreds. They are called discount brokers or deep-discount brokers. If they are online brokers, they are also called e-brokers. You see commercials for them all the time. Funny ones, where the hip twenty-year-old teaches his sixty-year-old boss how to trade online, then invites him to the bash at his house after work. Or the women who just get in from an early-morning jog and go to their computer to make a trade. Little-known fact, our actress Chick Cheryl did a commercial for a discount broker not too long ago. She was adorable. Her dog's name was Max, and she pretended to be a single woman trading online in her lofty apartment. Funny thing is, it wasn't too far from the truth. She has a big clumsy dog *and* makes trades online from home. Only difference, she is not single. (Another little-known fact: Chick Cheryl used to be on *General Hospital*. She misses the spotlight. I'm thinking we should petition for her to get back on another soap. She was Jenny Quartermaine, and I think she was married a couple of times. I didn't watch then. After Luke and Laura left, I got serious about college.)

Hey, Karin, I was huge. I got fan letters every week! HUGE! Anthony Geary, Luke (beating heart be still), was my brother. I was married to Ned, with Paul on the side. I was on the cover of Soap Opera Digest! *I was at the daytime Emmys! How could you have not watched me?*

You see? Poor Cheryl. Still living the actress life. This is probably the most logical decision you're going to get to make as a club—I mean, it's easy to get all the facts about these brokers and brokerages—but how do you sift through all of these brokerage houses to find one that suits you? Should it be the easiest to use? The cheapest? Who has the best customer service? Is it worth a couple more dollars to have a fast reply to a stock order? Is it important that my e-broker also have telephone transacting available? Do I need everything these guys offer, or are some of them still too full-service?

Well, let's talk about just what a discount broker does, and what the differences are between discount brokers and full-price competitors. First, let me tell you that in the all-important transaction phase of making a stock purchase, there is no difference at all. In fact, some of the discount brokers use the same clearance desks—that's the people who actually buy and confirm the purchase of the stock—as the full-price brokers. Yet you will pay the full-price broker up to twenty times more to make the same transaction. You are probably asking yourself, "Yeah, discount brokers may be cheaper, but are they insured like the full-price broker?" Yes. The same government-sponsored Securities Investor Protection Corporation (SIPC) covers the discount brokers. All accounts are insured up to $100,000 in cash and up to $400,000 in other assets, and can be insured for more if you ask. So why wouldn't someone use a discount broker?

First, it goes back to my uncle John Locke's quote about people being resistant to change. If people are afraid to use their credit card online (and plenty are), why should we assume they'll cozy up to having a broker online? Having a broker out there in cyberspace, with no human face to contact in case of an Internet shutdown, may seem more than a little scary. Still, the fastest-growing group of stock traders are the ones trading online. Increasingly, online trading has become the norm.

Despite all that, the Chicks do not use an Internet-only investment account. Why? Because when we started investing, this concept of no human contact was a bit difficult for my mother to grasp. She was not at all comfortable with an Internet-only investment account. She liked knowing that she could talk with a human being if the Internet shut down or if there was a problem with our account. Since she was going to be the one making the trades and dealing with the broker, she had to be comfortable, so we narrowed our search to companies that had local brick-and-mortar offices with Internet trading available. She has since become accustomed to the online transactions and no longer feels uncomfortable with not seeing a person (as long as there is one at the other end of the phone).

There's another thing that keeps the full-service brokers going. It's always been pretty cool to be able to say, "My broker gave me a hot tip." Old-school investors still see it as the only way to purchase a stock. I see it as highway robbery and ignorance. That broker's hot tip may well be coming your way because he has a stock of the day that he's being given a bonus for unloading, and even if he doesn't, he loves getting the transaction fee—both when you buy it *and* when you sell it.

So, whenever I hear people bragging about a hot tip, I question their intelligence. Why aren't they doing their own investment research? Do they enjoy gambling their future on hot tips? Do they enjoy paying more for a transaction? To tell you the truth, I don't know why anyone would use a full-service broker, unless they didn't care about the extra fees involved or wouldn't mind eating a Filet-O-Fish when what they wanted was a Quarter-Pounder.

How does a discount e-broker work? First, get an application packet from the company. You can do this by either visiting the website or local office, or calling them on the phone. A couple of questions to ask of your prospective discount broker:

1. How much does it cost to make a trade? (I use the word "trade" because it's broker lingo. It means to either buy or sell. You trade money for stock. I want you to be able to use the correct lingo when asking your questions. Always thinking of you.)
2. Is there a minimum amount we have to keep in the account?
3. Are there free trades every so often?
4. Are you a member of the Securities Investor Protection Corporation (SIPC)?
5. How soon will you notify me after a trade has taken place?
6. Do you let me know via e-mail that the trade has been executed, or do you just update the account?
7. Do you offer free real-time quotes? (Not extremely important, but some club members may insist on it.)
8. Does your money market account offer free checking?

After you think you have found an e-broker you are comfortable with, you need to fill out the application for your investment club. This is the point where you'll need your EIN number and a signed copy of your operating procedures. You are opening an account for a partnership, not an individual. When all your paperwork is filled in, all *i*'s dotted and *t*'s crossed, write a check for your deposit amount and send it in. It will be deposited into a money market account until you actually do something with it. Don't forget to attach the copy of your operating procedures. Within days, your online account will be established. It's that simple.

Once your account is all set up, you will be given a password to access it. You can decide who will know the password within your club. Most of the time a broker will create dual passwords for a club: one to access the account, and another password to make a trade. Add this to your questions list:

9. Do you have a different password to access the account than you do to make the trade? (This is called dual passwords.)

Why is this important, you ask? Because you will want only one person to make the trades for the club, but all members should be able to access the account. This is how we do it, and it's highly recommended. The only person who makes our trades is my mother, the Egg Carton. The rest of us Chicks just like to see when the trade is executed and what we actually paid for the stock. We also like to check the status of the account and see if it matches our portfolio tracker at www.chickslayingnesteggs.com. We can easily find out by logging on to the broker's website and accessing our account.

Once all of this is done, the broker is just waiting for you to say go. What do you want to buy and how many shares? What would you like to order?

When you do buy a stock, it is called placing an order. The e-broker then either notifies you via e-mail that your transaction has taken place, or updates your account. The timeliness of this differs greatly from broker to broker, ranging from one minute—which some brokers guarantee or your trade is free—to twenty-four hours.

Below are the online rankings from www.money.com, which originally was in *Money* magazine.

SCORECARD: OUR RANKINGS

Broker	Ease of Use	Customer Service	System Responsiveness	Products and Tools	Cost	Total Score
Fidelity	★★★★★	★★★★★	★★	★★★★½	★★	★★★★★
Ameritrade	★★★★	★★★★★	★★★★	★★★½	★★★★★	★★★★★
Merrill Lynch	★★★	★★★★★	★★★★★	★★★★★	★★	★★★★½
Datek Online	★★★	★★★★½	★★★★	★★	★★★★	★★★★½
Charles Schwab	★★★★	★★★★	★★★★	★★★★½	★★	★★★★
JB Oxford & Co.	★★★★	★★★★	★★★	★★★	★★★	★★★★
Quick & Reilly	★★	★★★★½	★★★½	★★★½	★★★	★★★★
DLJdirect	★★★½	★★	★★★★½	★★★★½	★★★	★★★½
Morgan Stanley Dean Witter	★★★	★★	★★★★★	★★★★★	★★	★★★
Suretrade	★★	★★★	★★★	★★★★	★★★★★	★★★
Web Street Securities	★★	★★★★★	★½	★★★★	★★★★½	★★★
E*Trade	★★★	★★½	★★½	★★★★★	★★★	★★½
TD Waterhouse	★★★½	★★	★★½	★★★★★	★★★★½	★★½
A.B. Watley	★★★	★★	★★★½	★★★	★★★★★	★★
National Discount Brokers	★★★½	★	★★★	★★★★½	★★★	★★
American Express	★	★★★★	★★	★★★★	★★★★★	★★
Muriel Siebert & Co.	★★	★	★★★	★★★★	★★★★	★
Mydiscountbroker.com	★	★★★	★★	★★★½	★★★★	★
Dreyfus	★½	★	★★★★½	★★	★★★★	★
Scottrade	★★½	★	★½	★★★	★★★★½	★

The table details how the twenty largest e-brokers rated in five categories. We weighted each differently (with the mainstream investor in mind) to arrive at the total score—ease of use, customer service, and system responsiveness count for more than the availability of products and tools, and low-cost trades.

Cheryl did a commercial for mydiscountbroker.com and immediately opened an account with them. She thinks that they're one of the easiest brokers to use. I have another account at AmericanExpress.com, and trades are free if you have a balance of at least $20,000.

Chapter Summary

O It ain't Chicky to use a full-price/full-service broker.

O Blue Bugs do not necessarily a Filet-O-Fish fan make.

O Discount e-brokers are the way to go to make your stock transactions.

O Consider the questions you want to ask your broker.

O Check out www.chickslayingnesteggs.com for the latest in investment club brokers.

O Making a transaction is simple, and your broker should be too.

O Retin-A in the early stages burns.

O Make *sure* your broker is covered by the SIPC.

chick chat

TITLE: PARIS
From: Lynn

Thank you all so much for your prayers. We are back from Paris, and I have never been happier to be home with my husband . . . WHO IS ALIVE! It turns out what probably caused Craig to slip into the coma was the new high blood pressure medicine he was on. No one can be sure, but he seems to be doing better on this new drug. He is going to take a little leave of absence from work, and we are going to spend some time resting together. I missed you all!

Smooches,
Lynnie, now fluent in French

TITLE: **ORACLE
From: Kristin

I know we have a meeting coming up this Sunday night, and I just wanted to make sure that everyone knew I was going to do a report on Oracle. I'm serious, Chickies, their numbers are incredible, and the

·more I look at them, I can't believe I don't own more. Just wanted to forewarn you that I'm going to be putting on the big push.

Kristin

TITLE: **ORACLE
From: *Jana*

Speaking of pushing, I'm not yet. But this pregnancy has me sleeping even more than I'm gaining weight. (Not that I'm gaining a lot. I'm twenty-five weeks and only gained an ounce. Lying.) I wanted to add to Kristin's Oracle post. I absolutely love the company, and you all have heard how my stock has done. (I have owned it since 1989 and kicked some bootie. I'm trying to talk like Cheryl now.) If there is anything Larry Ellison wants, it is to succeed, at all costs. Gotta like that in a CEO. Can hardly wait to hear your report, Kristin!

Jana

TITLE: **S&P REPORT
From: *Cheryl*

I finally feel like I can do an S&P Report without crying. Sheez, it's been a roller coaster here lately. Jana, give us some more of your pregnancy stories to pick us up a bit!

Here is the S&P report for the last week:

Our Chick portfolio is up 52.53% vs. the market's 21.48%
AOL up 256.52% vs. 21.02%
CSCO up 58.93% vs. 10.03%
NOK up 42.84% vs. 6.36%
GPS down 12.95% vs. 6.9%
PFE up 5.22% vs. 37.60%
KO down 8.07% vs. 37.60%

17

All Accounted For?

From birth to age 18, a girl needs good parents.
From 18 to 35, she needs good looks.
From 35 to 55, she needs a good personality.
From 55 on, she needs good cash.

—SOPHIE TUCKER

Sophie ain't kidding. By the time women subtract work years from all the time we spend raising children, the inequality in salaries, and the fact that we live longer than men, we better know what the heck we are doing with our money when we *are* making it. It is estimated that baby boomers are going to need between $1 million and $2 million at retirement to maintain a middle-class lifestyle. Yikes! Get on the ball if you ever want to cruise the Riviera! A woman may have her money invested, but if it isn't performing for you, as in doing back flips across Wall Street, you'd better take a closer look at it.

The only way to tell whether your investments are behaving the way they should is by keeping good accounting records. The point here is to beat the market, so keep score. Making a profit is nice, but you shouldn't be satisfied with $1,100 after having invested $1,000 two years ago. It doesn't make any sense to boast that your car gets eight miles to the gallon if the industry standard is nineteen. You want to track your portfolio against a benchmark, and as we learned earlier, that benchmark is the S&P 500 Index. It's particularly difficult within a club to tell if you are beating the market when everyone owns different amounts and new members are coming and going. Accounting isn't easy, but it is important. In this chapter, we will look at how to track your club's portfolio. In the beginning, your club may have the same number of people all contributing the same amount, but through the years, you will inevitably lose a member, or someone will need some of her cash. What do you do then? What do you do when you have $40,000 in your club account and one member wants to withdraw her $5,000? Do you let another club member enter at the same price? Do you sell stock to pay her off? Do you give her some stock in that amount? Any way you look at it, inequality is going to arise. If the member who buys in at $5,000 wants to follow along with the portfolio tracking, it is a little difficult because her $5,000 is fresh. She wants to track it against the S&P from the day she purchased it, not from the club's history.

Or what do you do when the majority of the club decides to use the club as their main source of investing and want to put in more than $50 a month? What if someone wants to put in $1,000 a month and the others want to put in $75, and the rest are content at $50? Who wants to do those books and maintain the club theme? Keep it simple, sister.

I'll start with the simplest and work forward. If you're serious about your investment club being for life, or if you'd like to contribute unequal amounts, I'd advise getting a software package that is able to do your accounting for you. Trying to keep a per-unit value system is time-consuming when doing it all by hand; it's too easy to make mistakes, and besides, who has *more* time? There are several programs that can do this for you, but the software that the Chicks prefer because of its simplicity and cost-effectiveness is the Know Your Club software. (Know Your Club is available on our website at www.chickslayingnesteggs.com.)

If you are a martyr and insist on doing your club accounting by hand, I'll explain it, as best I can. Remember, I am not an accountant, and I do not play one on TV. Matter of fact, I do not play anything on TV, but just let me have the dream. If you are planning on getting an accounting software program, skip this, because it's going to be really boring.

If you plan on doing the accounting by hand, you need to develop a "unit" accounting system (the software does this automatically). Units are a must when you have members coming and going, or if members are contributing unequally.

Think of each member of your investment club buying shares of the club as a whole. So if I were to invest $50 and Lorene $100, she would get twice the number of shares. If each share, which we call a unit, is worth $50, I would get one unit, and Lorene would get two. With an investment club of five people and each unit being worth $50, here is how it would look:

Name	Amount Invested	Number of Units
Lorene	$100	2
Karin	$50	1
Jeanette	$150	3
Susie	$75	1.5
Lynn	$500	10

The total number of shares in the club is 17.5, and they are worth $875. Let's say that was month one. Now month two looks like this:

Name	Amount Invested	Number of Units	Total Number Owned (Adding to Last Month's)
Lorene	$200	4	6
Karin	$50	1	2
Jeanette	$50	1	4
Susie	$75	1.5	3
Lynn	$400	8	18

At the beginning of the year, the portfolio has $875, and each unit is worth $50. Then the contributing continues like above. After twelve months, and the same kind of sporadic and unequal investing, pretend the portfolio is worth $17,600. Also, there are two hundred units owned. How much would each unit be worth?

$17,600 ÷ 200 = 88. Each unit is worth $88!

Let's say our investment club unit ownership looks like this:

Name	Total Number Units Owned
Lorene	65
Karin	15
Jeanette	25
Susie	20
Lynn	75

To figure out how much each member owns in a dollar figure, you would multiply her unit ownership by the value of the unit on that given date. Here is what that would look like:

Name	Total Number Units Owned	Value on Given Day (× $88)
Lorene	65	$5,720
Karin	15	$1,320
Jeanette	25	$2,200
Susie	20	$1,760
Lynn	75	$6,600

This is the process you would have to go through each time you wanted to know your value in the club. You would have to multiply each member's units by the value of each unit at that moment. (To figure out the value of each unit, divide the portfolio's total worth by the number of units owned.) With the stock market changing every minute, and this method being so time-consuming, it would be tough to do this more than once a month. This is the only system that will allow for a member to leave and a new one to start purchasing her own units at the going rate, instead of having to buy in at the same price the exiting member is going out with.

I'm going to be honest with you. I have not tried to do this at home. Just writing this was enough for me to know I would screw it up. I am not a numbers person, and I don't want to be. There are some numbers people out there who might actually enjoy this process, but I'd still advise you to get a computer to back you up. In my humble, unnumbered opinion. Now just to test you. If this made-up investment club were yours, would you be able to figure out what your rate of return was for the past year?

A) 17.5 percent
B) 76 percent
C) .76
D) This is enough to encourage me not to use this method.

The answer would be B, 76 percent. We took the end-of-year price of each unit ($88) and subtracted the price from the beginning of the year ($50).

$$88.00 - 50.00 = 38.00$$

Then we take that and divide it by the beginning-of-the-year stock price ($50):

$$\frac{\$38.00}{\$50.00} = .76$$

Then we multiply that by 100 to get a percent:

$$.76 \times 100 = 76 \text{ percent}$$

So that's it, unit accounting. Stand up, be accounted for, and do the numbers this way only if you are really good at it *and* enjoy it. If you are, will you come to my house for dinner too? My eighth grader needs some help with her math, and I'm hiding.

chick chat

TITLE: MEGAN'S LIFE
From: Megan

The Michigan job fell through. No job, no job, no job, no job! I am just sweating! We go through this every year, but three teams folded this year, and the jobs are scarce. I love that everyone thinks this is so glamorous . . . such a joke.

And to top it all off, I am fat. Eating everything that is put in from of me—I can't stop. Oh, and it's my anniversary today. My husband is probably shaking his head, saying, "Ew!" On top of it all, I can't decide between Oracle, Martha Stewart, Intel, Broadcom (I'm still on the bandwagon), or GE for our next purchase. So now that I have rambled about nothing of any importance whatsoever, I'll have mercy on all of you and say . . . adios!

FrkdOutInME,

Megan

TITLE: MEGAN'S LIFE
From: Megan

I am wondering if they have AOL in London? I'm sure they have Oracle. It even sounds English. True story—job prospect in London for Kevin. Good God. I'm planning my sister's wedding, and she's decided to move up her wedding date to October 2 of this year instead of August of next year. (No, she's not pregnant, just in serious LOVE!) She wants to get married in Maine and she currently resides in New Jersey, so little sister gets to help, which is my forte, so I am psyched, besides whatever it takes to dull the pain of unemployment and the possibility of moving to London . . .

WshICldStyN1Plce,

Megan

TITLE: **ORACLE
From: Jeanette

Just wanted to keep you girls posted on the meeting and our latest purchase. Nice job, Chick Kristin, on your Oracle research. We bought this morning at the bell. Details are in your e-mailbox.

Jeanette

TITLE: **S&P REPORT
From: Cheryl

Wooo-Hooo . . . what a way to start a new purchase! I shouldn't be jumping up and down, but that guy from Iowa knew what he was talking about on that plane to my husband years ago. Imagine if we had invested THEN in Oracle. Doesn't matter, we're Chicks, and I'm happy to own them today! Please don't mention my commercial in the book, Karin. I'm so embarrassed.

Here is our S&P Report for the end of this month:
Our portfolio is up 67.95% vs. S&P up 23.28%: yeeeeeehaaaaaa!
AOL up 253% vs. 26.26%
CSCO up 103.74% vs. 14.8%
GPS up 4.18% vs. 11.53% (at least GPS is UP!)
KO down 8.86% vs. 43.56%
NOK up 122.08% vs. 8.97%
ORCL up 43.33% vs. 3.23%
PFE down 2.32% vs. 43.56%

Question: our first two stock picks happen to be our biggest losers. Are we getting better at this, or is it just the market? Go Chickies!

Cheryl

18

Tax Return

I recommend walking around naked in your living room.
— ALANIS MORRISETTE

I'm going to say this in the first sentence: don't bother trying to read this chapter until it is time to actually do your taxes—unless you want to go to sleep. The one thing I figured out while I was working on this chapter was that humor and taxes just don't mix. What's funny about filling out forms? I will, though, provide the only jokes I know. They are for those of us, investment clubs included, who must answer to Uncle Sam. If you are an IRS employee or a political figure, I don't blame you for taxation without relaxation. Really. I don't. And no, I am not just trying to cover my behind; I really do think that we could be friends if we met. This humor is just for the people that don't enjoy the month of April.

My Best Tax Jokes

○ A lot of people still have the first dollar they ever made. Uncle Sam has the rest.
○ A harp is a piano after taxes.
○ The way the cost of living and taxes are today, you might as well marry for love.

0 Behind every successful man stands a woman and the IRS. One takes the credit, the other takes the cash.

0 Income tax has made more liars out of the American people than golf.

0 The wealth of experience is the one possession that hasn't been taxed . . . yet.

0 What the present income tax form needs is a section that would explain the explanations.

I have come to help explain the forms in Chick lingo. Believe me, this is not fun, but I'm only doing it for my new buds, Governor Jesse and Judy at the Internal Revenue Service.

Every investment club must file a tax return, or else expect a body slam. It is not a difficult form, and if I walk you through it, one of your club members will be able to whip it up in less than an hour. Disclaimer: I am *not* a tax expert. One reviewed this section, but if you or your club has any doubts or feel your club has an unusual circumstance, then have your return reviewed by a tax adviser. (In any case, having an expert check your work isn't a bad idea.) This step-by-step tutorial shows you how our group, a normal, average investment club without a lot of complications, filled out a tax form.

The IRS defines a partnership as a syndicate, group pool, joint venture, or other unincorporated organization that carries on any business, financial operation, or venture and is not classified as a corporation, trust, or estate. An investment club fits in here. This is the simplest way to do your return. If you have formed a corporation for your investment club, you are going to have to fill out different forms. Since I have suggested you form a partnership, I am assuming that you took me at my word, so the tax form you fill out is the 1065.

The due date of the 1065 is April 15. To make it easier on your club, just plan on having it done by February 15. Get it over with. This way, you have plenty of time to send each member her own page for personal taxes: the K-1.

Don't leave me now. This is very important. These forms need to be looked at. Don't close the book and turn out the light. I'll be quick. We'll dash through the 1065, Schedule D, and the K-1, and then we'll be on to the next thing. Maybe I'll even throw in another joke at the end of the chapter.

This is what the first page of the tax form looks like. The 1065 has four pages. A downloadable copy of all of these forms is available at www.irs.gov. This is how we filled our return out for our club, but if you feel you have different or unusual circumstances, consult a tax professional.

Page One—Instructions

U.S. Partnership Return of Income

Step 1—Look at the heading, upper left-hand corner, Box A: Principal Business Activity. We wrote the word "investing."

Step 2—Box B: Principal Product or Service. We wrote "stocks."

Step 3—Box C: Must include the business code assigned by the IRS. So we plugged in our investment club code, 523900. (You can call your local tax office and ask for the code for an investment club on form 1065. The government changes these things at will.)

Step 4—We completed the main box in the heading by filling in the name of our investment club and its address.

Step 5—Box D: We filled in the Employer Identification Number that we got from the IRS when we filled out our SS4 form at the beginning of the club's existence.

Step 6—Box E: This is the date our club started.

Step 7—Box F: We left this one blank since we could answer yes to the following questions: 1) The partnership's total tax receipts for the tax year were less than $250,000; 2) The partnership's total assets at the end of the tax year were less than $600,000; 3) Schedules K-1 are filed with the return and furnished to the partners on or before the due date (including extensions) for the partnership return.

Step 8—G: We checked the applicable boxes.

Step 9—H: Like most investment clubs, we checked "cash."

Step 10—I: Each of our members got a K-1. (Remember, this might be more or less than the number of members in your club at present if you've had some departures or additions.)

Form **1065**			U.S. Partnership Return of Income		OMB No. 1545-0099

Department of the Treasury
Internal Revenue Service

For calendar year 1999, or tax year beginning .... , 1999, and ending .... , ...
▶ **See separate instructions.**

1999

A Principal business activity	Use the IRS label. Other-wise, please print or type.	Name of partnership	D Employer identification number
B Principal product or service		Number, street, and room or suite no. If a P.O. box, see page 12 of the instructions.	E Date business started
C Business code number		City or town, state, and ZIP code	F Total assets (see page 12 of the instructions) $

G Check applicable boxes: **(1)** ☐ Initial return **(2)** ☐ Final return **(3)** ☐ Change in address **(4)** ☐ Amended return
H Check accounting method: **(1)** ☐ Cash **(2)** ☐ Accrual **(3)** ☐ Other (specify) ▶ ....
I Number of Schedules K-1. Attach one for each person who was a partner at any time during the tax year ▶ ....

Caution: *Include only trade or business income and expenses on lines 1a through 22 below. See the instructions for more information.*

Income

1a Gross receipts or sales	1a		
b Less returns and allowances.	1b	1c	
2 Cost of goods sold (Schedule A, line 8)		2	
3 Gross profit. Subtract line 2 from line 1c.		3	
4 Ordinary income (loss) from other partnerships, estates, and trusts *(attach schedule)*.		4	
5 Net farm profit (loss) *(attach Schedule F (Form 1040))*		5	
6 Net gain (loss) from Form 4797, Part II, line 18.		6	
7 Other income (loss) *(attach schedule)*.		7	
8 **Total income (loss).** Combine lines 3 through 7		8	

Deductions (see page 14 of the instructions for limitations)

9 Salaries and wages (other than to partners) (less employment credits).		9	
10 Guaranteed payments to partners.		10	
11 Repairs and maintenance.		11	
12 Bad debts.		12	
13 Rent.		13	
14 Taxes and licenses.		14	
15 Interest.		15	
16a Depreciation (if required, attach Form 4562)	16a		
b Less depreciation reported on Schedule A and elsewhere on return	16b	16c	
17 Depletion **(Do not deduct oil and gas depletion.)**		17	
18 Retirement plans, etc.		18	
19 Employee benefit programs.		19	
20 Other deductions *(attach schedule)*		20	
21 **Total deductions.** Add the amounts shown in the far right column for lines 9 through 20		21	
22 **Ordinary income (loss)** from trade or business activities. Subtract line 21 from line 8		22	

Please Sign Here

Under penalties of perjury, I declare that I have examined this return, including accompanying schedules and statements, and to the best of my knowledge and belief, it is true, correct, and complete. Declaration of preparer (other than general partner or limited liability company member) is based on all information of which preparer has any knowledge.

▶ Signature of general partner or limited liability company member   ▶ Date

Paid Preparer's Use Only	Preparer's signature ▶	Date	Check if self-employed ▶ ☐	Preparer's SSN or PTIN
	Firm's name (or yours if self-employed) and address ▶		EIN ▶	
			ZIP code ▶	

For Paperwork Reduction Act Notice, see separate instructions.   Cat. No. 11390Z   Form **1065** (1999)

The rest of page one (Lines 1a—22) pertains to money earned by a trade or business (such as a machine shop or beauty salon), not by an investment club, so we skipped to the end of page one.

Step 11—Our club member who filled out this form signed and dated the return as a general partner.

Page Two—Instructions

Schedule A—Cost of Goods Sold (not applicable)
Schedule B—Other Information

Step 1—Under Schedule B, Question 1: we checked General Partnership box.

Step 2—All of our answers to the Schedule B questions (1–11) were no, except for number 5, which we already went over: this answer was yes, because even though we had a great year, we didn't strike it rich and our club still isn't worth more than $600,000. (But that day will come!) How does the joke go? Ambition in America is still rewarded . . . with high taxation.

The only likely exception in Schedule B that might have been a yes is number 11, if our club had had a partial or full withdrawal of a member during the year.

Step 3—bottom of page two: the Tax Matters Partner (TMP) is the same person who signed on page one. She entered her social security number where it calls for the identifying number of the TMP, then filled in the address blank.

Page Three—Instructions

Schedule K: Partners' Shares of Income, Credits, Deductions, etc.

Page three is the place where you get to put in your numbers. For most investment clubs, the income usually comes from three sources:

Schedule A   Cost of Goods Sold (see page 17 of the instructions)

1 Inventory at beginning of year	1	
2 Purchases less cost of items withdrawn for personal use	2	
3 Cost of labor	3	
4 Additional section 263A costs (attach schedule)	4	
5 Other costs (attach schedule)	5	
6 **Total.** Add lines 1 through 5	6	
7 Inventory at end of year	7	
8 **Cost of goods sold.** Subtract line 7 from line 6. Enter here and on page 1, line 2	8	

9a Check all methods used for valuing closing inventory:
  (i) ☐ Cost as described in Regulations section 1.471-3
  (ii) ☐ Lower of cost or market as described in Regulations section 1.471-4
  (iii) ☐ Other (specify method used and attach explanation) ▶ _____
 b Check this box if there was a writedown of "subnormal" goods as described in Regulations section 1.471-2(c) . . . ▶ ☐
 c Check this box if the LIFO inventory method was adopted this tax year for any goods (if checked, attach Form 970) . ▶ ☐
 d Do the rules of section 263A (for property produced or acquired for resale) apply to the partnership? . . . ☐ Yes   ☐ No
 e Was there any change in determining quantities, cost, or valuations between opening and closing inventory? ☐ Yes   ☐ No
   If "Yes," attach explanation.

Schedule B   Other Information

	Yes	No
1 What type of entity is filing this return? Check the applicable box:		
a ☐ General partnership b ☐ Limited partnership c ☐ Limited liability company		
d ☐ Limited liability partnership e ☐ Other ▶ _____		
2 Are any partners in this partnership also partnerships?		
3 Is this partnership a partner in another partnership?		
4 Is this partnership subject to the consolidated audit procedures of sections 6221 through 6233? If "Yes," see **Designation of Tax Matters Partner** below		
5 Does this partnership meet **ALL THREE** of the following requirements?		
a The partnership's total receipts for the tax year were less than $250,000;		
b The partnership's total assets at the end of the tax year were less than $600,000; **AND**		
c Schedules K-1 are filed with the return and furnished to the partners on or before the due date (including extensions) for the partnership return.		
If "Yes," the partnership is not required to complete Schedules L, M-1, and M-2; Item F on page 1 of Form 1065; or Item J on Schedule K-1		
6 Does this partnership have any foreign partners?		
7 Is this partnership a publicly traded partnership as defined in section 469(k)(2)?		
8 Has this partnership filed, or is it required to file, **Form 8264,** Application for Registration of a Tax Shelter? . .		
9 At any time during calendar year 1999, did the partnership have an interest in or a signature or other authority over a financial account in a foreign country (such as a bank account, securities account, or other financial account)? See page 18 of the instructions for exceptions and filing requirements for Form TD F 90-22.1. If "Yes," enter the name of the foreign country. ▶ _____		
10 During the tax year, did the partnership receive a distribution from, or was it the grantor of, or transferor to, a foreign trust? If "Yes," the partnership may have to file Form 3520. See page 18 of the instructions		
11 Was there a distribution of property or a transfer (e.g., by sale or death) of a partnership interest during the tax year? If "Yes," you may elect to adjust the basis of the partnership's assets under section 754 by attaching the statement described under **Elections Made By the Partnership** on page 7 of the instructions		

Designation of Tax Matters Partner (see page 18 of the instructions)
Enter below the general partner designated as the tax matters partner (TMP) for the tax year of this return:

Name of designated TMP ▶		Identifying number of TMP ▶	
Address of designated TMP ▶			

Schedule K   Partners' Shares of Income, Credits, Deductions, etc.

	(a) Distributive share items		(b) Total amount	
	1 Ordinary income (loss) from trade or business activities (page 1, line 22)	**1**		
	2 Net income (loss) from rental real estate activities *(attach Form 8825)*	**2**		
	3a Gross income from other rental activities **3a**			
	b Expenses from other rental activities *(attach schedule)* **3b**			
	c Net income (loss) from other rental activities. Subtract line 3b from line 3a	**3c**		
	4 Portfolio income (loss):			
	a Interest income	**4a**		
	b Ordinary dividends	**4b**		
Income (Loss)	**c** Royalty income	**4c**		
	d Net short-term capital gain (loss) *(attach Schedule D (Form 1065))*	**4d**		
	e Net long-term capital gain (loss) *(attach Schedule D (Form 1065)):*			
	(1) 28% rate gain (loss) ▶ .... **(2)** Total for year ▶	**4e(2)**		
	f Other portfolio income (loss) *(attach schedule)*	**4f**		
	5 Guaranteed payments to partners	**5**		
	6 Net section 1231 gain (loss) (other than due to casualty or theft) *(attach Form 4797)*	**6**		
	7 Other income (loss) *(attach schedule)*	**7**		
Deduc-tions	**8** Charitable contributions *(attach schedule)*	**8**		
	9 Section 179 expense deduction *(attach Form 4562)*	**9**		
	10 Deductions related to portfolio income (itemize)	**10**		
	11 Other deductions *(attach schedule)*	**11**		
	12a Low-income housing credit:			
	(1) From partnerships to which section 42(j)(5) applies for property placed in service before 1990	**12a(1)**		
	(2) Other than on line 12a(1) for property placed in service before 1990	**12a(2)**		
	(3) From partnerships to which section 42(j)(5) applies for property placed in service after 1989	**12a(3)**		
Credits	**(4)** Other than on line 12a(3) for property placed in service after 1989	**12a(4)**		
	b Qualified rehabilitation expenditures related to rental real estate activities *(attach Form 3468)*	**12b**		
	c Credits (other than credits shown on lines 12a and 12b) related to rental real estate activities	**12c**		
	d Credits related to other rental activities	**12d**		
	13 Other credits	**13**		
Invest-ment Interest	**14a** Interest expense on investment debts	**14a**		
	b (1) Investment income included on lines 4a, 4b, 4c, and 4f above	**14b(1)**		
	(2) Investment expenses included on line 10 above	**14b(2)**		
Self-Employ-ment	**15a** Net earnings (loss) from self-employment	**15a**		
	b Gross farming or fishing income	**15b**		
	c Gross nonfarm income	**15c**		
	16a Depreciation adjustment on property placed in service after 1986	**16a**		
Adjustments and Tax Preference Items	**b** Adjusted gain or loss	**16b**		
	c Depletion (other than oil and gas)	**16c**		
	d (1) Gross income from oil, gas, and geothermal properties	**16d(1)**		
	(2) Deductions allocable to oil, gas, and geothermal properties	**16d(2)**		
	e Other adjustments and tax preference items *(attach schedule)*	**16e**		
	17a Type of income ▶			
	b Name of foreign country or U.S. possession ▶			
Foreign Taxes	**c** Total gross income from sources outside the United States *(attach schedule)*	**17c**		
	d Total applicable deductions and losses *(attach schedule)*	**17d**		
	e Total foreign taxes (check one): ▶ ☐ Paid ☐ Accrued	**17e**		
	f Reduction in taxes available for credit *(attach schedule)*	**17f**		
	g Other foreign tax information *(attach schedule)*	**17g**		
	18 Section 59(e)(2) expenditures: **a** Type ▶ .... **b** Amount ▶	**18b**		
	19 Tax-exempt interest income	**19**		
Other	**20** Other tax-exempt income	**20**		
	21 Nondeductible expenses	**21**		
	22 Distributions of money (cash and marketable securities)	**22**		
	23 Distributions of property other than money	**23**		
	24 Other items and amounts required to be reported separately to partners *(attach schedule)*			

Form **1065** (1999)

1. Interest—money market account
2. Dividends—on stock owned
3. Sale of stock—a gain or a loss

We reported these amounts on page three, items 4a, 4b, 4d, and 4e, under Schedule K.

Step 1—4a: We reported the interest we received for the year from our money market account.

Step 2—4b: Then we entered dividend totals for the year received from our stock ownership.

Step 3—4d: We reported any short-term gain or loss. Short-term means anything held a year or less.

Step 4—4e: Here's where we would report any long-term gain or loss. Long-term means anything held over a year, meaning a year and a day or more. The government taxes us at a much lower percentage on our long-term gains. The amount we would have reported as a gain or loss in 4d and 4e would have been the difference between what we sold the stock for (minus commissions) and what we purchased it for (minus commissions). Statements from your brokerage firm are usually sent to the partnership address in January for the previous year's transactions. If not, call them or check your online account for this information. (We didn't sell anything this year.)

Step 5—8–11: Deductions and expenses. Any money that our club gave away, and any expenses that were club-related (mailings, fees, investment club software), were entered on this line.

Step 6—14b (1) The total of lines 4a + 4b + 4c + 4f from above.
   —14 (2) The sum of expenses on line 10.

We didn't fill out the following lines because they didn't apply to us. Uncommon Schedule K items:

O Lines 17a–17g apply if the partnership had foreign income, deductions, or losses, or has paid or accrued foreign taxes.

O Lines 22–23 apply if the investment club had a partner who left the club with some or all of her money, or with stock.

Page Four—Instructions

Analysis of Net Income
Line 1—We entered the sum of Income (Loss).
Line 2—We classified all General Partners (Chicks) as Active, and entered
our total from line 1.

Schedule L, M-1, and M-2
We answered question five on Schedule B (above on page two) no, so we
got to leave the rest of this page blank. If we had answered it yes, this is
where we'd have spent our extra hours. (Congrats on your success to any
of you who do have to spend those hours.)

On the following pages is a fictitious partnership return. I have filled
it out already, but let's see if you can follow along. The ABC Investment
Club consisted of four girls: Henny Penny, Chicken Little, Daisy Duck,
and Ducky Doo. During 1998 they received $20 in interest income, $188
in dividend income, and sold the following stock:

Stock	Purchase Date	Cost	Date Sold	Price
40 shares of ABC	09-03-95	$400	01-12-98	$780
21 shares of DEF	10-31-97	$870	04-09-98	$1,102
100 shares of GHI	05-11-96	$1,250	07-02-98	$1,098
64 shares of KLM	05-11-96	$1,280	01-02-98	$1,300

If this were your investment club, and those were your transactions,
try and go through the fifteen steps it takes to fill out the 1065.

Schedule D

Capital Gains and Losses
If your club has sold any investments during the past year, you will also
have to fill out Schedule D. The IRS needs you to separate your gains
from your losses. A sample of the Schedule D is below, filled out for our
ABC Investment Club.

Analysis of Net Income (Loss)

1	Net income (loss). Combine Schedule K, lines 1 through 7 in column (b). From the result, subtract the sum of Schedule K, lines 8 through 11, 14a, 17e, and 18b				**1**	688 00

2	Analysis by partner type:	(i) Corporate	(ii) Individual (active)	(iii) Individual (passive)	(iv) Partnership	(v) Exempt organization	(vi) Nominee/Other
	a General partners						
	b Limited partners						

Schedule L — Balance Sheets per Books (Not required if Question 5 on Schedule B is answered "Yes.")

		Beginning of tax year		End of tax year	
	Assets	(a)	(b)	(c)	(d)
1	Cash				
2a	Trade notes and accounts receivable				
b	Less allowance for bad debts				
3	Inventories				
4	U.S. government obligations				
5	Tax-exempt securities				
6	Other current assets (attach schedule) . . .				
7	Mortgage and real estate loans				
8	Other investments (attach schedule)				
9a	Buildings and other depreciable assets . . .				
b	Less accumulated depreciation				
10a	Depletable assets				
b	Less accumulated depletion				
11	Land (net of any amortization)				
12a	Intangible assets (amortizable only)				
b	Less accumulated amortization				
13	Other assets (attach schedule)				
14	**Total assets**				
	Liabilities and Capital				
15	Accounts payable				
16	Mortgages, notes, bonds payable in less than 1 year .				
17	Other current liabilities (attach schedule) . . .				
18	All nonrecourse loans				
19	Mortgages, notes, bonds payable in 1 year or more .				
20	Other liabilities (attach schedule)				
21	Partners' capital accounts				
22	Total liabilities and capital				

Schedule M-1 — Reconciliation of Income (Loss) per Books With Income (Loss) per Return
(Not required if Question 5 on Schedule B is answered "Yes." See page 29 of the instructions.)

1	Net income (loss) per books		6	Income recorded on books this year not included on Schedule K, lines 1 through 7 (itemize):	
2	Income included on Schedule K, lines 1 through 4, 6, and 7, not recorded on books this year (itemize):			a Tax-exempt interest $	
3	Guaranteed payments (other than health insurance)		7	Deductions included on Schedule K, lines 1 through 11, 14a, 17e, and 18b, not charged against book income this year (itemize):	
4	Expenses recorded on books this year not included on Schedule K, lines 1 through 11, 14a, 17e, and 18b (itemize):			a Depreciation $	
a	Depreciation $				
b	Travel and entertainment $		8	Add lines 6 and 7	
	....		9	Income (loss) (Analysis of Net Income (Loss), line 1). Subtract line 8 from line 5	
5	Add lines 1 through 4				

Schedule M-2 — Analysis of Partners' Capital Accounts (Not required if Question 5 on Schedule B is answered "Yes.")

1	Balance at beginning of year		6	Distributions: a Cash	
2	Capital contributed during year			b Property	
3	Net income (loss) per books		7	Other decreases (itemize):	
4	Other increases (itemize):				
	....		8	Add lines 6 and 7	
5	Add lines 1 through 4		9	Balance at end of year. Subtract line 8 from line 5	

Capital Gains and Losses

▶ Attach to Form 1065.

OMB No. 1545-0099

1999

Name of partnership	Employer identification number
ABC Investment Club	41

Part I Short-Term Capital Gains and Losses—Assets Held 1 Year or Less

(a) Description of property (e.g., 100 shares of "Z" Co.)	(b) Date acquired (month, day, year)	(c) Date sold (month, day, year)	(d) Sales price (see instructions)	(e) Cost or other basis (see instructions)	(f) Gain or (loss) ((d) minus (e))	
1 21 shares of DEF	10-31-97	04-09-98	1102.00	870.00	232.00	

2	Short-term capital gain from installment sales from Form 6252, line 26 or 37 . .	2	
3	Short-term capital gain (loss) from like-kind exchanges from Form 8824 . . .	3	
4	Partnership's share of net short-term capital gain (loss), including specially allocated short-term capital gains (losses), from other partnerships, estates, and trusts . . .	4	
5	**Net short-term capital gain or (loss).** Combine lines 1 through 4 in column (f). Enter here and on Form 1065, Schedule K, line 4d or 7	5	232.00

Part II Long-Term Capital Gains and Losses—Assets Held More Than 1 Year

(a) Description of property (e.g., 100 shares of "Z" Co.)	(b) Date acquired (month, day, year)	(c) Date sold (month, day, year)	(d) Sales price (see instructions)	(e) Cost or other basis (see instructions)	(f) Gain or (loss) ((d) minus (e))	(g) 28% rate gain or (loss) *(see instr. below)
6 40 shares of ABC	09-03-95	01-12-98	780.00	400.00	380.00	
100 shares of GHI	05-11-96	07-02-98	1098.00	1250.00	(152.00)	
64 shares of JKL	05-11-96	01-02-98	1300.00	1280.00	20.00	

7	Long-term capital gain from installment sales from Form 6252, line 26 or 37 . .	7	
8	Long-term capital gain (loss) from like-kind exchanges from Form 8824 . . .	8	
9	Partnership's share of net long-term capital gain (loss), including specially allocated long-term capital gains (losses), from other partnerships, estates, and trusts . .	9	
10	Capital gain distributions	10	
11	Combine lines 6 through 10 in column (g). Enter here and on Form 1065, Schedule K, line 4e(1) or 7	11	
12	**Net long-term capital gain or (loss).** Combine lines 6 through 10 in column (f). Enter here and on Form 1065, Schedule K, line 4e(2) or 7	12	248.00

'**28% rate gain or (loss)** includes all "collectibles gains and losses" as defined in the instructions.

Note: when we hold a stock for a year or less, the tax percentage charged to us would depend on our tax brackets. The average tax bracket is anywhere from 28 percent to 39.6 percent. If we decided that we wanted to buy and sell stocks within the same year, any gains we had on those stocks would have been taxed at our individual personal rate. Anything that we hold over a year is taxed at a lower 20 percent rate.* The government is giving us a bit of break if we are long-term buy-and-holder Chicks! Let me say that again: the government is giving Chicks a break!

The Schedule D is filled out above for the ABC Investment Club.

Schedule K-1 (Form 1065)

Partner's Share of Income, Credits, Deductions, etc.

This is it—the last form—almost there! It hasn't even been an hour, and you are almost proficient in investment club partnership returns! Tell Uncle Sam to bring it on.

The 1065 K-1 form is filled out for each member of your club. You need to know everyone's social security number and address. Please try to get the K-1 form to all members as early as possible so they can get on with preparing their own returns. I am going to attach samples of the ABC Investment Club's Schedule K-1 for two members, but four actually need to be filled out for their club, since it has four members.

Step 1—Boxes A: check General Partner

Step 2—Box B: write Individual, or "I."

Step 3—Box C: check Domestic.

Step 4—Box D requires math. If the ABC Investment Club has four members, each member is an equal 25 percent (100 percent ÷ 4 = 25 percent). They are equal members in profit sharing, loss sharing, and ownership of capital. If there are ten Chicks in your club, each

---

*Unless, of course, your personal tax bracket is lower; then that would apply instead of the 20 percent.

SCHEDULE K-1 (Form 1065)	Partner's Share of Income, Credits, Deductions, etc.	OMB No. 1545-0099

SCHEDULE K-1 (Form 1065)
Department of the Treasury
Internal Revenue Service

Partner's Share of Income, Credits, Deductions, etc.

▶ See separate instructions.

For calendar year 1999 or tax year beginning , 1999, and ending ,

OMB No. 1545-0099

1999

Partner's identifying number ▶ 475-25-8383	Partnership's identifying number ▶ 41:30476138
Partner's name, address, and ZIP code Penny Saver 4624 Colored Egg Drive Easter Morning, Iowa 12346	Partnership's name, address, and ZIP code ABC Investment Club 111-11th Avenue South Ames, Iowa 12345

A This partner is a ☑ general partner ☐ limited partner
  ☐ limited liability company member
B What type of entity is this partner? ▶ I
C Is this partner a ☑ domestic or a ☐ foreign partner?
D Enter partner's percentage of:

	(i) Before change or termination	(ii) End of year
Profit sharing	25 %	25 %
Loss sharing	25 %	25 %
Ownership of capital	25 %	25 %

E IRS Center where partnership filed return: **Kansas City, MO**

F Partner's share of liabilities (see instructions):
  Nonrecourse . . . . $ ....
  Qualified nonrecourse financing . . $ ....
  Other . . . . $ ....
G Tax shelter registration number . ▶ ....
H Check here if this partnership is a publicly traded partnership as defined in section 469(k)(2) . . . . . ☐
I Check applicable boxes: (1) ☐ Final K-1 (2) ☐ Amended K-1

J Analysis of partner's capital account:

(a) Capital account at beginning of year	(b) Capital contributed during year	(c) Partner's share of lines 3, 4, and 7, Form 1065, Schedule M-2	(d) Withdrawals and distributions	(e) Capital account at end of year (combine columns (a) through (d))
			( )	

	(a) Distributive share item		(b) Amount	(c) 1040 filers enter the amount in column (b) on:
Income (Loss)	**1** Ordinary income (loss) from trade or business activities . . .	1		See page 6 of Partner's Instructions for Schedule K-1 (Form 1065).
	2 Net income (loss) from rental real estate activities	2		
	3 Net income (loss) from other rental activities	3		
	4 Portfolio income (loss):			
	a Interest	4a	5.00	Sch. B, Part I, line 1
	b Ordinary dividends	4b	47.00	Sch. B, Part II, line 5
	c Royalties	4c		Sch. E, Part I, line 4
	d Net short-term capital gain (loss)	4d	58.00	Sch. D, line 5, col. (f)
	e Net long-term capital gain (loss):			
	(1) 28% rate gain (loss)	e(1)	62.00	Sch. D, line 12, col. (g)
	(2) Total for year.	e(2)		Sch. D, line 12, col. (f)
	f Other portfolio income (loss) (attach schedule)	4f		Enter on applicable line of your return.
	5 Guaranteed payments to partner	5		See page 6 of Partner's Instructions for Schedule K-1 (Form 1065).
	6 Net section 1231 gain (loss) (other than due to casualty or theft) .	6		
	7 Other income (loss) (attach schedule)	7		Enter on applicable line of your return.
Deductions	**8** Charitable contributions (see instructions) (attach schedule) . .	8		Sch. A, line 15 or 16
	9 Section 179 expense deduction	9		See pages 7 and 8 of Partner's Instructions for Schedule K-1 (Form 1065)
	10 Deductions related to portfolio income (attach schedule) . . .	10		
	11 Other deductions (attach schedule)	11		
Credits	**12a** Low-income housing credit:			
	(1) From section 42(j)(5) partnerships for property placed in service before 1990	a(1)		Form 8586, line 5
	(2) Other than on line 12a(1) for property placed in service before 1990	a(2)		
	(3) From section 42(j)(5) partnerships for property placed in service after 1989	a(3)		
	(4) Other than on line 12a(3) for property placed in service after 1989	a(4)		
	b Qualified rehabilitation expenditures related to rental real estate activities	12b		
	c Credits (other than credits shown on lines 12a and 12b) related to rental real estate activities.	12c		See page 8 of Partner's Instructions for Schedule K-1 (Form 1065).
	d Credits related to other rental activities	12d		
	13 Other credits	13		

For Paperwork Reduction Act Notice, see Instructions for Form 1065.   Cat. No. 11394R   Schedule K-1 (Form 1065) 1999

(a) Distributive share item	(b) Amount	(c) 1040 filers enter the amount in column (b) on:

Investment Interest

14a Interest expense on investment debts **14a**		Form 4952, line 1
b (1) Investment income included on lines 4a, 4b, 4c, and 4f . . **b(1)**	52.00	See page 9 of Partner's Instructions for Schedule K-1 (Form 1065).
(2) Investment expenses included on line 10. . . . . . . **b(2)**		

Self-employment

15a Net earnings (loss) from self-employment **15a**		Sch. SE, Section A or B
b Gross farming or fishing income. **15b**		See page 9 of Partner's Instructions for Schedule K-1 (Form 1065).
c Gross nonfarm income. **15c**		

Adjustments and Tax Preference Items

16a Depreciation adjustment on property placed in service after 1986 **16a**		
b Adjusted gain or loss **16b**		See page 9 of Partner's Instructions for Schedule K-1 (Form 1065) and Instructions for Form 6251
c Depletion (other than oil and gas) **16c**		
d (1) Gross income from oil, gas, and geothermal properties . . **d(1)**		
(2) Deductions allocable to oil, gas, and geothermal properties **d(2)**		
e Other adjustments and tax preference items *(attach schedule)* **16e**		

Foreign Taxes

17a Type of income ▶		Form 1116, check boxes
b Name of foreign country or possession ▶		
c Total gross income from sources outside the United States *(attach schedule)* **17c**		Form 1116, Part I
d Total applicable deductions and losses *(attach schedule)*. . . **17d**		
e Total foreign taxes (check one): ▶ ☐ Paid ☐ Accrued . . . **17e**		Form 1116, Part II
f Reduction in taxes available for credit *(attach schedule)* . . . **17f**		Form 1116, Part III
g Other foreign tax information *(attach schedule)* **17g**		See Instructions for Form 1116

Other

18 Section 59(e)(2) expenditures: a Type ▶		See page 9 of Partner's Instructions for Schedule K-1 (Form 1065).
b Amount **18b**		
19 Tax-exempt interest income **19**		Form 1040, line 8b
20 Other tax-exempt income **20**		
21 Nondeductible expenses **21**		See pages 9 and 10 of Partner's Instructions for Schedule K-1 (Form 1065)
22 Distributions of money (cash and marketable securities) . . . **22**		
23 Distributions of property other than money **23**		
24 Recapture of low-income housing credit:		
a From section 42(j)(5) partnerships **24a**		Form 8611, line 8
b Other than on line 24a. **24b**		

Supplemental Information

25 Supplemental information required to be reported separately to each partner *(attach additional schedules if more space is needed):*

⊛   Schedule K-1 (Form 1065) 1999 member's ownership percentage is ten (100 percent ÷ 10 = 10 percent). Fifteen members, 6.67 percent (100 percent ÷ 15 = 6.67 percent). And so on. Skip Boxes F–J.

In the Income (Loss) section, you need to answer 4a, 4b, 4d, and 4e for the ABC Investment Club, so you need to go back to the 1065 Form, page three. Under Schedule K on that form are the numbered questions 4a, 4b, 4d, and 4e. These numbers need to be divided by each partner's percentage of ownership for the K-1. If ABC Investment Club members each have a quarter stake in the club, the numbers on the 1065 Form, page three, will be divided by four.

For example: For ABC Investment Club, on page three of the 1065, under 4a, we wrote 20. To split it up individually, for each member of ABC, we divide it by four: 20 ÷ 4 = 5. On Penny Saver's K-1 form, we put 5 in 4a. For the amount entered into 4b, we take the amount from 4b on page three of the 1065 (188) and divide it by four: 188 ÷ 4 = 47. Same goes for 4d: 232 ÷ 4 = 58. Ditto for 4e: 248 ÷ 4 = 62.

The purpose of a K-1 form is to equally divide the profit sharing and loss among all members so they each can claim it on a personal income tax return. Each member of your investment club is required to file a K-1 form with her tax return.

I hope I have simplified the partnership tax return a bit. It's hard to believe that America was founded to avoid high taxation. Can you imagine if you were a corporation? A partnership form is as uncomplicated as tax forms get, and it still destroys a gazillion brain cells. There is one last little detail in filing your partnership return. You should call your local tax office and ask what your state requires for a partnership tax filing. Each state is different, but they usually match what we did here, if not make it simpler. Your state's requirements can be found at www.chickslayingnesteggs.com or www.irs.gov.

Now, here's your reward—more tax humor:

0 Congress does some strange things. It puts a high tax on liquor and then raises the other taxes that drive people to drink.

0 About the time a man is cured of swearing, another income tax is due.

O The latest income tax form has been greatly simplified. It consists of only three parts:

A) How much did you make last year?———

B) How much have you got left?———

C) Send in amount listed on line B.

Chapter Summary

O It's hard to find tax jokes funny.

O For federal forms, you will need 1065, Schedule D, and the K-1 (Form 1065).

O The 1065 is the club's return as a whole; Schedule D differentiates between your club's gains and losses; and the K-1 form divides the 1065 into equal parts for each member of the club.

O Be organized and have partnership forms filled out by February 15.

O It should take you about an hour to do the club's return (for everyone).

O I'll bet you're elated that we're through with this chapter. So am I.

chick chat

TITLE: MEGAN'S LIFE
From: Megan

Well, the deal is done. The Kaminskis have decided to head to Providence . . . can you believe it? Okay, the good things are: A) Newport is right there; B) New mall featuring Nordstrom and Saks. The bad things are: A) Rink is too far from Newport; B) Not enough money to shop at the new mall.

Go figure.

BgBnWllHv2Wait,

Megan

TITLE: GOLF COURSE
From: Julie

I decided to leave the name of my course Brockway since you guys couldn't really come up with anything better. I'm sorry it sounds weird by now.

Julie

TITLE: MEGAN'S WORLD
From: Megan

And just when you thought I was moving to Providence, we got traded to Orlando. "Hey Megan, what are you doing this afternoon?"

"I'm going to Disney World!"

Megan

TITLE: **S&P REPORT
From: Cheryl

It seems like yesterday that I posted the last S&P report. Sheez, we've purchased GE since then and are kicking some serious bootie. (Whenever you get sick of that phrase, I'll make up a new one.) I'm so glad

·that GE was the majority vote getter in our last meeting because now we are "bringing good things to life." It's like Martha Stewart and a soap opera all in one. Oooh, and Karin, I watched your friend on *One Life to Live,* Darlene, I mean Melanie McGyver. She's great. Here's our S&P Report:

Our whole portfolio is up 81.51% vs. the market's 25.09%

AOL up 219.87% vs. 30.31%

CSCO up 185.04% vs. 18%

GE up 12.26% vs. 7.61%

GPS up 3.33% vs. 15.11%

KO down 27.74% vs. 48.16% (loser)

NOK up 161% vs. 12.47%

ORCL up 122% vs. 6.53%

PFE up 16.88% vs. 48.16%

TITLE: MARY LEE HOUSLEY

From: Karin

Phil's mother passed away about an hour ago. We were all able to make it back to Minnesota to say good-bye.

Karin

19

You Gotta Have Heart

> *Never doubt that a small group of thoughtful,*
> *committed citizens can change the world;*
> *indeed, it's the only thing that ever has.*
> — MARGARET MEAD

I have this picture of the Ohio State women's rugby team hanging above my desk. I don't even know anyone on the team. Every once in a while, I look up at it and ponder, "What were they thinking? I wonder if I would have? Are they crazy? Was it worth it? Were they cold? Hmm." In November 1999, the picture made it into newspapers around the world. The women shocked the public. They were in Washington, D.C., to play the American University rugby team the next day. During their team photo at the Lincoln Memorial, they wanted to do something crazy that would help them bond as a team; kind of like a blood oath. Moments before the photographer snapped the picture, they ripped off their jerseys. Bare-naked breasts everywhere.

Can you imagine? With Mr. Lincoln looking on in the background? Topless women! On the steps to his memorial! Unthinkable, but they did it. They also clobbered American University the next day.

As an investment club, you need this kind of bond. But keep your shirts on. You don't have to go this far. An essential element that many clubs lack is the heart. The feeling of belonging and being accounted for. You want people to notice if you miss a meeting. You really want to *know* the women in your club. You want to like them, have fun with them, and share common goals. If you don't, your club will not last. If it does last, you won't really care about the success of the club or its members. It's a female thing. An all-men club would chuckle at this whole chapter. To them, it's all about the money. Women don't do anything just for money. Which is why someone said a long time ago, "The hand that rocks the cradle is the hand that rules the world." We know that there is so much more to life than money; there are love, humanity, health, spirituality, and friendships. These rate higher than money, and they should.

Karin, Karin, Karin, do we have to go into this? You know some of us are very private about our giving of ourselves. We don't have to boast to the world that we are good people on top of being smart. If you are going to talk about this, I'm going out to hit some balls.

Julie is so funny. In the beginning of our club, we decided to implement another Chick Rule. Each of us was to perform one Random Act of Kindness per month and post it to our message board. We were to do one really nice thing for someone, anyone, and post about it. Reading other Chicks' Random Acts would inspire us all. Julie went missing.

After numerous RAOK posts about how nice we had been—from Chick Jana leaving money for the guy behind her at the tollbooth to Chick Lorene buying magazines from the man at the door then sending them to the Ronald McDonald House—Julie was still missing.

During our monthly meeting, we badgered her. What was she doing? Was she not a nice person? Did she need help thinking of ideas? Did she think we were a bunch of silly women and she wanted to stick to investing? Maybe since RAOK had nothing to do with the stock market, she wasn't going to listen. We were befuddled.

In our stone-throwing process, we found out that Julie was a very private person. Giving back to her community, her employees, and her friends was part of her daily routine. She didn't want to share this because she felt it was tacky. After we thought about it, it kind of was, though to this day we still continue posting our RAOK, knowing how tacky it is. But we enjoy the stories. We excuse Julie.

After many months of RAOK, we decided to do something more. The RAOK had inspired us. We each came up with a charity that we could give a percentage of our profit to. We discussed them all at our next face-to-face meeting. In the sifting process, we realized we all had our own personal charities. One of us is a big participant in the Alzheimer's Foundation. One gives regularly to the American Cancer Society. One runs marathons for breast cancer research. No one charity looked better than the next. We changed our minds. We are not giving cash. We are going to give of ourselves physically.

Along came Habitat for Humanity. Chick Cheryl popped in on her husband at work one day. Unbeknownst to her, he was having lunch with the director of public affairs for Habitat. Cheryl (remember, she enjoys attention) had no difficulties in sharing the Chicks' dilemma and asked what Habitat was all about. Lo and behold, they had just started an arm of Habitat called Women Build. Women building houses for other women. Chicks building nests for other Chicks: how perfect!

Nationally, 47.5 percent of Habitat's homes are built for women heads of household. But sadly, because of a woman's training, we make up only 15 percent of the build's actual labor. We don't do it because *we don't know how.* What did I say was the reason I never invested in the stock market? Mission accomplished.

The Chicks jumped into the stock market not knowing a thing. It was a rooster's world. We had never had the opportunity to get our beaks in there in a way we felt comfortable. Once we did, through the club, it wasn't hard at all. We had to do it to learn. Right now, it's hard to remember a day when we didn't know how to do it; it's become that familiar. But building houses? Could it be possible?

Why not? Especially with your club? Why couldn't Chicks build Nests? Why does building a house seem so difficult? Because you've never done it! What happens during a Women Build is the same thing that happens when you conquer the stock market; it's empowering beyond words. You are doing something that you never dreamed you'd be able to, in an environment where you feel completely comfortable. Chicks all around. Girls giggling. Starbucks shared. Hard work being accomplished while experiencing life like never before.

Julie got excited. This she could do. This she would be proud to do. This she had been dying to do! All Habitat said we needed was a hammer and a tool belt. Julie started to design Chicks Laying Nest Eggs tool belts.

Women Build gave us a perfect opportunity to use our Chick motto—"Girls just wanna have fun . . . Chicks wanna learn something along the way."

Women want to be empowered in a nonthreatening environment. Like an all-female investment club, Women Build gave us the opportunity to learn. Even more important, it gave us a chance to give back. And with that, you've come full circle.

Once your club gets up and running, seriously think about how you could give back to your community as a group. Take one day a year to work at a soup kitchen. Wrap gifts at the mall during Christmas for charity. Volunteer at a hospital. Visit a nursing home. Cook a meal for a less fortunate family during Thanksgiving. Do something *together*. Your club needs heart. It just feels good.

It's up to you if you want to take your shirts off.

For further information on the Women Build program, contact:

Habitat for Humanity
    Women Build Department
    121 Habitat Street
    Americus, GA 31709-3498
    or call 912-924-6935

chick chat

TITLE: NEXT FACE-TO-FACE
From: Karin

We have a meeting this Sunday night and the only thing on the agenda is where our next face-to-face meeting should be. Do you mind if I miss it? Phil has gone to Russia to play for Team USA in the World Championships, and I am going to meet him there with the kids. I know Miss Rotten Egg Patrol Megan will have some terrible punishment for me. I am going to stop off in Helsinki at Nokia Headquarters, so does this count as an investment club–related trip? May I be excused? Maybe we could plan our next face-to-face in Finland! Please post your good dates for next September, and a spot you think we should go. Oh, and one more thing, post a company's name that you would like to research. We buy again in a month.

Karin

TITLE: BABY AUSTIN
From: Jana

Add another small, small baby to our small, small world! Our little prince was born this afternoon at twelve-thirty P.M. It's a BOY! Austin Lee, 7 pounds 15 ounces, 21 inches long.

Jana

Diane's Story ... Updated

Dear Karin and Chicks,

Thank you so much for helping me out! I read absolutely everything in this book. For the people who are reading this right now, I've known Karin since I was a little girl. She gave me the chapters of this book as she wrote them. I was her guinea pig. It's not the first time. She has been doing this to me for years: "Hey, Diane, you wanna try this shake that I just made? It has ice cream, grape pop, spearmint leaves, and pixie sticks in it. Come on, try it. Tell me what you think?" Most of the time her creations were disasters, but I never had the heart to tell her because she was so enthusiastic. So the day she asked me to read the book and give her some feedback, I had to bite my tongue.

After zooming through the first four chapters, I wanted more. I called her every day to say, "Are you done yet? I have eight women ready to go . . . what next? Hurry hurry!"

Eventually I had twelve women who wanted to join my club, and Karin let us *all* read the book. She called us the Guinea Chicks, but we officially named ourselves Club Chick—a swanky place where you go to relax (and learn). We've been together only a few months, but we're up and going full speed. We buy every two months and know exactly what we are doing. (Our husbands are begging for a chance to spy on our meetings.) It was so easy, thanks to the step-by-step instructions! (Though I am not looking forward to the tax return part. I'll beg Nancy to do it.)

I just want to thank all of you Chicks Laying Nest Eggs for the wonderful book, for empowering all of us in Club Chick, and to you especially, Karin. You can make me a shake anytime. (Oh, and Linda wants to know if we can come build with you.)

Diane

P.S. By the way, I am still very young. It didn't take Karin that long to write the book, so start to finish, I aged, what, three hours?

Glossary

AMEX: American Stock Exchange.

Annualized rate of return: Average return over a designated period of time (usually years), taking into account the effect of compounding.

Back-end Load: Sales charge that is deducted from the *selling* price of mutual fund shares.

Balance sheet: The part of a company's financial statement that depicts how it is doing over the long term.

Bond: A debt security with a maturity of greater than one year; a corporate or government IOU. You buy a piece of paper from a corporation with the understanding that they will pay you back in a certain amount of time. In that amount of time, they will pay you a guaranteed amount of interest, which is usually paid every six months.

Broker: Any person registered by the National Association of Securities Dealers and/or a state's securities regulation authority to take customer orders on the sale of a security.

Capital gain: Gain (or profit) from the sale of securities (or assets).

Capital loss: Loss on capital invested.

Certified tax identification number: IRS requirement for all investment accounts; social security number or tax ID number.

Close: The price at which a security closed on a given trading day.

Compounding: Earning additional interest on previously earned interest; interest on interest.

Cost basis: The purchase price you paid for your stock; you need this for tax purposes.

Desktop computer: The larger computers that sit on a desk and are not mobile.

Discount broker: A broker who will buy and sell securities for a reduced rate, usually between $5 and $30.

Diversify: To spread your assets among various types of investments.

Dividend: Payment by a fund (or stock) you've invested in.

Dow Jones: Thirty of the largest corporations in America.

Dow Jones Industrial Average: The stock index consisting of thirty of the largest American corporations.

Download: The process of getting computer files from the Internet and loading them onto your computer.

E-broker: A broker who is able to make a stock trade for his or her customers via the Internet.

EIN: Employer Identification Number; how your club is identified to Uncle Sam.

E-tail: Retail on the Internet.

Equity: How much you would walk away with if you sold something.

Equity security: Ownership in a corporation; common stock and preferred stock.

Fiscal year: Accounting period of 365 days.

Front-end load: Sales charge that is deducted from the *purchase* price of mutual fund shares.

Government security: Debt obligation issued by the U.S. government.

Gross margins: Percentage of gross profit relative to revenue.

Home page: A place on the Internet that can be tailored to identify you or, in this case, your club. It can contain pictures and information unique to you.

Income statement: The part of a company's financial statement that depicts how a company is doing in the short term.

Index: Benchmark against which to measure performance.

Index fund: Mutual funds whose portfolio matches the components of a particular index; most popular is the Vanguard S&P 500 Fund.

Initial public offering (IPO): The first day a stock goes on sale to the public.

Internet: The World Wide Web, cyberspace, the global computer network that's changing everything.

Internet service provider: The company that gets your computer talking to other computers on the Internet; the middleman.

IPO: Initial public offering (see above).

ISP: Internet service provider (see above).

Java: Coffee. (Okay, in Sun Microsystems buildings, it's a computer language.)

Laptop computer: The smaller notebook-type computers that are portable.

Load fund: Mutual fund that deducts a sales charge, or "load," from the net asset value of an investment.

Market capitalization: The total value of a company's stock.

Marketable securities: Stocks or other securities that are as good as liquid.

Market order: An order that instructs a broker to execute a buy as quickly as possible at the best price available.

Modem: The device inside your computer that dials and connects your computer to the Internet.

Money market account: An account in which money is invested in various short-term securities; seeks to maintain $1 per share value.

Money market fund: A highly liquid mutual fund that invests in short-term securities and seeks to maintain a stable net asset value of $1 per share.

Mutual fund: An investment company that pools money from shareholders and invests in a variety of securities, such as stocks and bonds.

NASDAQ: National Association of Securities Dealer Automated Quotations system, designed to facilitate over-the-counter stock trading.

Net margins: Also known as profit margins; the actual amount a company makes on each dollar after all expenses are deducted.

NYSE: New York Stock Exchange.

Online: Being hooked up to the Internet.

Online broker: A broker who is able to make a stock trade for his or her customers via the Internet.

Open: The price at which a security opened for trading on a given day.

Order: Just like at McDonald's, a command to supply something; in the stock market lingo, it means a command to supply a stock—you place an order.

Portfolio: Three-ring binder made up of your securities, or stock holdings.

Preferred stocks: A class of stock with a claim on the company's earnings before payment is made to the common stock holders if the company declares bankruptcy.

Profit margins: Also known as net margins (see above).

Public stock: Stock that is made available to the public for purchase through one of the stock exchanges.

Principal: The amount of money that is financed, borrowed, or invested.

Russell 2000: The index that tracks two thousand of the smaller companies in America.

Screen name: How you are identified in the cyberworld, or on the computer.

Snapshot: A brief overview of a company.

Stock: A piece-of-paper ownership in a company.

Quarter: Every three months of a fiscal year.

Quarterly reports: The financial report that a U.S. corporation must file with the Securities and Exchange Commission (SEC) every three months or quarter.

Quorum: A minimum number of members that must be present at a meeting to make it valid.

Security type: A type of security, such as a stock, bond, or mutual fund.

Securities and Exchange Commission (SEC): Agency of the U.S. government, responsible for enforcement of federal securities laws in the United States.

Share: Unit of ownership.

Shareholder: Owner of shares.

Shares outstanding: Shares of a company that are owned by the public.

SIPC: Securities Investor Protection Corporation, a government-sponsored insurance that covers discount brokers.

Ticker symbol: The letters used to designate a security/stock for trading.

Total return: Annual return on an investment. This is measured by the sum of an appreciation plus all dividends, interest, and reinvested gains.

Treasury bill: A short-term debt security of the U.S. government, known as a "T-bill."

Treasury note: A mid-term debt security of the U.S. government, with maturities ranging from two to ten years, that pays a fixed rate of interest every six months and returns its face value at maturity.

Treasury security: Debt obligations of the U.S. government that are issued through the Department of the Treasury. Since they are backed by the full faith and credit of the U.S. government, they are considered virtually free from risk of default.

Upload: The process of sending computer files from your computer to cyberspace.

Venture capitalist: A person with extra cash lying around who is willing to invest in your company to help it get started in exchange for some preferred stock or ownership.

Vested: The percentage of ownership in a retirement plan's assets.

Volume: The daily number of shares traded in a security.

Web: Short for World Wide Web.

Wilshire 5000: The index that tracks six thousand American companies of any size.

World Wide Web: The most widely used portion of the Internet.

www.: The prefix that comes before almost all website addresses; stands for World Wide Web.

12b1 plan: Expense under which a certain percentage of fund assets can be used to pay distribution and marketing expenses. *Be sure to check these on your mutual funds.*

401(k): Corporate retirement plan that allows employees to contribute pretax dollars in an investment plan.

403(b): A qualified retirement plan similar to a 401(k), designed for non-profit organizations.

52-week high: The highest price at which a security has traded within the previous fifty-two weeks.

52-week low: The lowest price at which a security has traded within the previous fifty-two weeks.

Acknowledgments

Good night, Mom. I love you so much.
— TAYLOR HOUSLEY

Ooof. How do people write more than one book? How do they do it and try to maintain a life? During the writing of this book, so many people made sacrifices on my behalf; mostly, my family. My routine was to sneak off into my bathroom (turned office, don't ask) when things had settled down after dinner, to write. My husband would then get the kids to bed, if he was home. If he wasn't, I would put the youngest down at eight P.M. and let the others stay up until nine, but I still snuck off to my bathroom. At nine, I would yell, "Go to bed . . . now!" At nine-thirty, I would yell, "And I mean it!" Everyone was forced to fend for him- or herself in my absence.

How bad was it? One night I found a note from my daughter Taylor, typed smack dab in the middle of chapter 13, in bold: **Good night, Mom. I love you so much.** Not only did I make her late to a zillion soccer games and miss four orthodontist appointments, now we were saying good night via my laptop. I had to finish the book.

My husband would take a bath right next to me while I wrote. I didn't even notice. To make it worse, I forgot his birthday. My baby still hasn't had her first haircut. She's two. My son wants to know if I'm *ever* going to let him have a friend sleep over. My middle daughter wants to know why I don't accompany her on her field trips anymore. I'm sure her teachers are wondering too.

I want to thank my kids so much for putting up with me and bringing me water, tea, and Diet Coke whenever I pushed the pager button on the phone. Once they even brought me a Dairy Queen Blizzard. Thank you Taylor, Reide, Wilson, and Avery. I love you sooooooo much. And to Phil, my husband of forever. I did good. Not too many men would stand for what you have. 'Specially about the birthday present. I love you.

To Suzanne Gluck, Chick of all Chicks. Her name even sounds Chicky. Gluck, Gluck, Gluck. Thanks for finding me, or did I find you? To Mecoy, ya freak. (He's my editor.) Thanks for all your advice and being so patient with me, your small-town first-time writer. Could you stop it with the foo-foo drinks, though? We aren't ever going to be invited back to the Anheuser-Busch box at Madison Square Garden if you keep it up. Thanks to Lori Lipsky for all of her excitement about the book. I was more than thrilled!

To Tom Gardner, my idol. I'll never be as good a writer as you, or as skinny, but I'll always keep trying. Thanks for your encouragement on this project, and for not bugging me during the process.

To Mr. and Mrs. Rock Newman, thank you for your unbelievable hospitality toward the Chicks in Vegas. We'll have to do it again . . . only with you there next time!

To Tom and Kim Christiansen, I Know Your Club. Thank you for your advice, wisdom, and software. Both of you.

To Karen, Rob, and Tricia for helping me with the kids. (Yes, my cleaning lady moonlights as a baby-sitter.) I couldn't have done any of this without help from you guys.

To George, thanks for all the connections. I owe you.

To money honey Chick Celeste, thanks so much for all your help with the accounting, counting, and recounting. (Again, it's obvious I'm not a numbers person.)

To the Chicks. Thanks so much to each of you for all your research and hard work on this book. I never could have thought of doing it without you, and I never would have finished it had you not tortured me. Thank you for being such great friends and putting up with me. To Jana, my baby sister, for setting up timelines for each chapter. I should have paid attention.

To my older sister, Kirsten, and her family, thanks so much for helping me with the kids.

To Phil's parents, Leroy and Mary Lee (Mary Lee didn't live long enough to see this book go to print; she was a great Chick), thanks for giving me your son and welcoming me into your family. Even if I was twelve. I love you both.

To my parents, Pete and Jeanette. What can I say? You have taken me from crayons to perfume. I mean . . . crayons to a *book!* Can you even? Thanks for continually reminding me what is important in life: going to church; being on time for church; and getting those kids to church. Do you think now that I'm thirty-six we can skip the Sunday checkup calls? Thanks for being my parents; I know it couldn't have been easy. I love you so much. Dad? Is it too late to become Miss America?

index

About the Author

KARIN HOUSLEY lives in St. Paul, Minnesota, and Calgary, Alberta. She is married to professional hockey player Phil Housley and has four children and a website (www.chickslayingnesteggs.com).